Recent Research in Psychology

Global Report on Student Well-Being

Published Volumes

Volume I: Life Satisfaction and Happiness
Volume II: Family, Friends, Living Partner, and Self-Esteem

Forthcoming Volumes

Volume III: Employment, Finances, Housing, and Transportation
Volume IV: Religion, Education, Recreation, and Health

Alex C. Michalos

Global Report on Student Well-Being

Volume II: Family, Friends, Living Partner, and Self-Esteem

Springer-Verlag

New York Berlin Heidelberg London Paris
Tokyo Hong Kong Barcelona Budapest

Alex C. Michalos, Ph.D.
Professor
University of Guelph
Guelph, Ontario N1G 2W1
Canada

Library of Congress Cataloging-in-Publication Data
Michalos, Alex C.
    Global report on student well-being / Alex C. Michalos.
      p.   cm. — (Recent research in psychology)
    Includes bibliographical references and index.
    Contents: v.2. Family, friends, living partner, and self-esteem
    ISBN 0-387-97666-3 (New York : v. 1 : alk. paper). — ISBN
3-540-97663-3 (Berlin : v. 1 : alk. paper)
      1. College students. 2. College students—Psychology. I. Title.
    II. Series.
    LA186.M49   1991 v.2
    378.1'98—dc20   90-19335

Printed on acid-free paper.

Camera-ready prepared by the author.
Printed and bound by Edwards Brothers, Inc., Ann Arbor, MI.
Printed in the United States of America.

9 8 7 6 5 4 3 2 1

ISBN 0-387-97666-3 Springer-Verlag New York Berlin Heidelberg
ISBN 3-540-97666-3 Springer-Verlag Berlin Heidelberg New York

To
Frank M. Andrews and Wolfgang Zapf
with
Admiration, Appreciation, and Affection

Preface

I suppose that most of the people reading this volume will have read or have access to Volume One of my *Global Report on Student Well-Being*. Therefore, I will not review the background literature relevant to multiple discrepancies theory (MDT), the theory itself or the essential features of the international university undergraduate data-set on which this whole report is based. Anyone familiar with my earlier papers (Michalos 1985, 1987, 1988) will have a good idea of MDT. However, one really has to have a look at the first volume of this study in order to appreciate the richness of a data-set consisting of over 18,000 cases drawn from 39 countries. As I indicated at the beginning of that volume, the data-set is available for a very modest cost to anyone who wants it and I do hope others will take advantage of it.

Contents

1

Literature Review

1.1 Introduction

Nye (1988) wrote an excellent introduction to our subject. In it he reviewed all the papers related to family research that were published in the *Journal of Marriage and the Family, American Sociological Review, American Journal of Sociology, Social Forces*, and *Sociology and Social Research* in the years 1937, 1947, 1957, 1967, 1977 and 1986. Among other things, he found that "the most popular subject of family research over the 50-year period" was "family and premarital relationships", and "The largest subcategory within this general grouping is marital happiness, unhappiness, and conflict..." (p.308). His most remarkable finding was that about 80% of the projects reported over the entire period employed "no type of theory" and in the final year, 1986, a full 75% were still atheoretical (p.311). Glenn's (1990) more recent review confirms this assessment. Clearly, the positivist knife has made a very deep cut in this area!

    His most gratifying comment was the following. "Early on, Burgess and Cottrell (1939) took every individual characteristic they could think of and correlated it with marital success, producing an R of about .50 and an R^2 of .25, or 25% of the variance in the dependent variable. Not a bad start, but we have not progressed much beyond that point in 50 years" (p.315). The comment is gratifying because, as you will see in some detail below, on average MDT is able to explain over 50% of the variance in people's satisfaction with their family, living partner and friendships. Although none of these dependent variables is identical to marital success, and I think Glenn (1990) is right in denying that marital success is identical to marital quality, satisfaction with one's living partner and family must share some of the connotation and denotation of the concepts of marital success and marital quality. However one operationalizes the ideas of marital success and marital quality, some account must be taken of people's reported satisfaction with their family and living partner. Therefore, I suppose MDT has substantially increased our explanatory power since 1939, and that is some kind of progress.

1.2 Marriage and the Family

Several studies have shown that people's reported satisfaction levels
with their family and/or marital relationships are typically higher than
their reported satisfaction levels with any other domains of life, e.g.,
Campbell, Converse and Rodgers (1976); Andrews and Withey (1976);
Michalos (1982a, 1983); Zapf *et al.* (1987), and Oppong, Ironside and
Kennedy (1988). Andrews and Withey said the reports from their
national samples of Americans "were so favorable that it is easy to be
disbelieving" (p.265). They speculated that the relatively high
assessments might be the result of people's reluctance to be critical
of their family relationships in the presence of a total stranger with
an interview schedule. Campbell, Converse and Rodgers speculated
that the absence of an external and objective standard regarding
family relationships might allow people's assessments to rise more
easily (pp.345-346). If you look at Exhibit 7.1 in the first volume
of this study, you will find that for my global sample of
undergraduates satisfaction with one's family life had the highest
average ratings for all 12 domains and life as a whole. So, here again
results obtained from convenience samples of university students are
very similar to results obtained from national probability samples of
adults. More importantly, from my point of view, in Section 2.3 of
the next chapter it will be shown that MDT is able to explain over
half the variance in such satisfaction. Given the similarity of
satisfaction ratings between the student and adult samples, it is
probably a good bet that MDT would also explain most of the
variance in family satisfaction levels for adults.

Schmitt and Kurdek (1985) found that their relatively small
sample of college men (N<100) were significantly more dissatisfied
than college women with their relationships with family and friends.
This is consistent with results reported below in Chapters 2 and 3.
On the contrary, Zapf *et al.* (1987) found that German women were
less satisfied with their family life than German men. More
particularly, German women were also less satisfied with their
"marriage/cohabitation" than German men, and cohabiting singles
were "not quite as satisfied with their partners as married persons"
(p.100). For my sample of German students, unlike the general
population, females were more satisfied than males with their family
life (Exhibit 2.2), but like the general population, married students
expressed higher levels of satisfaction with their living partners than
unmarried students (Exhibits 6.6 and 6.7).

Many studies have shown that married people report higher

levels of life satisfaction and happiness as well as better mental and physical health, fewer suicides, and generally lower mortality rates than unmarried people (Veenhoven 1983; Haring-Hidore, Stock, Okun and Witter 1985; Michalos 1986; Farrell and Markides 1985; Markides and Farrell 1985; Broman 1988; Trovato and Lauris 1989; Anson 1989). Results reported in Chapter 6 are certainly consistent with these studies. While most research suggests that higher life satisfaction and so on are consequences of being married (i.e., the social integration hypothesis), there is certainly some causality in the opposite direction too (i.e., the social selection hypothesis).

Contrary to a fairly popular belief that the importance of marriage is declining, at least in industrialized countries, Veenhoven (1983) produced an impressive amount of evidence "suggesting that marriage is becoming an increasingly indispensable 'haven' in an increasingly 'privatizing' world". His evidence included the facts that "the differences in well-being between unmarried and married persons are becoming greater rather than smaller. In the Netherlands - between 1950 and 1980 - suicide rates have risen far more among the unmarried than among the married. Furthermore, the differences in happiness between unmarried and married persons appear greatest in the most modern European countries [Denmark and the Netherlands], whereas almost no differences exist in the most traditional ones [Italy and Ireland]. Secondly, married persons appear to have become more dependent on the relationship with their spouse rather than less. During the last few decades in the Netherlands the overall happiness of married people has become more closely associated with their satisfaction with marriage" (p.48).

Further support for Veenhoven's thesis is provided by Jones, Marsden and Tepperman (1990) who claimed that for most Canadians "marriage remains a desired state" (p.9). According to Veevers (1988), in Canada in 1981 roughly two-thirds of everyone 16 years or older was married, and about 90% of all men and 92% of all women would marry at least once before the age of 80.

1.3 Correlates of Family and Marital Satisfaction

There is considerable evidence that family life and marital satisfaction increases with income for white and black Americans (Berry and Williams 1987; Ball and Robbins 1986; Glenn and Weaver 1979; Spanier and Lewis 1980). Berry and Williams (1987) found that for their sample of 252 wives, marital satisfaction increased with income satisfaction. There was no relation between these variables for their sample of 195 husbands. For wives the most important predictor of satisfaction with a spouse was communication, while for husbands the most important predictor was disagreement over finances.

Good communication among partners is a well-known major contributor toward marital satisfaction (Michalos 1986). In an interesting study of 318 married individuals, Holman and Jacquart (1988) found that "the cliche 'The family (or couple) that plays together, stays together' should be amended to include: '...if they have a great deal of communication while they play.' With our couples, at least, joint leisure without high levels of perceived communication has at best no association with, and at worst a negative association with, marital satisfaction" (p.76).

Moffitt, Spence and Goldney (1986, pp.72-73) found that for their sample of 33 Australian couples, "wives who are more happily married tend to be good communicators (or to view their marital communication as good), to be comfortable in affiliating with others, and to have good mental health. They also seem to have husbands who are happy with them--it is interesting that wives' happiness is not associated with any husbandly trait, other than happiness, in our sample. Husbands...who are more happily married tend to be either good communicators or seem to think the marital communication is good and tend to be socially conforming and not very extroverted. In their wives, the maritally happy husbands seem to find good levels of communication, happiness and mental health."

Kurdek and Schmitt (1987, pp.212-213) claimed that the facilitation of "communication, understanding and empathy" was behind the variety of studies confirming the homogamy hypothesis that predicts that likes marry likes. Support for the hypothesis has been found "For demographic characteristics such as age, race, socioeconomic status, and religion,...[and]...for cognitive style and for personality characteristics such as impulsivity, reasoning accuracy, vocabulary, field independence, sensation seeking, masculinity, femininity, extroversion, dominance, quarrelsomeness, and ingenuousness".

Halford, Hahlweg and Dunne (1990) compared small samples (N<50) of Australian and German couples searching for cultural correlates of communication. They found that the German couples used significantly more negative verbal responses than the Australian couples. However, for our purposes their most interesting finding was that "The data from both cultures suggest that the most outstanding feature of unhappy couples is their inability to terminate negative interaction, particularly in nonverbal communication. Unhappy couples are very predictable: once a partner reciprocates a negative response an aversive escalation process is almost inevitable. In contrast, happy couples manage to deescalate such a process or refrain from starting it at all" (p.499). Similarly, Jones and Gallois (1989) claimed that although many studies had documented the fact that "conflict is ubiquitous in marriage... .How conflict is managed, rather than how much conflict there is, may be the important variable in distinguishing happy from unhappy couples" (p.957).

There are empirical and theoretical grounds for believing that the traditional marriage model of a male bread winner and a female housekeeper provides more benefits for husbands than for wives, e.g., Michalos (1982) and Eichler (1983). Fortunately for women, in many countries that model is being seriously eroded (Spitze 1988). Unfortunately for women, the traditional model is often being replaced by one of male and female bread winners but still only female housekeepers (Eichler 1983).

According to a recent literature review, "No matter what technique is used to measure household division of labor, wives typically do much more than husbands... .Study after study has shown that attitudes and shared norms continue to define household work as 'women's work,' and most wives seem satisfied with the small amount of housework their husbands do" (Thompson and Walker 1989, p.854). Nevertheless, these authors also emphasize the fact that the more each partner perceives that the other is doing a fair share of housework, the more satisfied they are with their marriage (p.858).

The trouble is that partners collectively construct their perceived reality in ways that tend to benefit men at the expense of women. Regarding parenting, for example, Thompson and Walker claim that "Partners seem to collaborate to sustain the belief that fathers are intimately involved with their children and 'fairly' sharing child care when mothers actually are doing the daily parenting... .Partners tend to view men's minimal help with raising children as substantial, and women's substantial help with provision as minimal" (pp.863-864).

Mastekaasa (1990) examined results of national surveys in 19 developed countries, and found that husbands and wives reported very similar levels of life satisfaction and happiness. The relationship between marital status and psychological well-being was also "about equally strong for men and women" (p.13). These results are not entirely consistent with those that will be reported below in Chapter 6.

Besides doing most of the housework in the obvious sense of

this term, i.e., cleaning, cooking, shopping, etc., wives also do most of the psychological work required to keep a household together. According to Thompson and Walker (1989, pp.848-849), "Wives...usually have more responsibility than their husbands for monitoring the relationship, confronting disagreeable issues, setting the tone of the conversation, and moving toward resolution when conflict is high." Besides having greater responsibility in this area, "wives usually are more expressive and send clearer messages than husbands in marital communication. Since most wives are better senders, most husbands, especially the happily married, have an advantage over wives in receiving messages." Apparently, then, husbands and other household members are probably lucky that wives do have a disproportionate share of the responsibility in this area.

Long and Andrews (1990) studied the impact of "perspective taking, defined as the imaginative tendency to put oneself in another person's place" on 239 American married couples who had been together an average of 24 years. Other studies had found a positive association between relationship satisfaction and self-reported perspective taking. Long and Andrews found that people who are married to competent perspective takers are relatively well adjusted in their marriages. As in the case of competence in communication mentioned in the previous paragraph, wives had higher scores on perspective-taking scales and both partners recognized that wives were more competent perspective takers.

Several studies have shown that married women are less lonely than unmarried women. Essex and Nam's (1987) study of 480 Wisconsin women over 50 showed that married and never-married women were lonely the least often and formerly married women were lonely most often.

There are many studies showing that parents have lower levels of marital satisfaction than nonparents and there are fewer studies showing the reverse (Campbell 1981; Glenn and McLanahan 1982; Michalos 1986; Zapf *et al.* 1987, and Pittman and Lloyd 1988). After reviewing some of the evidence regarding the impact of children on marital quality, Veevers (1979, p.14) expressed the view that "The crucial variable in maintaining marital morale may be the ability to have as many children as one wants to have, whatever number that may be... ." In our terms, she guessed the crucial variable involved a self/wants discrepancy. As we will see in Chapters 2, 4 and 6, while this variable is very influential for family and living partner satisfaction, social comparison is even more important.

Glenn (1990) cited a few longitudinal studies showing a decline in marital satisfaction over time for couples with and without children. He claimed, correctly I think, that such studies indicate that at least some of the decline in marital satisfaction that has usually been regarded as a parenting effect may be more appropriately intepreted as a "duration-of-marriage effect".

Callan (1987, p.847) studied a small sample of mothers, voluntarily childless wives and infertile women, and found that the infertile women "reported more loving marital relationships" and "were generally more satisfied with their marriage than were mothers and the voluntarily childless. In contrast to other women, the voluntarily childless reported more time with their husbands, more exchanges of ideas, and higher levels of consensus."

Wright, Matlock and Matlock (1985) compared the lives of 42 parents of handicapped children with those of 42 parents of nonhandicapped children, and found that the former group "were six times as likely as parents of the nonhandicapped to indicate that their children caused marital problems" (p.38). Still, there were no significant differences between the two groups of parents in reported life satisfaction.

Marital satisfaction seems to reach its lowest level when young children are in the home, and then it rises slightly after they leave. "The postparental period is one of the happiest and most satisfying stages of life" (Cassidy 1985, p.435), although retirement brings a new range of problems. For example, Cassidy (1985) cited studies showing that women with retired husbands often report a loss of personal freedom. Her own research on 190 postparental women over 55 showed that the marital satisfaction of employed women but not of retired women was significantly affected by the prestige associated with the employed women's and their husbands' occupations.

Margolin and White (1987) studied the impact of "decreases in physical appearance normally associated with aging" in a national sample of 1509 married Americans under 60 years of age. Such changes affected husbands more than wives. Husbands' "sexual interest, happiness in the sexual relationship, and, to a lesser extent, unfaithfulness" were all unfavourably affected. Feingold (1990) applied meta-analyses to several studies involving 5 different research paradigms, and concluded that "men place greater value on physical attractiveness than do women" (p.981).

From the point of view of MDT and this project, the most interesting suggestion coming out of Margolin and White's research concerns the importance of social comparison. "The pattern of effects noted in this study," they wrote (p.26), "suggests that a simple gender effect is inadequate to explaining the importance of attractiveness for marital sexuality. If men as a category place more emphasis on partner's attractivenes (because of conditioning or because of biological predisposition), then we should expect to find that response to spouse's aging was independent of one's own aging. Instead, the results suggest a more complex exchange model in which changes in relative physical assets are more critical than absolute changes. That this change is more important for men suggests that there is, in fact, a double standard of aging and that men attach more importance than women to the changing balance of physical assets."

1.4   Exchange and Equity

Some people tend to have an exchange orientation in their interpersonal relationships, including their marriages. For these people their relationship and marital satisfaction is a function of the perceived equity of the exchange. For those with a communal orientation, considerable inequities might be tolerated without any significant effect on their relationships.

Clark and Reis (1988) cited studies showing that people reacted negatively when they thought they were in a communal relationship and received compensation for favours as if they were in an exchange relationship. Broderick and O'Leary (1986, p.516) found that for their sample of 50 couples, "Higher levels of positive feelings, commitment, and positive behavior were associated with higher levels of marital satisfaction. Conversely, greater exchange orientation and higher frequencies of negative behavior on the part of the spouse were correlated with lower levels of marital satisfaction." The moderate correlation they found between an exchange orientation and marital dissatisfaction was similar to that found by Jacobson (1983).

According to Clark and Reis (1988), equity theorists have identified at least 17 rules of exchange that some people perceive as just or fair, including such things as meeting one's own needs first, distribution by contribution and distribution by mutual need. Different rules may be invoked by people depending on the particular relationships involved, on particular goals, circumstances, gender, tasks and roles. As a result of this great complexity regarding the nature of equitable exchanges and distributions, the interpretation of equity assessments is extremely difficult, to say the least. At a minimum it requires one to be very cautious about the meaning of purported claims regarding the impact of equity on satisfaction or anything else.

Besides diverse rules of equitable exchange, there are a variety of things to be exchanged, again varying with circumstances, particular relationships, personalities and so on. For example, as a rule self-disclosure contributes to satisfying personal relationships, but the disclosure of feelings has a greater impact than the disclosure of information on marital satisfaction. In relationships defined by the participants "in an emotionally distanced manner", intimate self-disclosure may be harmful (Clark and Reis 1988, p.637).

In a study of 131 heterosexual student couples, Franzoi, Davis and Young (1985) showed that the more detailed and accurate information people have about themselves, the more they are inclined to self-disclosure and, consequently, the more satisfaction they are able to get out of social relations. They also reported that "Although self-disclosure increased the discloser's satisfaction, it had little impact on the recipients' feelings of satisfaction in the relationship. Together, these findings suggest that revealing private self-aspects to one's partner is a more important factor influencing satisfaction than is listening to similar disclosure from one's partner" (p.1592). Perhaps their most intriguing finding was that female attempts to appreciate the point of view of their male partners affected the latters' satisfaction, but male attempts to reciprocate had "no impact on female satisfaction". The traditional nurturers (females) were apparently unable to get any measurable satisfaction from being nurtured, while the traditionally nurtured (males) apparently enjoyed the full benefits of their role.

In the first volume of this treatise I reported several studies showing that equitable relationships are generally perceived to be more satisfying than inequitable relationships. Clark and Reis (1988) reported that people in such relationships are more confident of staying together, more content in the relationship and less likely to have extramarital sexual affairs. Women tend to be more distressed than men by being "overbenefited" and men tend to be more distressed than women by being "underbenefited". As well, they claimed that inequity tends to have a greater impact on men's than on women's emotions. Some support for this claim was reported in Volume One regarding life satisfaction and happiness, and further support is reported below regarding satisfaction with friendships and living partners. However, interesting disconfirmations are also reported below regarding satisfaction with one's friendships and one's own self-esteem. Some researchers have reported that the absolute level of benefits obtained by a partner is at least as important as the perceived equity that those benefits represent (Cate, Lloyd and Long 1988).

1.5   Roles and Expectations

Role theorists have tested several kinds of gap hypotheses. For example, it has been shown that marital satisfaction is to some extent a function of the perceived consistency between people's self-concepts and their various role requirements. In my terminology, such consistency would be described as a relatively small discrepancy between what one thinks about oneself and what is needed for some particular role. In short, role theorists are concerned with some sort of a self/needs gap.

Chassin, Zeiss, Cooper and Reaven (1985) hypothesized that one's own marital satisfaction might be affected by how much of a perceived gap one's spouse finds between oneself and one's role in marriage. For a sample of 83 dual-worker couples, these authors found that "the highest marital satisfaction was found for couples in which both spouses viewed themselves as either congruent or incongruent with the spouse role. If only one of the spouses showed self-spouse role congruence, marital satisfaction was lowered" (p.307). In another study involving 100 dual-worker couples, Cooper, Chassin and Zeiss (1985) found marital satisfaction positively associated with congruence between spouses sex-role attitudes.

Anson (1989, p.186) noted that "Marital status is related to social integration through the attaining of valued social roles and statuses and through the fulfillment of social expectations. At a certain age, 'married' is the socially preferred status and the socially valued role. Failure to acquire or maintain this status is a failure to live up to social norms and expectations".

Mashal (1985, p.41) claimed that "The sociological literature on marital role expectations and marital satisfaction has shown clearly that couples are happy if their marriage conforms to their own ideal of marriage...and if the spouses agree on the ideal form of the marriage... ." Mashal's own study of 20 couples revealed that "neither a patricentric nor a matricentric authority structure was associated with greater marital happiness. Joint power sharing, however, was strongly related to marital satisfaction. In regard to the couples' views of ideal power, the closer the approximation of actual authority and outcome power to their ideal, the greater was the marital happiness for both husbands and wives. Contrary to predictions, however, congruence of the spouses' view of the ideal authority distribution was unrelated to their conjugal harmony" (p.44).

Using a sample of 301 married Americans, Sabatelli and Pearce (1986) studied the relationships between the expectation and importance of 32 dimensions of married life. The dimensions covered such things as a partner's willingness to listen, trust, displayed affection, household responsibilities and sexual activity. There was considerable variation among the dimensions, with trust, for example, being most expected and important while jealousy expressed by a partner was least expected and moderately important. For females, but not for males, there were significant negative associations between expectations and age, length of marriage and number of marriages. For males, but not for females, there was a significant positive association between expectations and education. For both groups there was a significant positive association between expectations and perceived commitment to the marriage. In another study of expectations, Sabatelli (1988, p.220) provided evidence suggesting that "the relatively high and idealistic relationship expectations held by individuals before marriage may contribute to the drop in marital satisfaction typically noted after the 'honeymoon' period is past... ."

Thornton (1989) reviewed the National Opinion Research Center's General Social Survey of Americans from the late 1950s to the middle 1980s and found marked increases in egalitarian sentiments regarding sex roles and the family. He also found significant "weakening of the normative imperative to marry, to remain married, to have children, to restrict intimate relations to marriage, and to maintain separate roles for males and females" (p.873).

1.6   Self-Esteem and Satisfaction

While the primary focus of MDT is on the seven perceived discrepancies that to some extent mediate the impact of external circumstances on and cause reported subjective well-being, other partial mediators and causal influences have been investigated, extensively reviewed in Volume One, Chapter 2.4, and included in the theory. For example, several studies have noted the impact of self-esteem on subjective well-being (Robertson and Simons 1989), and MDT is designed with the causal arrows running in this direction. However, as indicated in Volume One, Chapter 2.4, a more realistic and complicated theory would have virtually all causal arrows running in both directions. That is to say, the systems I am attempting to understand and model are much more interactive than my theory shows. A good illustration of this point may be found by comparing the results of a fine study by Pelham and Swann (1989) to those reviewed in Robertson and Simons. Using a sample of 501 American undergraduates, Pelham and Swann showed that self-esteem was partly determined by the perceived "discrepancy between people's actual and ideal self-views". In my terminology, they showed that self-esteem was partly determined by the self/wants gap, which is the reverse of the relationship usually found and the one posited in MDT. In Chapter 5 it will be shown that MDT can be used to explain satisfaction with one's own self-esteem.

As indicated in Volume One, Chapter 6.2, separate measures of self-esteem and social support were taken in 8 of my country samples, but there was severe multicollinearity $(r=.88)$ between the scores for these variables. Further analyses raised so many unanswerable questions that I decided to leave the two measures out of the rest of the volumes in this treatise and deal with them in separate studies.

Research has shown that people with relatively low self-esteem tend to have relatively low performance expectancies on a variety of tasks, to avoid competition and diagnostic comparisons with others (Campbell, Fairey and Fehr 1986), to "experience more pain in response to negative feedback and more pleasure in response to positive feedback", to "overgeneralize the implications of negative feedback to other aspects of their identities" (Kernis, Brockner and Frankel (1989, p.707), and to be "generally more susceptible to the effects of self-relevant social cues" than are people with relatively high self-esteem (Campbell 1990, pp.539-539). Swann, Pelham and Krull (1989) designed some clever experiments showing that people are inclined to seek positive feedback (self-enhance) as much as they are inclined to seek accurate feedback (self-verify) about themselves, whether they are high or low in self-esteem. Confirming my own and others' findings (Volume One, Chapter 6.3) that most people perceive themselves to be at least as good as others on most attributes, even those with very low self-esteem in Swann, Pelham and Krull's sample of 486 American undergraduates "gave themselves above average ratings on most of the SAQ [Self-Attributes Questionnaire]" (p.784).

There is also evidence indicating that people compare themselves to others in fairly self-serving ways in order to make themselves feel better (Michalos 1985). Using a sample of 162 undergraduates, Campbell, Fairey and Fehr (1986) found that relatively high self-esteem subjects got more satisfaction from out-performing friends than they did from merely performing tasks well. Just as others have found in the case of satisfaction with one's salary or wages, relative superiority to some relevant other person or group is more important than any absolute values (Michalos 1986). Clark and Reis (1988) cited studies showing that the discovery that one's performance on a task is superior to that of a friend may be more or less satisfying depending on the perceived relevance of the task to one's self-definition.

In a study of 57 heterosexual undergraduate couples, Hendrick, Hendrick and Adler (1988) found that self-esteem was a positive predictor of relationship satisfaction for men but not for women. Men's, but not women's, self-esteem was also positively related to their partners' satisfaction. A follow-up review of a subsample of 30 of the couples two months after the original data were collected found that, among other things, couples who remained together were higher in self-esteem and relationship satisfaction than couples who broke up.

According to Snowden, Schott, Awalt and Gillis-Knox (1988), self-esteem belongs to a family of concepts including such things as self-confidence, self-efficacy and hardiness that give one hope and, in the words of Lazarus and Folkman (1984), "sustain coping efforts in the face of the most adverse conditions". Miller and Kirsch (1987) reviewed 200 studies dealing with a variety of marital problems and found no important gender differences in coping.

2

Satisfaction with One's Family Relations

2.1 Introduction

In this chapter MDT is used to explain satisfaction with one's family relations. In the next section (2.2), I review mean satisfaction scores for the world balanced sample, relatively developed and less developed countries, 39 countries, males and females. In Sections 2.3 and 2.4 family satisfaction is explained by MDT, respectively, for the world balanced sample taken as a whole, and for males and females taken separately. Section 2.5 summarizes results of using MDT to explain family satisfaction in 38 countries, including relatively developed and less developed countries, males and females. In the final section (2.6), MDT's prediction success ratios are reviewed for all the explanations offered in Section 2.5.

2.2 Descriptive Statistics for World Sample, Males and Females

On my questionnaire "family relations" were specified as the "kind of contact and frequency of contact you have with your family members. This includes personal contact, phone calls and letters". As indicated in Volume One, Chapter 3.3, all satisfaction ratings were obtained from my revised 7-step delightful-terrible scale that was originally developed by Andrews and Withey (1976). So, while I usually just talk about satisfaction, strictly speaking my data consist of reported numerical scores indicating students' perceived net satisfaction levels. In order to simplify the discussion, I usually refer to differences among the means of such scores without indicating whether or not the differences are statistically significant. Broadly speaking, one may assume that the difference between any two mean scores considered here is statistically significant at the .05 level if for each group N > 200, their standard deviations are sd = 1.2 and the difference is at least .3, or for each group N > 350, sd = 1.2 and the difference is at least .2. Because differences of .1 between two mean scores are statistically significant at the .05 level whenever N>2000 and sd=1.2 for each group, all of the differences referred to regarding my world balanced sample scores are statistically significant.

Exhibit 2.1 lists the mean and standard deviation scores,

Exhibit 2.1 Participating countries' mean and standard deviation scores, and sample sizes for satisfaction with one's family life

Country	Mean	SD	N
Austria	5.0	1.3	345
Bahrain	5.8	1.4	281
Bangladesh+	5.6	1.3	263
Belgium	5.1	1.2	150
Brazil	5.6	1.3	281
Cameroon	4.8	1.1	182
Canada	5.4	1.2	1634
Chile	5.3	1.2	263
Colombia	5.2	1.1	91
Egypt+	5.4	1.4	279
Finland	5.7	1.1	268
Germany	5.0	1.2	797
Greece	5.4	1.1	257
Hungary	5.3	1.0	228
India+	5.5	1.2	256
Israel	5.6	1.2	317
Japan	5.0	1.3	1189
Jordan	5.7	1.3	296
Kenya+	5.2	1.2	270
Korea	5.1	1.4	449
Mexico	5.3	1.1	244
Netherlands	5.3	1.3	352
New Zealand	5.2	1.3	323
Norway	5.2	1.1	230
Philippines	5.4	1.2	1004
Portugal	5.4	1.1	388
Puerto Rico	5.5	1.1	306
Singapore	4.8	1.1	256
S. Africa	5.5	1.1	285
Spain	4.9	1.0	276
Sweden	5.4	1.1	265

Exhibit 2.1 (continued)

Country	Mean	SD	N
Switzerland	5.2	1.2	340
Taiwan	5.2	1.1	2476
Tanzania+	5.4	1.0	227
Thailand	5.5	1.3	581
Turkey+	5.1	1.3	297
U. Kingdom	5.5	1.0	223
USA	5.5	1.3	1343
Yugoslavia	5.3	1.3	332
Total Mean	5.3	1.2	458
Dev.C.Mean	5.3	1.2	493
L.D.C.Mean	5.4	1.2	265
World	5.3	1.2	8998

+ Below 142-country median on per capita GNP and literacy rate.

and sample sizes for satisfaction with one's family relations for my 39 participating countries. The last row of the table gives the figures for my balanced world sample. The family satisfaction mean and standard deviation for this sample are 5.3 and 1.2, respectively, with an N=8998. In fact, those are the same figures for the means of the mean and standard deviation scores for the 39 countries, indirectly representing a total sample of N=17,844. On the 7-step scale, a score of 5 is labeled "satisfying" and a score of 6 is labeled "very satisfying".

The two rows above the last give the results of separating out the 6 less developed countries (LDCs) from the 33 relatively developed countries (RDCs). The mean family satisfaction score of the LDCs (5.4) is slightly higher than the mean score of the RDCs and the world mean (5.3), while the standard deviations are all the same (1.2). Only 2 (33%) of the 6 LDCs (Turkey=5.1, Kenya=5.2) had mean family satisfaction scores below the world mean, while 14 (42%) RDCs had such scores.

These results differ from those reported by others (Volume One, Chapter 1.5) showing a tendency for people in economically relatively well-off countries to report higher levels of life satisfaction and happiness or, more generally, subjective well-being than people in countries that are economically relatively less well-off. Given the relatively greater importance of family cohesion in less than in more relatively greater importance of family cohesion in less than in more industrialized countries, I suppose one might have expected students in the former countries to get more satisfaction from their family relations than students in the latter countries. These data confirm that expectation.

Rather than attempt to comment on the scores for each of the 39 countries, I will continue the practice adopted in Volume One of mentioning those in about the top and bottom 10%. (Usually there are more than 4 countries (10% of 39) to be mentioned at the top and bottom because of matching scores.) There were 6 countries clustered around the top 10% for mean family satisfaction scores, namely, Bahrain=5.8, Finland and Jordan=5.7, and Bangladesh, Brazil and Israel=5.6. Bangladesh's family satisfaction score was 42% of one standard deviation above the world mean.

There were also 6 countries clustered around the bottom 10% for family satisfaction scores, namely, Cameroon and Singapore=4.8, Spain=4.9, and Austria, Germany and Japan=5.0. Cameroon and Singapore's score of 4.8 was 42% of one standard deviation below the world mean.

Exhibit 2.2 lists the mean and standard deviation scores, and sample sizes for satisfaction with one's family relations for males and females in my 39 countries. The last row of the table gives the figures for my balanced world sample. The family satisfaction mean and standard deviation for this sample of males (N=4594) are 5.3 and 1.2, respectively, and for females (N=4404) the corresponding figures are 5.4 and 1.2. Thus, females seem to have slightly more family satisfaction than males, although this is qualified below.

The fourth row from the last in this exhibit (total mean) shows that the means of the mean and standard deviation scores for the 39 countries for males and females are exactly the same as the figures for the world balanced sample. However, the sample sizes indirectly represented by the figures in the fourth row from the last are about twice as big as those for the last row. For the former, there were N=8968 males and N=8860 females.

The two rows above the last give the results of separating out the 6 LDCs from the 33 RDCs. For males, the mean of the family satisfaction scores of the LDCs (5.4) is higher than the world mean (5.3) and higher still than the mean of the RDCs (5.2). For females, the mean of the family satisfaction scores of the LDCs (5.3) is lower than the world mean and the mean of the RDCs (5.4).

For males, only one (17%) of the 6 LDCs (Turkey=5.2) had a family satisfaction score below the world mean, while 13 (39%) RDCs had such scores. For females, 4 (66%) of the 6 LDCs

Exhibit 2.2 Participating countries' mean and standard deviation
scores, and sample sizes for satisfaction with one's family life for
males and females

Country	Males Mean	SD	N	Females Mean	SD	N
Austria	4.9	1.3	138	5.1	1.3	207
Bahrain	6.0	1.3	57	5.8	1.4	224
Bangladesh+	5.5	1.4	175	5.7	1.2	88
Belgium	4.9	1.3	84	5.4	1.1	66
Brazil	5.5	1.4	113	5.6	1.3	168
Cameroon	4.6	1.1	143	5.1	1.0	39
Canada	5.4	1.2	629	5.4	1.2	1001
Chile	5.3	1.2	143	5.3	1.1	120
Colombia	5.1	1.1	55	5.3	1.1	36
Egypt+	5.4	1.3	157	5.3	1.5	122
Finland	5.4	1.0	107	5.9	1.1	161
Germany	4.9	1.1	433	5.1	1.3	364
Greece	5.5	1.1	144	5.4	1.0	113
Hungary	5.1	1.0	59	5.4	1.0	169
India+	5.4	1.3	158	5.5	1.2	98
Israel	5.6	1.2	163	5.6	1.2	154
Japan	5.0	1.3	973	5.2	1.3	216
Jordan	5.7	1.3	237	5.8	1.2	59
Kenya+	5.3	1.1	154	5.0	1.4	116
Korea	5.2	1.4	354	5.0	1.5	95
Mexico	5.3	1.0	172	5.4	1.2	71
Netherlands	5.4	1.1	159	5.3	1.4	193
New Zealand	5.2	1.3	116	5.2	1.3	207
Norway	5.3	1.0	87	5.2	1.1	143
Philippines	5.5	1.2	320	5.3	1.2	684
Portugal	5.3	1.1	201	5.4	1.1	184
Puerto Rico	5.6	1.0	170	5.4	1.1	136
Singapore	4.4	1.5	43	4.9	1.0	213
S. Africa	5.4	1.2	126	5.5	1.0	159
Spain	4.7	1.1	136	5.0	1.0	140
Sweden	5.3	1.2	139	5.5	1.1	126
Switzerland	5.1	1.2	172	5.4	1.2	168
Taiwan	5.2	1.1	1282	5.2	1.1	1194
Tanzania+	5.4	1.0	156	5.3	0.8	71
Thailand	5.3	1.3	265	5.6	1.3	316

Exhibit 2.2 (continued)

Country	Males			Females		
	Mean	SD	N	Mean	SD	N
Turkey+	5.2	1.3	198	5.1	1.4	91
U. Kingdom	5.3	1.0	104	5.7	0.9	119
USA	5.3	1.3	469	5.5	1.3	874
Yugoslavia	5.3	1.3	177	5.3	1.3	155
Total Mean	5.3	1.2	230	5.4	1.2	227
Dev.C.Mean	5.2	1.2	242	5.4	1.2	251
L.D.C.Mean	5.4	1.2	166	5.3	1.3	98
World	5.3	1.2	4594	5.4	1.2	4404

+ Below 142-country median on per capita GNP and literacy rate.

(Kenya=5.0, Turkey=5.1, Egypt and Tanzania=5.3) had scores below the world mean, while 15 (46%) RDCs had such scores.

Generally speaking, then, on the basis of the figures in the previous two paragraphs, it seems fair to say that the family satisfaction of females in LDCs is probably lower than that of females in RDCS, while the reverse is true for males, i.e., the family satisfaction of males in LDCs is probably higher than that of males in RDCs. It also seems fair to say that the family satisfaction of females in RDCs is probably higher than that of males in RDCs, while the reverse is true for LDCs, i.e., the family satisfaction of females in LDCs is lower than that of males in LDCs. Thus, it may be the case that the slightly higher female family satisfaction scores in the world balanced sample is the result of the fact that 85% of the countries in the sample are RDCs. However, before one endorses this conclusion, one ought to recall that in Volume One, Exhibits 4.4 and 4.5 it was shown that females have slightly higher life satisfaction and happiness scores than males in the world balanced sample, the total sample, RDCs and LDCs. Hence, it may also be the case that things are as they first appeared to be, namely, that on average around the world females have slightly higher levels of family satisfaction than males. If I had to bet, I would favour the hypothesis that my world balanced sample scores reflect some RDC bias. Nevertheless, in the absence of any other information, I would still regard my world balanced sample scores for the whole group and for males and females taken separately as a plausible set of *norms* for university undergraduates until a better set is obtained.

For males, the 4 countries in the top 10% for family satisfaction scores were Bahrain=6.0, Jordan=5.7, Israel and Puerto Rico=5.6. For females, the 5 top countries were Finland=5.9, Bahrain and Jordan=5.8, Bangladesh and the United Kingdom=5.7. For males, Bahrain's score was 58% of one standard deviation above the world mean, and for females Finland's score was 42% of a standard deviation above the world mean.

For males, there were 6 countries clustered around the bottom 10% for family satisfaction scores, namely, Singapore=4.4, Cameroon=4.6, Spain=4.7, and Austria, Belgium and Germany=4.9. For females, the 4 bottom countries were Singapore=4.9, Kenya, Korea and Spain=5.0. The Singapore scores were 75% and 42% of one standard deviation below the world means for males and females, respectively.

Considering the results reported in the previous two paragraphs together, it is clear that male family satisfaction scores had a wider range (6.0-4.4=1.6) than their female counterparts (5.9-4.9=1.0).

2.3 Satisfaction Explained by MDT for World Sample

Exhibit 2.3 is the correlation matrix for the variables employed in this chapter. Definitions of all the abbreviations in this and other tables may be found in Appendix 1. There are 7 cases of moderate (r>.50) multicollinearity among the predictors. As indicated in Volume One, although multicollinearity does not have any impact on the squared multiple correlation coefficients, it can seriously distort regression coefficients and even reverse their signs. With respect to all of the discrepancy variables except self/future, I have never encountered a case in which the signs of these variables' regression coefficients were negative. The sign for self\future is often negative because, I think, the item was poorly worded. Maybe there is some shifting of the apparent influence of some of these variables in some of my samples, but it is unlikely that there is serious distortion regarding their influence in the world sample.

Exhibit 2.4 gives the results of using MDT to explain satisfaction with one's family relations in the world balanced sample. In the left side column under S there are listed the numbers of students in the sample (N) for the whole group, and males and females taken separately. Each of the nine columns from that labeled

Exhibit 2.3 Correlation matrix for satisfaction with one's family relations*

	SX	AG	WS	LD	B	SO	SD	SN	SP	SF	SB	SW
SX	-											
AG	9	-										
WS	ns	12	-									
LD	2	36	ns	-								
B	ns	4	14	5	-							
SO	2	5	2	3	3	-						
SD	ns	6	3	ns	ns	52	-					
SN	ns	6	4	ns	ns	55	62	-				
SP	5	2	3	ns	2	49	49	55	-			
SF	ns	ns	6	5	4	22	30	30	32	-		
SB	6	ns	5	2	ns	43	41	44	56	29	-	
SW	3	2	4	ns	3	63	46	51	46	22	43	-
FA	3	4	2	ns	3	63	46	50	46	20	42	67

* Decimal points omitted; underlined figures indicate negative correlations; P = .05 or better; N = 9092; ns = not significant.

S to that labeled SB gives the results of a stepwise regression of the labeled item on the variables listed below it. A single application of MDT requires 8 regressions. A complete set runs from S to SB. The squared multiple correlation coefficient (R^2) is given below each distinct N, indicating a separate regression equation. For example, in the column under S (in this context, for "satisfaction with one's family relations") we find a total sample N of 7934 students, including 3994 males and 3940 females. MDT explained 55% of the variance in reported family satisfaction scores for the whole group, 54% for males and 56% for females.

As explained in Volume One, we are interested in the percent of variance explained in satisfaction scores by all the predictors collectively and the relative impacts of the various predictors individually. The impacts with which we are especially concerned are the sums of direct and indirect effects, which are called total effects or effect coefficients (Pedhazur 1982). The *direct effects* of a predictor variable on a dependent variable are indicated by the beta values of the predictors when the dependent variable is regressed on them. The

Exhibit 2.4 Satisfaction with one's family relations
(decimal points omitted)

World
Total Balanced Sample

	S	SW	SO	SD	SN	SP	SF	SB	TES	TESW
N	7934	7990	8675	8603	8702	8678	8623	8686	-	-
R^2	55	47	1	1	1	1	1	1	-	-
Pred										
Sex	0	0	0	0	0	0	0	6	1	1
Age	0	3	-8	-6	-6	5	0	0	-4	-1
WS	0	0	0	-3	-3	-3	6	-5	-2	-1
LED	0	-3	6	0	0	0	4	3	2	0
ETH	-4	4	-3	0	0	2	-3	0	-3	3
SO	26	43							44	43
SD	5	8							8	8
SN	7	14							13	14
SP	6	7							9	7
SB	5	11							10	11
SW	41								41	
Males										
N	3994	4025	4417	0	4437	0	4402	0	-	-
R^2	54	46	1	0	1	0	1	0	-	-
Age	0	4	-8	0	-6	0	0	0	-3	0
WS	0	0	0	0	-4	0	4	0	0	-1
LED	0	-4	6	0	0	0	7	0	1	-1
ETH	-4	5	0	0	0	0	-5	0	-2	5
SO	26	45							44	45
SD	5	7							8	7
SN	6	13							11	13
SP	6	4							8	4
SB	5	13							10	13
SW	40								40	
Females										
N	3940	3965	4258	4213	0	0	4221	0	-	-
R^2	56	47	1	1	0	0	1	0	-	-
Age	0	0	-6	-6	0	0	0	0	-3	-3
WS	0	0	0	-3	0	0	8	0	0	0
LED	0	0	6	0	0	0	0	0	3	3
ETH	-4	4	-6	0	0	0	0	0	-5	2
SO	27	41							44	41

Exhibit 2.4 (continued)

	S	SW	SO	SD	SN	SP	SF	SB	TES	TESW
SD	4	8							7	8
SN	8	15							14	15
SP	6	10							10	10
SF	3	0							3	0
SB	6	9							10	9
SW	41								41	

indirect effects of a predictor on a dependent variable are indicated by the joint product of the path coefficients (beta values) connecting the predictor variables to the dependent variable via mediating variables. The *total effects* are measured by the sum of the direct and all indirect effects. (A more detailed account of direct, indirect and total effects may be found in Volume One, Chapter 6.2.) In Exhibit 2.4 these figures are given in the column under TES, which in this context is short for "total effects on satisfaction with one's family relations scores". TESW is short for "total effects on self/wants gap scores".

Most of the column entries in Exhibit 2.4 are standardized regression coefficients or beta values, with decimal places omitted. The zeros in the columns from S to SB indicate that an explanatory variable had no direct effect on the dependent variable statistically significant at the 95% level of confidence or better. Any zeros in the last two columns (under TES and TESW) indicate that an explanatory variable had no total effect on the dependent variable. When an explanatory variable had no influence on anything, it was simply deleted from the table.

For example, all things considered, for the group as a whole, age has a negative impact on satisfaction with one's family relations (-.04, TES column) and on the gap between what one has and wants regarding such relations (-.01, TESW column). Because the variables in the regression equations are standardized with means of zero and standard deviations of one, the -.04 figure literally means that an increase of one standard deviation in age scores produces a decrease of 4 percent of one standard deviation in family satisfaction scores, when the values of all the other variables in the equation are held constant. Figuratively speaking, if the impact of all other variables is held constant, one could say that as one's age increases a full step, one's family satisfaction decreases four percent of a step and the gap between what one has and wants regarding family relations decreases one percent of a step. Clearly, these results are very different from those that would have been found if one considered only direct effects. In the latter case one would have said that age has no effect on family satisfaction (0, S column) and a positive effect on the self/wants gap (.03, SW column). However, age has a significant negative impact on the gaps regarding self/others (-.08), self/deserved (-.06) and self/needs (-.06), as well as a positive impact on self/progress (.05), and all of these impacts must be calculated into the total effect of age on family satisfaction. When that calculation is made, the overall impact of age on family satisfaction for university undergraduates is shown to be modest and negative.

One might have expected age to be negatively related to the gaps concerning social comparisons, equity and needs. Regarding social comparisons, the role and consequences of being an undergraduate student might put more strain on one's family relations as one's age increases, e.g., a 20 year old undergraduate is not but a 40 year old undergraduate is unusual and appears so to his or her peers. Because of their unusual circumstances, older students might also feel that they deserve more sympathy and encouragement than they get from their families, and they might have unmet family needs or other responsibilities that younger undergraduates do not have. On the other hand, as a student's age increases, he or she should have been able to make a relatively more accurate estimate three years earlier of how his or her family life would be at the later point in time. So, one should have expected a positive association between age and the self/progress gap, which is just what we found.

Reading down the TES column in Exhibit 2.4, one finds that besides age, the number of hours students work per week (WS=-.02) and their country of birth (ETH=-.03) also have negative impacts on family satisfaction. The impact of the work status variable for students is understandable. The more time one must devote to paid employment, the less time one has for other things, including family relations.

As explained in Volume One, Chapter 6.2, for the world sample, ethnicity (ETH) was measured by country of birth, and each country was assigned a numerical value based on its alphabetical rank order from Austria to Yugoslavia. If the country list in Volume One, Exhibit 3.2 is divided in half, with countries from Austria to Kenya in one half and those from Korea to Yugoslavia in the second half, those in the latter group are relatively advantaged compared to those in the former group. The mean rank order of 1983 per capita GNP for the latter group is 44, compared to 53 for the former, and the mean literacy rate rank order for the latter group is 34, compared to 49 for the former. Thus, what the total effect figure of -.03 in Exhibit 2.4 tells us is consistent with what we found in the previous section. In that section we found that students in LDCs probably had slightly higher levels of family satisfaction than students in RDCs. Here we fine that being born in a country with a relatively superior per capita GNP and literacy rate has a modest and negative impact on satisfaction with one's family relations.

Rounding out the demographic picture, the total effects of one's sex (SEX=.01) and level of university education (LED=.02) are also relatively low, but positive. The former figure is consistent with what we found in the previous section. In my analysis, males were scored as one point and females as two. So, the TES figure for sex tells us that being female has a slightly positive impact on one's family satisfaction. The TES figure for level of university education is not comparable to any figures previously cited.

The relatively modest importance of demographic variables as predictors becomes even more apparent in the presence of discrepancy variables. All things considered, with regard to family satisfaction, the self/others gap (SO=.44) has the greatest impact, followed by self/wants (SW=.41). So, in the given set of predictors, social comparisons are 11 times more important to family satisfaction than the most influential demographic variable, age, and aspirations are 10 times more important. Self/needs (SN=.13) enters in third place, followed by a cluster running in succession from self/best (SB=.10) to self/progress (SP=.09) to self/deserved (SD=.08). Thus, in the given set of discrepancy predictors, equity considerations have the smallest impact and fulfilled expectations are only slightly more important to family satisfaction. The self/future gap had no impact on family satisfaction or anything else. So, it (SF) is not listed among the predictors.

Having determined the relative influence of the various predictors on family satisfaction for the group as a whole, our next task is to examine their relative influence on the perceived gap between the sort of family relations students have and want. From the column under SW it is clear that my set of predictors explains 47% of the variance in self/wants scores. Returning to TESW, one finds that it is social comparison scores (SO=.43) that dominate the lot of predictors. The next most influential predictors occur in two clusters. First, there are self/needs (SN=.14) and self/best (SB=.11), and then self/deserved (SD=.08) and self/progress (SP=.07).

The impact of the demographic variables is again relatively

modest, although there is one surprise. Ethnicity (operationalized as country of birth) has a positive rather than a negative impact on the self/wants gap (ETH=.03). Recall (from Volume One, Chapter 3.3) that the self/wants items asked students to indicate how well their lives or various domains of their lives measured up to what they wanted. In the present case, for example, a score of one indicated that their current family relations were not at all what they wanted, a score of four indicated that their relations were running about half as well as what they wanted, and a score of seven indicated that their current relations matched or were better than what they wanted. Thus, all things considered, the ETH=.03 figure here indicates that being born in a relatively advantaged country is positively related to closing the gap between what one has and wants regarding family relations. That is confusing because closing the self/wants gap is also positively related to family satisfaction, while being born in a relatively advantaged country is negatively related to such satisfaction. It is easy to see that the differences in the ethnicity figures in the TES and TESW columns merely reflect the direct effect differences shown in the S and SW columns, but I cannot explain the latter diffferences.

Considering the total effects listed in the columns under TES and TESW for the group as a whole, it is fair to say that social comparisons and aspiration/achievement gaps are generally the two most influential contributors to satisfaction with one's family relations. The self/needs gap, which roughly represents the basic hypothesis of person-environment fit theory (Volume One, Chapter 2.2), comes in a fairly distant third. In the given set of predictors, each of the first two variables is three times as influential as the self/needs gap, and four times as influential as the gaps regarding self/best, self/progress and self/deserved.

2.4 Satisfaction Explained by MDT for Males and Females

Age and ethnicity have relatively small negative impacts on satisfaction with one's family relations for males (Age=-.03; ETH=-.02) and females (Age=-.03; ETH=-.05). Level of university education has a modest positive impact for males (LED=.01) and females (LED=.03), and work status has no impact at all for the two groups considered separately.

Considering perceived discrepancies relative to family satisfaction, the rank orderings of the three most influential predictors for males and females are exactly the same as the ordering for the group as a whole. Indeed, the numerical values are almost the same. For males, we have self/others (SO=.44), self/wants (SW=.40) and self/needs (SN=.11), while for females we have SO=.44, SW=.41 and SN=.14. After these triads, for males self/best runs a distant fourth (SB=.10), followed by self/deserved and self/progress (SD=SP=.08). For females, following the initial triad we have self/best and self/progress tied (SB=SP=.10), then self/deserved (SD=.07) and finally self/future (SF=.03). In my analysis, self/future score values were reversed so that higher scores indicated a smaller perceived gap and a brighter future. So, a positive relation between self/future and family satisfaction scores indicates that the more a student expects to get out of his or her family relations in five years (the more promising or hopeful the relations seem to be), the more satisfaction he or she gets out of those relations at the time of the survey.

It is perhaps worth noting here that while the self/deserved variable was a bit more important than the self/needs variable for the life satisfaction and happiness of males (Volume One, Chapter 6.2), and the reverse was true for females, in the case of family satisfaction the self/needs variable is more important than the self/deserved variable for both groups. In fact, the equity variable comes in fifth for both groups, with almost the same numerical value in each case. Thus, from the point of view of satisfaction with one's family relations, the evidence here indicates that, relative to the other six discrepancies, equity considerations are not very important predictors.

Considering the relative impacts of my predictors on the gaps between what one has and wants regarding family relations, the self/others gap is three times as influential as its next rival for males (SO=.45) and almost three times as influential as its next rival for females (SO=.41). Self/needs and self/best are tied for second place for males (SN=SB=.13), while the former stands alone in second place for females (SN=.15). Equity comes in third for males (SD=.07), with ethnicity (ETH=.05) and self/progress (SP=.04) close behind. For females, third place is occupied by a cluster consisting of self/progress (SP=.10), self/best (SB=.09) and self/deserved (SD=.08).

2.5 Thirty-Eight Countries

Exhibit 2.5 shows the percent of variance explained by MDT in satisfaction with one's family relations scores for 38 countries,

Exhibit 2.5 Percent of variance explained by MDT in satisfaction
with one's family relations

Country	Total	Males	Females
Austria	72	72	71
Bahrain	44	-	46
Bangladesh+	63	59	69
Belgium	67	-	-
Brazil	58	59	56
Cameroon	50	57	-
Canada	64	62	65
Chile	49	50	49
Colombia	-	-	-
Egypt+	47	39	53
Finland	63	61	62
Germany	64	63	64
Greece	48	46	50
Hungary	61	-	61
India+	37	40	-
Israel	61	54	71
Japan	55	56	54
Jordan	43	43	-
Kenya+	58	44	70
Korea	59	56	-
Mexico	44	49	-
Netherlands	67	58	71
New Zealand	68	62	72
Norway	59	-	62
Philippines	57	62	54
Portugal	52	57	-
Puerto Rico	61	59	63
Singapore	72	-	70
S. Africa	34	33	37
Spain	55	58	51
Sweden	69	67	72
Switzerland	71	69	74
Taiwan	41	38	44
Tanzania+	42	46	-
Thailand	47	38	52
Turkey+	46	63	-
U. Kingdom	58	66	50

Exhibit 2.5 (continued)

Country	Total	Males	Females
USA	65	64	65
Yugoslavia	54	59	58
Total Mean	56	55	60
Dev.C.Mean	57	56	59
L.D.C.Mean	49	49	64
World	55	54	56

+ Below 142-country median on per capita GNP and literacy rate.

developed and less developed countries, and the world sample. The detailed regressions on which these figures are based are in Appendix 2. On average the total mean figures for all countries under-estimate the world sample figures by about 2 percentage points. The mean percent of variance explained in family satisfaction scores for 38 countries is 56%, compared to a world balanced sample figure of 55%. For males, the mean of the mean family satisfaction scores for 38 countries is 55%, compared to a world sample score of 54%. For females, the mean figure is 60%, compared to 56% for the global sample figure.

For the group as a whole and for males, MDT did a relatively better job accounting for family satisfaction in RDCs than in LDCs. For females, the reverse was true. On average the mean figures for RDCs for the whole group and males were 8 percentage points higher than those for LDCs, while for females the mean figure for RDCs was 5 percentage points lower than that for LDCs. Specifically, MDT accounted for an average of 57% of the variance in family satisfaction scores for the whole group of RDCs and 49% for LDCs. For males, the average percent of variance explained by MDT in RDCs was 56%, compared to 49% in LDCs. For females, MDT explained 59% of the variance in family satisfaction scores in RDCs and 64% in LDCs.

For the whole group, percents of variance explained in scores indicating satisfaction with one's family relations ranged from a high of 72% in Austria and Singapore to a low of 34% for South Africa. There was only one other country figure in the 70s (Switzerland=71%) and only one other in the 30s (India=37%). There were a full dozen country figures in the 60s. Altogether, there were 7 countries in which MDT accounted for over two-thirds of the variance in family satisfaction scores, namely, Austria and Singapore = 72%, Switzerland = 71%, Sweden = 69%, New Zealand = 68%, and Belgium and the Netherlands = 67%. The United States was close to these countries with 65%.

For males, family satisfaction percents of variance explained ranged from a high of 72% for Austria to a low of 33% for South Africa. There were no other male figures in the 70s, but there were 3 other male figures in the 30s, namely, Egypt = 39%, Taiwan and Thailand = 38%. Although there were 10 male figures in the 60s, only 3 of them reached the two-thirds level; Switzerland = 69%, Sweden = 67% and the United Kingdom = 66%. Altogether, then, 33% of the male figures were above 60% and 12% were above the two-thirds level.

For females, family satisfaction percents of variance explained ranged from a high of 74% for Switzerland to a low of 37% for South Africa. There were 7 other female figures in the 70s; New Zealand and Sweden = 72%, Austria, Israel and the Netherlands = 71%, and Kenya and Singapore = 70%. Altogether there were 16 female figures above 60% and 9 above the two-thirds level. Because there were only 29 countries with sufficient numbers of females to justify running regressions, 55% of the female figures were above 60% and 31% were above the two-thirds level.

Considering the results reviewed in this section, then, so far as explained variance in family satisfaction is concerned, it is clear that MDT performed much better for females than for males.

2.6 Prediction Success Ratios

Exhibit 2.6 lists the prediction success ratios for MDT in explanations of satisfaction with one's family relations for 38 countries, developed and less developed countries and the world balanced sample. Two ratios are presented for each case and these are entered in the exhibit in double columns. The first figure in each column gives the ratio of successful to total predicted *total effects*. I refer to such figures as "narrow prediction success ratios" or "narrow ratios" for short. If predictions made from MDT were 100% successful, then every relationship predicted by the theory would be statistically significant. So, if MDT were 100% successful, for every country there would be 12 hits in the column under TES for the country totals, and 11 hits for males and females. Thus, the 92% figure beginning the last row of Exhibit 2.6 indicates that in accounting for family satisfaction in the balanced world sample MDT made 11 hits out of 12 possibilities

Exhibit 2.6 Prediction success ratios for MDT in explanations of
satisfaction with one's family relations*

Country	Total		Males		Females	
Austria	75	28	55	18	73	24
Bahrain	42	15	-	-	36	18
Bangladesh+	58	19	55	13	46	18
Belgium	50	17	-	-	-	-
Brazil	50	19	36	13	46	13
Cameroon	42	11	46	13	-	-
Canada	67	32	73	22	64	29
Chile	42	13	36	11	46	16
Colombia	-	-	-	-	-	-
Egypt+	42	13	18	09	36	13
Finland	58	17	46	11	46	13
Germany	50	23	73	31	55	22
Greece	50	17	55	18	50	16
Hungary	58	21	-	-	55	20
India+	67	23	64	22	-	-
Israel	58	17	46	18	55	24
Japan	75	34	82	33	46	18
Jordan	42	13	36	18	-	-
Kenya+	58	13	36	09	36	16
Korea	67	21	55	16	-	-
Mexico	50	15	46	18	-	-
Netherlands	75	19	55	24	73	22
New Zealand	67	19	55	16	55	18
Norway	75	23	-	-	82	22
Philippines	58	30	46	13	46	27
Portugal	67	19	64	27	-	-
Puerto Rico	25	09	27	13	36	13
Singapore	50	21	-	-	55	16
S. Africa	42	17	46	16	46	13
Spain	58	19	46	13	46	16
Sweden	42	15	55	20	64	22
Switzerland	67	21	46	16	46	16
Taiwan	83	40	82	31	73	27
Tanzania+	25	17	27	18	-	-
Thailand	58	26	36	24	46	22
Turkey+	67	28	73	33	-	-
U. Kingdom	50	23	36	20	36	20
USA	100	34	55	18	91	33

Exhibit 2.6 (continued)

Country	Total		Males		Females	
Yugoslavia	67	26	82	29	55	18
Total Mean	57	21	51	19	53	20
Dev.C.Mean	58	21	52	19	54	20
L.D.C.Mean	53	19	46	17	39	16
World	92	59	82	49	91	44

* The first figures in each column give the ratio of successful to total predicted total effects. The second figures give the ratio of successful to total predicted direct effects in the 8 regressions required for an application of MDT.
+ Below 142-country median on per capita GNP and literacy rate.

(column under TES, Exhibit 2.4). That is, MDT had a narrow prediction success ratio of 92% for the world sample explanation of family satisfaction, taking males and females together. For males, MDT had a narrow ratio of 82% (9/11 hits, column under TES, Exhibit 2.4), and for females MDT was 91% successful (10/11 hits).

The second figure in each double column of Exhibit 2.6 gives the ratio of successful to total predicted *direct effects* in the 8 regression equations required for an application of MDT. I refer to such figures as "broad prediction success ratios" or simply "broad ratios". If MDT were 100% successful, for every country there would be 53 hits in the columns from S to SB for the country totals, and 45 hits for males and females. Thus, the 59% figure in the last row of the exhibit indicates that in accounting for family satisfaction in the world sample MDT made 31 hits out of 53 possibilities (columns under S to SB, Exhibit 2.4). That is, MDT had a broad prediction success ratio of 59% for the world sample explanation of satisfaction with one's family relations, taking males and females together. For males, MDT had a broad ratio of 49% (22/45 hits, columns under S to SB for males, Exhibit 2.4), and for females it had a broad ratio of 44%.

As explained in Volume One, since both direct and indirect effects are obtained in the interest of measuring total effects or effect coefficients, it is probably reasonable and fair to regard narrow prediction success ratios as more important than their broad counterparts. From this point of view, MDT looks very good. Its narrow prediction success ratio never dropped below 82% for the world balanced sample, and two-thirds of the time it was above 90%.

On the other hand, if one thinks that the broad prediction success ratios are as important as the others, then MDT does not look as good as it did. Still, the whole group figure of 59% for family satisfaction is probably good compared to average social scientific theories, and even the male and female figures of 49% and 44%, respectively, are probably at least average if not better than average.

Examination of the total mean prediction success ratios in Exhibit 2.6 (fourth row from the last) reveals a considerable drop in all figures compared to the world balanced sample figures. For example, instead of a family satisfaction narrow ratio of 92% for the whole, we have a total mean figure of 57%. The average total mean broad ratio is only 20%. The developed country mean prediction success ratios are all higher than the less developed country mean ratios.

In spite of the relatively low average performance of MDT for the 38 countries (compared to its performance in the world sample), there were some notable successes. With respect to family satisfaction for males and females together, MDT had a narrow prediction success ratio of 100% for the United States, 83% for Taiwan, and 75% for Austria, Japan, the Netherlands and Norway. Altogether narrow ratios above 60% were obtained in 13 (34%) countries. For males, MDT achieved narrow ratios of 82% for Japan, Taiwan and Yugoslavia, and 73% for Canada, Germany and Turkey. For females, the figures reached 91% for the United States, 82% for Norway, and 73% for Austria, the Netherlands and Taiwan. In 24% of the countries MDT obtained ratios above 60% for both male and female groups analyzed separately.

MDT's lowest narrow ratio for the whole group was 25% for Puerto Rico and Tanzania. For males, the lowest ratio was 18% for Egypt, and for females it was 36% for Bahrain, Egypt, Kenya, Puerto Rico and the United Kingdom.

The fact that the total mean prediction success ratios are so radically different from the world balanced sample ratios implies that the former would have provided a very misleading estimate of the latter. Because the world sample is so much more varied and larger than any of the country samples on which the total mean prediction success ratios are based, I believe results obtained from the world sample are probably more reliable and valid than those obtained from calculating averages of all the country samples. Hence, I did not calculate average total effect scores for all the predictors for all the countries. Along with the world sample percents of variance explained, I regard this sample's narrow prediction success ratios as our best estimates of MDT's acceptability as a theory of subjective well-being in general or of satisfaction and happiness in particular. The total effect scores for the various predictors in the world sample are our best estimates of the relative explanatory power of each predictor in the presence of the others.

3

Satisfaction with One's Friendships

3.1 Introduction

In this chapter MDT is used to explain satisfaction with one's friendships. In the next section (3.2), I review mean satisfaction scores for the world balanced sample, relatively developed and less developed countries, 39 countries, males and females. In Sections 3.3 and 3.4 friendship satisfaction is explained by MDT, respectively, for the world balanced sample taken as a whole, and for males and females taken separately. Section 3.5 summarizes results of using MDT to explain friendship satisfaction in 38 countries, including relatively developed and less developed countries, males and females. In the final section (3.6), MDT's prediction success ratios are reviewed for all the explanations offered in Section 3.5.

3.2 Descriptive Statistics for World Sample, Males and Females

On my questionnaire "friendships" were specified as the "kind of contact and frequency of contact you have with your friends. This includes personal contact, phone calls and letters". Again, all satisfaction ratings were obtained from my revised 7-step delightful-terrible scale.

Exhibit 3.1 lists the mean and standard deviation scores, and sample sizes for satisfaction with one's friendships for my 39 participating countries. The last row of the table shows that the friendship satisfaction mean and standard deviation scores for the world balanced sample are 5.2 and 1.2, respectively, with an N=8977. In fact, those are the same figures for the means of the mean and standard deviation scores for the 39 countries, indirectly representing a total sample of N=17,815.

The two rows above the last give the results of separating out the 6 less developed countries (LDCs) from the 33 relatively developed countries (RDCs). The mean friendship satisfaction score of the RDCs (5.3) is slightly higher than the mean score of the LDCs and the world mean (5.2). The standard deviation of the RDC scores

Exhibit 3.1 Participating countries' mean and standard deviation scores, and sample sizes for satisfaction with one's friendships

----

Country	Mean	SD	N
Austria	5.1	1.2	343
Bahrain	5.7	1.2	282
Bangladesh+	5.3	1.3	259
Belgium	5.5	1.0	151
Brazil	5.3	1.2	281
Cameroon	4.7	1.1	180
Canada	5.5	1.2	1641
Chile	5.2	1.1	261
Colombia	5.0	1.3	91
Egypt+	5.5	1.3	279
Finland	5.3	1.2	270
Germany	5.0	1.2	799
Greece	5.3	1.2	266
Hungary	4.6	1.0	228
India+	5.2	1.4	258
Israel	5.2	1.1	317
Japan	5.0	1.1	1203
Jordan	5.5	1.2	298
Kenya+	5.0	1.3	271
Korea	5.1	1.3	450
Mexico	5.1	1.0	245
Netherlands	5.5	1.2	357
New Zealand	5.4	1.0	323
Norway	5.3	1.1	233
Philippines	5.7	1.1	1004
Portugal	5.4	1.6	296
Puerto Rico	5.5	1.0	304
Singapore	5.3	1.0	255
S. Africa	5.3	1.1	286
Spain	5.2	0.9	279
Sweden	5.2	1.2	266
Switzerland	5.2	1.1	341
Taiwan	4.8	1.1	2477
Tanzania+	5.2	0.9	226
Thailand	5.1	1.1	580
Turkey+	4.8	1.2	297
U. Kingdom	5.4	1.0	224

Exhibit 3.1 (continued)

Country	Mean	SD	N
USA	5.6	1.1	1346
Yugoslavia	5.1	1.3	330
Total Mean	5.2	1.2	456
Dev.C.Mean	5.3	1.1	491
L.D.C.Mean	5.2	1.2	265
World	5.2	1.2	8977

+ Below 142-country median on per capita GNP and literacy rate.

(1.1) is slightly smaller than that of the LDC and world scores (1.2). One third of the LDCs (Turkey=4.8, Kenya=5.0) and the RDCs had mean friendship satisfaction scores below the world mean.

Again, rather than attempt to comment on the scores for each of the 39 countries, I will continue the practice adopted earlier of mentioning those in about the top and bottom 10%. There were 3 countries clustered around the top 10% for mean friendship satisfaction scores, namely, Bahrain and the Philippines=5.7, and the United States=5.6. Following close behind these countries, there was a cluster of 6 with mean scores of 5.5 consisting of Belgium, Canada, Egypt, Jordan, the Netherlands and Puerto Rico. The friendship satisfaction score of Bahrain and the Philippines was 42% of one standard deviation above the world mean.

There were 4 countries clustered around the bottom 10% for friendship satisfaction scores, namely, Hungary=4.6, Cameroon=4.7, and Taiwan and Turkey=4.8. Hungary's score of 4.6 was 50% of one standard deviation below the world mean.

Exhibit 3.2 lists the mean and standard deviation scores, and sample sizes for satisfaction with one's friendships for males and females in my 39 countries. The last row of the table indicates that the friendship satisfaction mean and standard deviation scores for the world balanced sample of males (N=4593) are 5.2 and 1.2, respectively, and for females (N=4384) the corresponding figures are 5.3 and 1.2. Thus, as in the case of family satisfaction, females seem to have slightly more friendship satisfaction than males.

The fourth row from the last in this exhibit (total mean) shows that the means of the mean friendship satisfaction scores for the 39 countries for males and females are exactly the same as the

Exhibit 3.2 Participating countries' mean and standard deviation scores, and sample sizes for satisfaction with one's friendships for males and females

Country	Males			Females		
	Mean	SD	N	Mean	SD	N
Austria	5.0	1.2	138	5.2	1.1	205
Bahrain	5.7	1.4	57	5.7	1.2	225
Bangladesh+	5.2	1.3	170	5.5	1.2	89
Belgium	5.6	1.1	85	5.4	0.9	66
Brazil	5.4	1.3	113	5.3	1.2	168
Cameroon	4.7	1.1	144	5.0	1.0	36
Canada	5.4	1.2	630	5.5	1.1	1007
Chile	5.1	1.2	142	5.3	1.0	119
Colombia	4.8	1.3	55	5.4	1.3	36
Egypt+	5.5	1.2	158	5.5	1.3	121
Finland	5.0	1.1	109	5.5	1.2	161
Germany	4.9	1.2	435	5.2	1.2	364
Greece	5.3	1.2	150	5.2	1.1	116
Hungary	4.5	0.9	59	4.9	1.0	169
India+	5.2	1.5	160	5.2	1.3	98
Israel	5.0	1.0	163	5.3	1.1	154
Japan	5.0	1.2	983	5.2	1.1	220
Jordan	5.5	1.2	239	5.3	1.5	59
Kenya+	5.0	1.3	154	4.8	1.3	117
Korea	5.2	1.3	355	4.7	1.4	95
Mexico	5.1	0.9	173	5.2	1.0	71
Netherlands	5.6	1.1	161	5.5	1.2	196
New Zealand	5.2	1.1	117	5.6	0.9	206
Norway	5.1	1.1	91	5.4	1.1	142
Philippines	5.7	1.1	320	5.7	1.0	684
Portugal	5.4	1.5	154	5.3	1.6	141
Puerto Rico	5.5	1.0	170	5.4	1.0	134
Singapore	5.1	1.0	43	5.3	1.0	212
S. Africa	5.3	1.1	124	5.3	1.1	162
Spain	5.2	0.9	138	5.2	0.9	141
Sweden	5.0	1.1	141	5.4	1.2	125
Switzerland	5.1	1.2	172	5.3	1.1	169
Taiwan	4.8	1.1	1283	4.9	1.0	1194
Tanzania+	5.2	1.0	155	5.1	0.8	71
Thailand	5.1	1.1	264	5.2	1.1	316
Turkey+	4.8	1.3	198	4.7	1.2	91

Exhibit 3.2 (continued)

Country	Males			Females		
	Mean	SD	N	Mean	SD	N
U. Kingdom	5.2	0.9	104	5.6	1.0	120
USA	5.5	1.1	470	5.6	1.1	876
Yugoslavia	5.1	1.3	176	5.1	1.2	154
Total Mean	5.2	1.2	230	5.3	1.1	226
Dev.C.Mean	5.2	1.1	241	5.3	1.1	250
L.D.C.Mean	5.2	1.3	166	5.1	1.2	98
World	5.2	1.2	4593	5.3	1.2	4384

+ Below 142-country median on per capita GNP and literacy rate.

figures for the world balanced sample. However, the sample sizes for the fourth row from the last indirectly represent N=8953 males and N=8830 females.

The two rows above the last give the results of separating out the 6 LDCs from the 33 RDCs. For males, the mean of the friendship satisfaction scores of the LDCs (5.2) is the same as the means of the world, the total sample and the RDCs. For females, the mean of the friendship satisfaction scores of the LDCs (5.1) is lower than the means of the world, the total sample and the RDCs (5.3).

For males, two (33%) LDCs (Turkey=4.8, Kenya=5.0) had friendship satisfaction scores below the world mean, while 17 (52%) RDCs had such scores. For females, 4 (66%) LDCs (Turkey=4.7, Kenya=4.8, Tanzania=5.1 and India=5.2) had scores below the world mean, while 12 (36%) RDCs had such scores.

Generally speaking, then, on the basis of the figures in the previous two paragraphs, it seems fair to say that the friendship satisfaction of females in RDCs is higher than that of females in LDCs. It also seems fair to say that the friendship satisfaction of females in RDCs is probably higher than that of males in RDCs, while the reverse is true for LDCs, i.e., the friendship satisfaction of females in LDCs is lower than that of males in LDCs. Thus, as in the case of family satisfaction, maybe the slightly higher female friendship satisfaction scores in the world balanced sample is the result of the fact that 85% of the countries in the sample are RDCs. All the same, in the absence of any other information, I would still regard my world balanced sample scores for the whole group and for males and females taken separately as a plausible set of *norms* for university undergraduates until a better set is obtained.

For males, the 4 countries in the top 10% for friendship satisfaction scores were Bahrain and the Philippines=5.7, Belgium and the Netherlands=5.6. For females, the 5 top countries were Bahrain and the Philippines=5.7, New Zealand, United Kingdom and the United States=5.6. For males, Bahrain's score was 42% of one standard deviation above the world mean, and for females it was 33% of a standard deviation above the world mean.

For males, there were 5 countries clustered around the bottom 10% for friendship satisfaction scores, namely, Hungary=4.5, Cameroon=4.7, Colombia, Taiwan and Turkey=4.8. For females, the 5 bottom countries were Korea and Turkey=4.7, Kenya=4.8, Hungary and Taiwan=4.9. Hungary's male score was 58% of one standard deviation below the world mean for males, while Korea and Turkey's female scores were 50% below the world mean for females.

Considering the results reported in the previous two paragraphs together, it is clear that male friendship satisfaction scores had a wider range (5.7-4.5=1.2) than their female counterparts (5.7-4.7=1.0).

3.3 Satisfaction Explained by MDT for World Sample

Exhibit 3.3 is the correlation matrix for the variables employed in this chapter. There are 6 cases of moderate ($r>.50$) multicollinearity among the predictors.

Exhibit 3.4 gives the results of using MDT to explain satisfaction with one's friendships in the world balanced sample. In the column under S (in this context, for "satisfaction with one's friendships") we find a total sample N of 8091 students, including 4105 males and 3986 females. MDT explained 50% of the variance in reported friendship satisfaction scores for the whole group, 49% for males and 51% for females.

All things considered, for the group as a whole, age has a negative impact on satisfaction with one's friendships (Age=-.07, TES column) and on the gap between what one has and wants regarding such relations (Age=-.04, TESW column). Figuratively speaking, if the impact of all other variables is held constant, one could say that as one's age increases a full step, one's friendship satisfaction decreases seven percent of a step and the gap between what one has and wants regarding friendships decreases four percent of a step.

Exhibit 3.3 Correlation matrix for satisfaction with one's friendships*

	SX	AG	WS	LD	B	SO	SD	SN	SP	SF	SB	SW
SX	-											
AG	9	-										
WS	ns	12	-									
LD	2	36	ns	-								
B	ns	4	14	5	-							
SO	ns	5	4	ns	ns	-						
SD	ns	5	2	ns	3	46	-					
SN	ns	8	4	2	ns	52	57	-				
SP	3	7	3	3	4	49	48	58	-			
SF	ns	5	5	4	6	22	26	30	31	-		
SB	3	6	5	ns	ns	44	40	46	58	29	-	
SW	5	5	5	4	7	58	43	51	50	22	44	-
FR	4	7	4	3	ns	59	39	47	47	18	42	64	-

* Decimal points omitted; underlined figures indicate negative correlations; P = .05 or better; N = 9092; ns = not significant.

Besides having a negative direct effect on friendship satisfaction (Age=-.03, S column), age has a negative impact on the gaps regarding self/others, self/needs and self/progress (Age=-.07; SO,SN,SP columns), and self/deserved and self/best (Age=-.05; SD,SB columns). Clearly, the older a student gets, the more ways he or she is liable to suffer from perceived discrepancies concerning friendships.

Reading down the TES column in Exhibit 3.4, one finds that aside from age, the demographic predictors have very little impact on satisfaction with one's friendships. The numerical values range from one to two percent.

All things considered, with regard to friendship satisfaction, the self/others gap (SO=.41) has the greatest impact, followed closely by self/wants (SW=.40). So, in the given set of predictors, social comparisons and aspiration/achievement gaps are nearly 6 times more important to friendship satisfaction than the most influential demographic variable, age. Self/progress (SP=.13) enters in a fairly distant third place, followed immediately by self/needs (SN=.12) and

Exhibit 3.4 Satisfaction with one's friendships
(decimal points omitted)

World
Total Balanced Sample

	S	SW	SO	SD	SN	SP	SF	SB	TES	TESW
N	8091	8129	8703	8631	8731	8728	8624	8692	-	-
R^2	50	44	1	1	1	1	1	1	-	-
Pred										
Sex	0	4	0	0	0	2	0	3	2	5
Age	-3	2	-7	-5	-7	-7	3	-5	-7	-4
WS	0	0	-3	0	-4	0	4	-5	-2	-2
LED	0	-3	4	0	0	0	3	0	1	-2
ETH	-2	6	0	4	0	4	-6	0	1	7
SO	27	36							41	36
SD	0	8							3	8
SN	6	15							12	15
SP	7	14							13	14
SF	2	0							2	0
SB	6	9							10	9
SW	40								40	
Males										
N	4105	4126	4454	0	4465	4463	4403	4455	-	-
R^2	49	43	1	0	1	1	1	1	-	-
Age	-2	0	-7	0	-8	-7	0	-7	-8	-5
WS	0	0	-3	0	-3	-5	4	-4	-2	-3
LED	0	0	6	0	0	0	6	0	3	2
ETH	0	7	0	0	0	4	-8	0	3	8
SO	30	37							44	37
SD	0	10							4	10
SN	6	12							10	12
SP	7	12							11	12
SF	3	0							3	0
SB	6	10							10	10
SW	37								37	
Females										
N	3986	4003	0	0	4266	0	4221	0	-	-
R^2	51	44	0	0	1	0	1	0	-	-
Age	-3	0	0	0	-7	0	3	0	-4	-1
WS	0	0	0	0	-4	0	5	0	-1	-1
LED	0	-3	0	0	0	0	0	0	-1	-3

Exhibit 3.4 (continued)

	S	SW	SO	SD	SN	SP	SF	SB	TES	TESW
ETH	-3	5	0	0	0	0	-3	0	-1	5
SO	24	35							39	35
SD	0	5							2	5
SN	6	18							14	18
SP	7	16							14	16
SB	5	8							8	8
SW	43								43	

then self/best (SB=.10). Gaps concerning equity (SD=.03) and the future (SF=.02) are even less important than age.

From the column under SW it is clear that my set of predictors explains 44% of the variance in scores indicating the perceived gap between the sort of friendships students have and the sort they want. Returning to TESW, one finds again that it is social comparison scores (SO=.36) that dominate the lot of predictors. The next most influential predictors occur in two clusters. First, there are self/needs (SN=.15) and self/progress (SP=.14), and then self/best (SB=.09) and self/deserved (SD=.08).

The impacts of the demographic variables are again relatively modest, except for ethnicity (operationalized as country of birth), which has a positive impact on the self/wants gap (ETH=.07). All things considered, the ETH=.07 figure here indicates that being born in a relatively advantaged country is positively related to closing the gap between what one has and wants regarding friendships. That is confusing (as in the case of family satisfaction) because closing the self/wants gap is also positively related to friendship satisfaction, while being born in a relatively advantaged country is negatively related to such satisfaction. Again, I can not explain these anomalous figures.

Considering the total effects listed in the columns under TES and TESW for the group as a whole, it is fair to say that social comparisons and aspiration/achievement gaps are generally the two most influential contributors to satisfaction with one's friendships. The self/needs gap (roughly representing person-environment fit theory and the self/progress gap (roughly representing expectancy theory) come in a fairly distant second place.

3.4 Satisfaction Explained by MDT for Males and Females

Of all the demographic variables, age has the greatest impact on satisfaction with one's friendships for males (Age=-.08) and females (Age=-.04). For males, work status (WS=-02), level of university education and ethnicity (LED=ETH=.03) are all of minor importance, while for females these variables are of even less importance (WS=LED=ETH=-.01).

Considering perceived discrepancies relative to friendship satisfaction, the rank orderings of the three most influential predictors for males is exactly the same as the ordering for the group as a whole. For males, we have self/others (SO=.44), self/wants (SW=.37) and self/progress (SP=.11). For females, the aspiration/achievement gap occupies first place. We have SW=.43, SO=.39, and SP=SN=.14. After these triads, for males self/needs and self/best run a close fourth (SN=SB=.10), while for females self/best (SB=.08) runs a more distant fourth.

As in the case of family satisfaction, the self/needs variable is more important than the self/deserved variable to friendship satisfaction for both males and females. The equity variable comes in sixth place for both groups, but the numerical figures indicate that in the context of the predictors used here, considerations of needs are 7 times more important than equity for females compared to 2 and a half times as important for males.

Considering the relative impacts of my predictors on the gaps between what one has and wants regarding friendships, the self/others gap is three times as influential as its next rival for males (SO=.37) and almost twice as influential as its next rival for females (SO=.35). Self/needs and self/progress are tied for second place for males (SN=SP=.12), while the former stands alone in second place for females (SN=.18). Equity and self/best are tied for third for males (SD=SB=.10), with ethnicity (ETH=.08) close behind. For females, third place is occupied by self/progress (SP=.16), followed by a distant self/best (SB=.08).

3.5 Thirty-Eight Countries

Exhibit 3.5 shows the percent of variance explained by MDT in satisfaction with one's friendships scores for 38 countries, developed and less developed countries, and the world sample. The detailed regressions on which these figures are based are in Appendix 3. The

Exhibit 3.5 Percent of variance explained by MDT in satisfaction
with one's friendships

Country	Total	Male	Female
Austria	60	65	57
Bahrain	37	-	38
Bangladesh+	53	53	53
Belgium	56	-	-
Brazil	50	48	53
Cameroon	40	40	-
Canada	55	53	57
Chile	39	35	48
Colombia	-	-	-
Egypt+	46	32	60
Finland	70	71	67
Germany	62	65	61
Greece	45	38	57
Hungary	60	-	58
India+	52	55	-
Israel	56	57	54
Japan	53	54	50
Jordan	41	41	-
Kenya+	44	33	60
Korea	62	60	-
Mexico	29	29	-
Netherlands	59	60	59
New Zealand	55	60	53
Norway	56	-	43
Philippines	38	47	34
Portugal	76	-	-
Puerto Rico	45	50	39
Singapore	54	-	52
S. Africa	34	40	34
Spain	48	54	39
Sweden	70	70	75
Switzerland	60	64	54
Taiwan	42	44	40
Tanzania+	22	27	-
Thailand	28	26	30
Turkey+	36	38	-
U. Kingdom	48	48	47
USA	55	49	59

Exhibit 3.5 (continued)

Country	Total	Male	Female
Yugoslavia	55	55	56
Total Mean	50	49	51
Dev.C.Mean	51	51	51
L.D.C.Mean	42	40	58
World	50	49	51

+ Below 142-country median on per capita GNP and literacy rate.

mean percents of variance explained in friendship satisfaction scores for 38 countries are exactly the same as those for the world balanced sample, namely, 50% for the whole group, 49% for males and 51% for females (fourth row from last).

For the group as a whole and for males, MDT did a relatively better job accounting for friendship satisfaction in RDCs than in LDCs. For females, the reverse was true. On average the mean figures for RDCs for the whole group and males were 10 percentage points higher than those for LDCs, while for females the mean figure for RDCs was 7 percentage points lower than that for LDCs. Specifically, MDT accounted for an average of 51% of the variance in friendship satisfaction scores for the whole group, males and females in RDCs. For LDCs, the mean percent of variance explained for the whole group was 42%, for males 40%, and for females 58%.

For the whole group, percents of variance explained in scores indicating satisfaction with one's friendships ranged from a high of 76% in Portugal to a low of 22% in Tanzania. There were two other country figures in the 70s (Finland and Sweden=70%) and two others in the 20s (Thailand=28%, Mexico=29%). There were five country figures in the 60s and five in the 30s.

For males, friendship satisfaction percents of variance explained ranged from a high of 71% for Finland to a low of 26% for Thailand. The only other male score in the 70s belonged to Sweden=70%, while Tanzania=27% and Mexico=29% also had scores in the 20s. Although there were 6 male figures in the 60s, none of them reached the two-thirds level; Austria and Germany=65%, Switzerland=64%, Korea, the Netherlands and New Zealand=60%. Altogether there were only 5 (16%) male figures above 60%.

For females, friendship satisfaction percents of variance

explained ranged from a high of 75% for Sweden to a low of 30% for Thailand. There were no other female figures in the 70s and only 4 in the 60s; Finland=67%, Germany=61%, and Egypt and Kenya=60%. Altogether there were only 3 (10%) female figures above 60%.

Considering the results reviewed in this section, then, so far as explained variance in friendship satisfaction is concerned, on average MDT performed better for females than for males, but there was a bigger share of male than female scores above 60%.

3.6 Prediction Success Ratios

Exhibit 3.6 lists the prediction success ratios for MDT in explanations of satisfaction with one's friendships for 38 countries, developed and less developed countries and the world balanced sample. The 100% figure beginning the last row of Exhibit 3.6 indicates that in accounting for friendship satisfaction in the balanced world sample MDT made 12 hits out of 12 possibilities (column under TES, Exhibit 3.4). That is, MDT had a narrow prediction success ratio of 100% for the world sample explanation of family satisfaction, taking males and females together. For males, MDT also had a narrow ratio of 100% (11/11 hits, column under TES, Exhibit 3.4), and for females MDT was 91% successful (10/11 hits).

The second figure in each double column of Exhibit 3.6 gives the ratio of successful to total predicted *direct effects* in the 8 regression equations required for an application of MDT, i.e., the broad prediction success ratios or simply the broad ratios. The 64% figure in the last row of the exhibit indicates that in accounting for friendship satisfaction in the world sample MDT made 34 hits out of 53 possibilities (columns under S to SB, Exhibit 3.4). That is, MDT had a broad prediction success ratio of 64% for the world sample explanation of satisfaction with one's friendships for the whole group. For males, MDT had a broad ratio of 58% (26/45 hits, columns under S to SB for males, Exhibit 3.4), and for females it had a broad ratio of 42%.

Examination of the total mean prediction success ratios in Exhibit 3.6 (fourth row from the last) reveals a considerable drop in all figures compared to the world sample figures. For example, instead of a friendship satisfaction narrow ratio of 100% for the whole group, we have a total mean figure of 60%. The average total mean broad ratio is only around 20%. The developed country mean prediction success ratios are all higher than the less developed mean ratios.

Exhibit 3.6 Prediction success ratios for MDT in explanations of satisfaction with one's friendships*

Country	Total		Males		Females	
Austria	67	23	55	16	46	18
Bahrain	42	13	-	-	55	16
Bangladesh+	75	25	64	18	73	18
Belgium	33	09	-	-	-	-
Brazil	50	19	46	13	55	20
Cameroon	50	13	36	16	-	-
Canada	83	47	73	29	64	36
Chile	42	13	27	11	46	16
Colombia	-	-	-	-	-	-
Egypt+	33	09	36	16	36	11
Finland	58	25	46	13	36	13
Germany	58	28	46	18	64	20
Greece	42	17	46	20	46	20
Hungary	50	15	-	-	36	13
India+	58	17	36	13	-	-
Israel	58	19	46	16	46	13
Japan	83	38	91	36	73	24
Jordan	58	23	46	29	-	-
Kenya+	67	15	18	16	55	16
Korea	67	21	73	24	-	-
Mexico	75	25	46	18	-	-
Netherlands	58	19	46	18	73	20
New Zealand	75	36	73	29	64	27
Norway	83	30	-	-	55	16
Philippines	58	23	55	18	73	31
Portugal	58	21	-	-	-	-
Puerto Rico	42	11	55	18	27	09
Singapore	58	19	-	-	73	24
S. Africa	42	13	46	13	64	18
Spain	67	21	46	18	46	13
Sweden	75	23	46	20	36	13
Switzerland	67	21	46	18	46	13
Taiwan	67	32	73	27	55	22
Tanzania+	25	19	27	22	-	-
Thailand	75	26	36	20	64	24
Turkey+	42	23	36	24	-	-
U. Kingdom	92	25	73	22	46	16

Exhibit 3.6 (continued)

Country	Total		Males		Females	
USA	83	38	64	33	82	40
Yugoslavia	58	23	64	20	73	27
Total Mean	60	22	51	20	56	20
Dev.C.Mean	62	23	54	21	56	20
L.D.C.Mean	50	18	36	18	55	15
World	100	64	100	58	91	42

* The first figures in each column give the ratio of successful to total predicted total effects. The second figures give the ratio of successful to total predicted direct effects in the 8 regressions required for an application of MDT.
+ Below 142-country median on per capita GNP and literacy rate.

In spite of the relatively low average performance of MDT for the 38 countries, there were still some notable successes. With respect to friendship satisfaction for the whole group, MDT had a narrow prediction success ratio of 92% for the United Kingdom, 83% for Canada, Japan, Norway and the United States, and 75% for Bangladesh, Mexico, New Zealand, Sweden and Thailand. Altogether narrow ratios above 60% were obtained in 16 (42%) countries. For males, MDT achieved narrow ratios of 91% for Japan, and 73% for Canada, Korea, New Zealand, Taiwan and the United Kingdom. For females, the figures reached 82% for the United States, and 73% Bangladesh, Japan, the Netherlands, the Philippines, Singapore and Yugoslavia. MDT obtained ratios above 60% for males in 9 (28%) countries, and for females in 12 (41%) countries.

MDT's lowest narrow ratio for the whole group was 25% for Tanzania. For males, the lowest ratio was 18% for Kenya, and for females it was 27% for Puerto Rico.

4

Satisfaction with One's Living Partner

4.1 Introduction

In this chapter MDT is used to explain satisfaction with one's living partner. In the next section (4.2), I review mean satisfaction scores for the world balanced sample, relatively developed and less developed countries, 39 countries, males and females. In Sections 4.3 and 4.4 living partner satisfaction is explained by MDT, respectively, for the world balanced sample taken as a whole, and for males and females taken separately. Section 4.5 summarizes results of using MDT to explain living partner satisfaction in 31 countries, including relatively developed and less developed countries, males and females. MDT could only be applied to 31 countries because, as indicated below, about a third of the students did not have living partners. In the final section (4.6), MDT's prediction success ratios are reviewed for all the explanations offered in Section 4.5.

4.2 Descriptive Statistics for World Sample, Males and Females

According to Clark and Reis 1988, p.647), "Just who qualifies for description as a friend or partner depends on the meaning attributed to those categories of relationships, and people differ systematically in the criteria they use in these judgments". On my questionnaire "living partner" was specified as including "a marriage partner; partner sharing intimate relations". Again, all satisfaction ratings were obtained from my revised 7-step delightful-terrible scale.

Exhibit 4.1 lists the mean and standard deviation scores, and sample sizes for satisfaction with one's living partner for my 39 participating countries. The last row of the table shows that the living partner satisfaction mean and standard deviation scores for the world balanced sample are 5.2 and 1.6, respectively, with an N=5809. This N is about 64% of the world sample of N=9092 (Volume One, Exhibit 3.5). The mean of the mean scores for the 39 countries is also

Exhibit 4.1 Participating countries' mean and standard deviation
scores, and sample sizes for satisfaction with one's living partner

Country	Mean	SD	N
Austria	5.4	1.6	265
Bahrain	5.9	1.5	117
Bangladesh+	4.8	1.7	96
Belgium	5.6	1.5	123
Brazil	5.3	1.6	204
Cameroon	4.7	1.4	154
Canada	5.4	1.5	927
Chile	5.3	1.1	93
Colombia	5.3	1.2	39
Egypt+	5.4	1.5	129
Finland	6.1	1.0	166
Germany	5.1	1.7	648
Greece	5.0	1.8	232
Hungary	5.6	1.5	157
India+	4.8	1.7	77
Israel	4.5	2.1	317
Japan	4.5	1.3	793
Jordan	4.9	1.8	150
Kenya+	4.8	1.4	199
Korea	5.0	1.3	432
Mexico	5.3	1.1	181
Netherlands	5.6	1.7	180
New Zealand	5.3	1.5	179
Norway	5.3	1.5	150
Philippines	5.1	1.2	199
Portugal	4.4	1.4	237
Puerto Rico	5.6	1.2	237
Singapore	4.9	1.3	43
S. Africa	5.2	1.4	225
Spain	5.2	1.2	176
Sweden	5.5	1.6	186
Switzerland	5.3	1.6	261
Taiwan	5.9	2.3	2412
Tanzania+	5.4	1.2	195
Thailand	4.9	1.1	402
Turkey+	4.8	1.5	274
U. Kingdom	5.0	1.8	75
USA	5.3	1.6	924

Exhibit 4.1 (continued)

Country	Mean	SD	N
Yugoslavia	4.5	1.9	247
Total Mean	5.2	1.5	310
Dev.C.Mean	5.2	1.5	337
L.D.C.Mean	5.0	1.5	162
World	5.2	1.6	5809

+ Below 142-country median on per capita GNP and literacy rate.

5.2, while the average standard deviation is 1.5. The total sample indirectly represented by these figures is N=12,101.

Although there is considerable statistical and anecdotal evidence indicating that many more people have living partners (as briefly defined here) than marriage partners, the 64% figure is surprisingly high. Tanfer (1987) reported that for her national sample of unmarried American women aged 20 to 29, 30% had cohabited sometime in their lives and 12% were living with their partner. About 32% of the sampled women from metropolitan areas had cohabited, compared to 22% of those from nonmetropolitan areas. Glick (1988, p.867) claimed that "By 1986, over 6% of all unmarried adults in the United States were cohabiting, but the level was far higher, 16%, among divorced persons in their late twenties. Four percent of all couples (married plus unmarried) living together were not married to each other. This proportion is only one-fourth as high as the level in Sweden in 1979". Jones, Marsden and Tepperman (1990, p.10) reported that in Canada "By 1984, roughly one adult respondent in six had been in a common-law partnership at one time or another... . Among young people aged 18 to 29, the proportion was much higher: about one man in five and one woman in four". Thus, on the basis of these figures, one might have expected to find at most about 30% of my sample with a living partner.

The two rows above the last in Exhibit 4.1 give the results of separating out the 6 less developed countries (LDCs) from the 33 relatively developed countries (RDCs). The mean living partner satisfaction score of the RDCs (5.2) is slightly higher than the mean score of the LDCs (5.0), while their average standard deviations (1.5) are the same. Two thirds of the LDCs (Bangladesh, India, Kenya and Turkey=4.8) and 28% of the RDCs had mean living partner satisfaction scores below the world mean.

There were 3 countries clustered around the top 10% for mean living partner satisfaction scores, namely, Finland=6.1, and Bahrain and Taiwan=5.9. Following these countries, there was a cluster of 4 with mean scores of 5.6 consisting of Belgium, Hungary, the Netherlands and Puerto Rico. Finland's living partner satisfaction score of 6.1 was 56% of one standard deviation above the world mean.

There were 4 countries clustered around the bottom 10% for living partner satisfaction scores, namely, Portugal=4.4, and Israel, Japan and Yugoslavia=4.5. Portugal's score of 4.4 was 50% of one standard deviation below the world mean.

Exhibit 4.2 lists the mean and standard deviation scores, and sample sizes for satisfaction with one's living partner for males and females in my 39 countries. The last row of the table indicates that the living partner satisfaction mean and standard deviation scores for the world balanced sample of males (N=3071) are 5.1 and 1.6, respectively, and for females (N=2738) the corresponding figures are 5.2 and 1.6. Thus, as in the cases of family and friendship satisfaction, females seem to have slightly more living partner satisfaction than males.

The fourth row from the last in this exhibit (total mean) shows that the mean of the mean living partner satisfaction scores for the 39 countries for males is exactly the same as that for the world balanced sample (5.1). For females, the mean for the 39 countries (5.3) is slightly above the world sample mean (5.2). The sample sizes for the fourth row from the last indirectly represent N=6365 males and N=5724 females.

The two rows above the last give the results of separating out the 6 LDCs from the 33 RDCs. For males, the mean of the living partner satisfaction scores of the RDCs (5.2) is higher than the means of the world and the total sample (5.1), and the LDCs (4.9). For females, the mean of the living partner satisfaction scores of the RDCs (5.3) equals that of the total sample, and is higher than the means of the world sample and the LDCs (5.2).

For males, 4 (66%) LDCs (Bangladesh=4.5, India=4.6, Kenya=4.8 and Turkey=4.9) had living partner satisfaction scores below the world mean, while 12 (31%) RDCs had such scores. For females, 2 (33%) LDCs (Kenya=4.9, Turkey=4.6) had scores below the world mean, while 12 (31%) RDCs had such scores.

Generally speaking, then, on the basis of the figures in the previous two paragraphs, it seems fair to say that the living partner satisfaction of males and females in RDCs is probably higher than

Exhibit 4.2 Participating countries' mean and standard deviation scores, and sample sizes for satisfaction with one's living partner for males and females

----

Country	Males Mean	SD	N	Females Mean	SD	N
Austria	5.2	1.7	109	5.5	1.5	156
Bahrain	5.7	1.8	34	5.9	1.4	83
Bangladesh+	4.5	1.8	61	5.5	1.4	35
Belgium	5.4	1.6	66	5.8	1.4	57
Brazil	5.4	1.5	84	5.3	1.6	120
Cameroon	4.7	1.4	119	4.8	1.3	35
Canada	5.2	1.6	346	5.5	1.4	579
Chile	5.4	1.1	53	5.2	1.1	40
Colombia	5.1	1.3	24	5.5	1.0	15
Egypt+	5.2	1.4	70	5.7	1.5	59
Finland	5.9	1.0	73	6.3	0.9	93
Germany	5.0	1.8	351	5.3	1.5	297
Greece	5.0	1.7	135	5.1	1.9	97
Hungary	5.7	1.5	44	5.5	1.5	113
India+	4.6	1.8	50	5.2	1.5	27
Israel	4.7	1.9	163	4.2	2.3	154
Japan	4.4	1.2	671	4.8	1.4	122
Jordan	4.8	1.7	118	5.1	1.9	32
Kenya+	4.8	1.4	109	4.9	1.5	90
Korea	5.1	1.3	340	4.8	1.4	92
Mexico	5.3	1.0	134	5.2	1.3	46
Netherlands	5.8	1.8	66	5.5	1.6	114
New Zealand	5.1	1.6	59	5.3	1.5	120
Norway	5.1	1.6	60	5.4	1.4	90
Philippines	5.2	1.4	81	5.1	1.2	118
Portugal	4.4	1.5	121	4.5	1.3	115
Puerto Rico	5.6	1.1	132	5.7	1.3	105
Singapore	5.0	1.7	10	4.8	1.2	33
S. Africa	5.2	1.5	97	5.1	1.3	128
Spain	5.0	1.2	92	5.4	1.3	84
Sweden	5.6	1.6	95	5.5	1.6	91
Switzerland	5.1	1.6	127	5.4	1.5	134
Taiwan	6.0	2.4	1249	5.7	2.1	1163
Tanzania+	5.4	1.2	131	5.3	1.2	64
Thailand	4.9	1.1	202	4.8	1.0	200

Exhibit 4.2   (continued)

Country	Males			Females		
	Mean	SD	N	Mean	SD	N
Turkey+	4.9	1.5	180	4.6	1.6	86
U. Kingdom	4.3	1.9	33	5.5	1.5	42
USA	5.2	1.5	339	5.3	1.6	585
Yugoslavia	4.5	2.0	137	4.6	1.8	110
Total Mean	5.1	1.5	163	5.3	1.5	147
Dev.C.Mean	5.2	1.5	175	5.3	1.5	163
L.D.C.Mean	4.9	1.5	100	5.2	1.5	60
World	5.1	1.6	3071	5.2	1.6	2738

+ Below 142-country median on per capita GNP and literacy rate.

that of males and females in LDCs.

For males, the 3 countries clustered around the top 10% for living partner satisfaction scores were Taiwan=6.0, Finland=5.9 and the Netherlands=5.8. For females, the 3 top countries were Finland=6.3, Bahrain=5.9 and Belgium=5.8. For males, Taiwan's score was 56% of one standard deviation above the world mean, and for females Finland's score was 69% of a standard deviation above the world mean.

For males, there were 5 countries clustered around the bottom 10% for living partner satisfaction scores, namely, the United Kingdom=4.3, Japan and Portugal=4.4, Bangladesh and Yugoslavia=4.5. For females, the 3 bottom countries were Israel=4.2, Portugal=4.5, Turkey and Yugoslavia=4.6. The United Kingdom's male score was 50% of one standard deviation below the world mean for males, while Israel's female score was 63% below the world mean for females.

4.3   Satisfaction Explained by MDT for World Sample

Exhibit 4.3 is the correlation matrix for the variables employed in this chapter. There are a chilling 15 cases of moderate ($r > .50$) multicollinearity among the predictors. However, there is still no evidence of serious distortion of any results.

Exhibit 4.3 Correlation matrix for satisfaction with one's living partner*

	SX	AG	WS	LD	B	SO	SD	SN	SP	SF	SB	SW
SX	-											
AG	9	-										
WS	ns	12	-									
LD	2	36	ns	-								
B	ns	4	14	5	-							
SO	4	12	ns	10	ns	-						
SD	ns	11	ns	5	ns	63	-					
SN	ns	11	3	5	ns	64	70	-				
SP	5	9	ns	6	3	69	65	70	-			
SF	ns	6	3	3	5	28	33	38	37	-		
SB	8	8	ns	7	ns	61	57	61	70	34	-	
SW	5	16	ns	9	4	75	62	65	67	30	60	-
LP	4	12	3	7	ns	74	57	60	64	26	58	76

* Decimal points omitted; underlined figures indicate negative correlations; P =.05 or better; N =9092; ns =not significant.

Exhibit 4.4 gives the results of using MDT to explain satisfaction with one's living partner in the world balanced sample. In the column under S (in this context, for "satisfaction with one's living partner") we find a total sample N of 4728 students, including 2493 males and 2235 females. MDT explained 67% of the variance in reported living partner satisfaction scores for the whole group, 64% for males and 71% for females.

All things considered, for the group as a whole, age has a positive impact on satisfaction with one's living partner (Age=.11, TES column) and on the gap between what one has and wants regarding one's partner (Age=.15, TESW column). Although age has no direct effect on living partner satisfaction (Age=0, S column), age has a positive impact on the gaps regarding self/others and self/deserved (Age=.11), self/needs (Age=.12), self/progress (Age=.09) and self/best (Age=.08). Clearly, the older a student gets, the more ways he or she is likely to be able to reduce discrepancies regarding a living partner.

Reading down the TES column in Exhibit 4.4, one finds that

Exhibit 4.4 Satisfaction with one's living partner
(decimal points omitted)

World
Total Balanced Sample

	S	SW	SO	SD	SN	SP	SF	SB	TES	TESW
N	4728	4962	5873	5857	6023	6071	6398	5984	-	-
R^2	67	64	2	1	1	1	1	2	-	-
Pred										
Sex	0	2	5	0	3	6	0	8	5	6
Age	0	5	11	11	12	9	-8	8	11	15
WS	2	0	0	0	-4	0	3	0	2	-1
LED	0	0	6	0	0	4	6	4	4	4
ETH	0	4	0	0	0	4	-4	0	2	5
SO	30	45							49	45
SD	0	10							4	10
SN	5	13							11	13
SP	8	14							14	14
SB	7	9							11	9
SW	42								42	
Males										
N	2493	2632	3121	3104	3205	3216	3394	3195	-	-
R^2	64	61	2	1	1	1	1	1	-	-
Age	0	7	10	12	12	9	-9	9	12	16
WS	0	0	0	0	-5	0	0	0	0	-1
LED	0	0	6	0	0	0	6	0	3	3
ETH	0	3	0	0	0	4	-6	0	2	3
SO	26	47							46	47
SD	7	11							12	11
SN	0	14							6	14
SP	9	10							13	10
SB	7	7							10	7
SW	42								42	
Females										
N	2235	2330	2752	2753	2818	2855	3004	2789	-	-
R^2	71	66	2	1	2	1	1	1	-	-
Age	0	3	12	11	11	8	-7	8	11	13
WS	3	0	0	0	0	0	4	0	3	0
LED	0	0	6	0	4	5	5	5	5	5
ETH	0	4	0	0	0	0	0	0	2	4
SO	34	42							52	42
SD	0	9							4	9

Exhibit 4.4 (continued)

	S	SW	SO	SD	SN	SP	SF	SB	TES	TESW
SN	5	13							11	13
SP	6	18							14	18
SF	3	0							3	0
SB	8	11							13	11
SW	42								42	

aside from age, the demographic predictors have very little impact on satisfaction with one's living partner. The numerical values never go above .05. For the group as a whole, males and females, ethnicity is always ETH=.02.

All things considered, with regard to living partner satisfaction for the whole group, the self/others gap (SO=.49) has the greatest impact, followed by self/wants (SW=.42). So, in the given set of predictors, social comparisons and aspiration/achievement gaps are about 4 times more important to living partner satisfaction than the most influential demographic variable, age. Self/progress (SP=.14) enters in a fairly distant third place, followed by self/needs and self/best (SN=SB=.11). The gap concerning equity (SD=.04) is less than half as important as age in the given set of predictors, and any gap regarding future expectations has no role to play at all.

From the column under SW one finds that my set of predictors explains 64% of the variance in scores indicating the perceived gap between the sort of living partner students have and the sort they want. Returning to TESW, one finds again that it is social comparison scores (SO=.45) that dominate the lot of predictors. The next most influential predictor is age (Age=.15). That is then followed closely by self/progress (SP=.14) and self/needs (SN=.13), and less closely by self/deserved (SD=.10).

4.4 Satisfaction Explained by MDT for Males and Females

Of all the demographic variables, age has the greatest impact on satisfaction with one's living partner for males (Age=.12) and females (Age=.11). For males, work status has no effect (WS=0) and level of university education (LED=.03) is of minor importance, while for females the corresponding variables are a bit more important, namely, WS=.03 and LED=.05.

Considering perceived discrepancies relative to living partner satisfaction, the rank orderings of the three most influential predictors for males and females are exactly the same as the ordering for the group as a whole. For males, we have self/others (SO=.46), self/wants (SW=.42) and self/progress (SP=.13), and for females we have SO=.52, SW=.42 and SP=.14. After these triads, for males self/deserved ties with age (SD=Age=.12) in fourth place, while for females self/best (SB=.13) stands alone in fourth place. Self/best (SB=.10) is fifth for males, and self/needs ties with age (SN=Age=.11) in fifth place for females. Self/needs (SN=.06) is only the sixth most important predictor of living partner satisfaction for males.

In the context of all the predictors used here, for males considerations of needs (SN=.06) are only half as important as considerations of equity (SD=.12), while for females considerations of needs (SN=.11) are nearly three times as important as considerations of equity (SD=.04). These findings regarding living partner satisfaction are particularly interesting because they are different from the cases of family and friendship satisfaction where we found that the self/needs variable was more important than the self/deserved variable for both males and females.

Considering the relative impacts of my predictors on the gaps between what students have and want regarding living partners, the self/others gap is almost three times as influential as its next rival for males (SO=.47) and over twice as influential as its next rival for females (SO=.42). For males, age (Age=.16) is the second most important predictor, followed closely by self/needs (SN=.14). For females, second place is occupied by the self/progress gap (SP=.18), which is followed by self/needs and age (SN=Age=.13).
Equity is less important than need fulfillment to self/wants gap scores for males (SD=.11) and females (SD=.09).

4.5   Thirty-One Countries

Exhibit 4.5 shows the percent of variance explained by MDT in satisfaction with one's living partner scores for 31 countries, developed and less developed countries, and the world sample. The detailed regressions on which these figures are based are in Appendix 4. The means of the mean percents of variance explained in living partner satisfaction scores for 31 countries are one percentage point short of the world percent for the whole group (66%) and males

Exhibit 4.5 Percent of variance explained by MDT in satisfaction
with one's living partner

Country	Total	Males	Females
Austria	79	82	79
Bahrain	-	-	-
Bangladesh+	69	-	74
Belgium	-	-	-
Brazil	70	-	75
Cameroon	55	56	-
Canada	72	73	72
Chile	-	-	-
Colombia	-	-	-
Egypt+	-	-	-
Finland	64	-	-
Germany	79	80	76
Greece	69	54	-
Hungary	81	-	83
India+	-	-	-
Israel	73	56	88
Japan	66	66	70
Jordan	51	-	-
Kenya+	57	-	-
Korea	66	63	-
Mexico	30	42	-
Netherlands	84	-	84
New Zealand	79	-	78
Norway	70	-	-
Philippines	58	-	-
Portugal	65	-	-
Puerto Rico	65	63	71
Singapore	-	-	-
S. Africa	45	-	-
Spain	64	-	-
Sweden	87	-	-
Switzerland	84	84	85
Taiwan	67	65	70
Tanzania+	61	67	-
Thailand	31	25	47
Turkey+	49	55	-
U. Kingdom	-	-	-

Exhibit 4.5 (continued)

Country	Total	Males	Females
USA	73	67	76
Yugoslavia	70	66	-
Total Mean	66	63	75
Dev.C.Mean	67	63	75
L.D.C.Mean	59	61	74
World	67	64	71

+ Below 142-country median on per capita GNP and literacy rate.

(63%), and 4 percentage points above the world percent for females (75%).

For the group as a whole, males and females, MDT did a relatively better job accounting for living partner satisfaction in RDCs than in LDCs. Specifically, MDT accounted for an average of 67% of the variance in living partner satisfaction scores for the whole group, 63% for males and 75% for females in RDCs. For LDCs, the mean percent of variance explained for the whole group was 59%, for males 61% and for females 74%.

For the whole group, percents of variance explained in scores indicating satisfaction with one's living partner ranged from a high of 87% in Sweden to a low of 30% in Mexico. There were 3 other country figures in the 80s (the Netherlands and Switzerland=84%, Hungary=81%) and only one other in the 30s (Thailand=31%). There were 9 country figures in the 70s and 2 in the 40s.

For males, living partner satisfaction percents of variance explained ranged from a high of 84% for Switzerland to a low of 25% for Thailand. There were 2 other male figures in the 80s (Austria=82%, Germany=80%), and no other male figures in the 20s or 30s. The only male score in the 70s belonged to Canada=73%. There were 7 male figures in the 60s and 4 of them reached the two-thirds level; Tanzania and the United States=67%, Japan and Yugoslavia=66%. Altogether there were 11 (65%) male figures above 60%.

For females, living partner satisfaction percents of variance explained ranged from a high of 88% for Israel to a low of 47% for Thailand. There were 3 other female figures in the 80s

(Switzerland=85%, the Netherlands=84% and Hungary=83%) and 10 in the 70s. Altogether there were 14 (93%) female figures above 60%.

Considering the results reviewed in this section, then, so far as explained variance in living partner satisfaction is concerned, on average MDT performed better for females than for males and there was a much bigger share of female than male figures above 60%.

4.6   Prediction Success Ratios

Exhibit 4.6 lists the prediction success ratios for MDT in explanations of satisfaction with one's living partner for 31 countries, developed and less developed countries and the world balanced sample. The 92% figure beginning the last row of the exhibit indicates that in accounting for living partner satisfaction in the balanced world sample MDT made 11 hits out of 12 possibilities (column under TES, Exhibit 4.4). That is, MDT had a narrow prediction success ratio of 92% for the world sample explanation of living partner satisfaction for the whole group. For males, MDT had a narrow ratio of 82%, and for females MDT was 100% successful.

The second figure in each double column of Exhibit 4.6 gives the ratio of successful to total predicted *direct effects* in the 8 regression equations required for an application of MDT, i.e., the broad prediction success ratios or simply the broad ratios. The 60% figure in the last row of the exhibit indicates that in accounting for living partner satisfaction in the world sample MDT made 32 hits out of 53 possibilities (columns under S to SB, Exhibit 4.4). That is, MDT had a broad prediction success ratio of 60% for the world sample explanation of satisfaction with one's living partner for the whole group. For males, MDT had a broad ratio of 51%, and for females 58%.

Examination of the total mean prediction success ratios in Exhibit 4.6 (fourth row from the last) reveals a considerable drop in all figures compared to the world sample figures. For example, instead of a living partner satisfaction narrow ratio of 92% for the whole group, we have a total mean figure of 53%. The average total mean broad ratio is only around 19%. The developed country mean prediction success ratios are all higher than the less developed mean ratios.

In spite of the relatively low average performance of MDT for the 31 countries, there were still some notable successes. With respect to living partner satisfaction for the whole group, MDT had

Exhibit 4.6 Prediction success ratios for MDT in explanations of
satisfaction with one's living partner*

Country	Total		Males		Females	
Austria	58	17	55	13	64	20
Bahrain	-	-	-	-	-	-
Bangladesh+	42	13	-	-	36	11
Belgium	-	-	-	-	-	-
Brazil	58	08	-	-	55	20
Cameroon	25	18	36	17	-	-
Canada	67	32	64	27	46	18
Chile	-	-	-	-	-	-
Colombia	-	-	-	-	-	-
Egypt+	-	-	-	-	-	-
Finland	50	15	-	-	-	-
Germany	67	30	64	33	64	24
Greece	58	21	73	24	-	-
Hungary	33	11	-	-	36	09
India+	-	-	-	-	-	-
Israel	50	21	46	20	46	13
Japan	83	32	82	31	64	20
Jordan	42	11	-	-	-	-
Kenya+	50	13	-	-	-	-
Korea	58	23	27	13	-	-
Mexico	58	21	55	24	-	-
Netherlands	75	25	-	-	64	20
New Zealand	58	19	-	-	55	18
Norway	42	21	-	-	-	-
Philippines	50	17	-	-	-	-
Portugal	42	13	-	-	-	-
Puerto Rico	25	11	36	11	46	13
Singapore	-	-	-	-	-	-
S. Africa	42	17	-	-	-	-
Spain	75	19	-	-	-	-
Sweden	42	15	-	-	-	-
Switzerland	58	15	55	16	55	16
Taiwan	75	32	64	33	64	33
Tanzania+	42	17	27	16	-	-
Thailand	50	21	55	20	36	13
Turkey+	50	15	36	16	-	-
U. Kingdom	-	-	-	-	-	-

Exhibit 4.6 (continued)

Country	Total		Males		Females	
USA	75	25	55	20	82	27
Yugoslavia	75	25	55	22	-	-
Total Mean	53	19	52	21	54	18
Dev.C.Mean	55	20	55	22	56	19
L.D.C.Mean	46	15	32	16	36	11
World	92	60	82	51	100	58

* The first figures in each column give the ratio of successful to total predicted total effects. The second figures give the ratio of successful to total predicted direct effects in the 8 regressions required for an application of MDT.
+ Below 142-country median on per capita GNP and literacy rate.

a narrow prediction success ratio of 83% for Japan, and 75% for the Netherlands, Spain, Taiwan, United States and Yugoslavia. Altogether narrow ratios above 60% were obtained in 8 (26%) countries. For males, MDT achieved narrow ratios of 82% for Japan and 73% for Greece. For females, the figures reached 82% for the United States. Altogether, then, MDT obtained ratios above 60% for males in 5 (29%) countries, and for females in 6 (40%) countries.

MDT's lowest narrow ratio for the whole group was 25% for Cameroon and Puerto Rico. For males, the lowest ratio was 27% for Korea and Tanzania, and for females it was 36% for Bangladesh, Hungary and Thailand.

5

Satisfaction with One's Self-Esteem

5.1 Introduction

In this chapter MDT is used to explain satisfaction with one's own self-esteem. In the next section (5.2), I review mean satisfaction scores for the world balanced sample, relatively developed and less developed countries, 39 countries, males and females. In Sections 5.3 and 5.4 self-esteem satisfaction is explained by MDT, respectively, for the world balanced sample taken as a whole, and for males and females taken separately. Section 5.5 summarizes results of using MDT to explain self-esteem satisfaction in 37 countries, including relatively developed and less developed countries, males and females. In the final section (5.6), MDT's prediction success ratios are reviewed for all the explanations offered in Section 5.5.

5.2 Descriptive Statistics for World Sample, Males and Females

On my questionnaire "self-esteem" was defined as "how you feel about yourself; your sense of self-respect". Again, all satisfaction ratings were obtained from my revised 7-step delightful-terrible scale.

Exhibit 5.1 lists the mean and standard deviation scores, and sample sizes for satisfaction with one's self-esteem for my 39 participating countries. The last row of the table shows that the self-esteem satisfaction mean and standard deviation scores for the world balanced sample are 5.1 and 1.2, respectively, with an N=8942. The figures for the means of the mean and standard deviation scores for the 39 countries are exactly the same, while the total sample indirectly represented by these figures is N=17,775.

The two rows above the last give the results of separating out the 6 less developed countries (LDCs) from the 33 relatively developed countries (RDCs). The mean and standard deviation self-esteem satisfaction scores of the RDCs (5.1,1.1) are slightly lower than the scores of the LDCs (5.2,1.2). Two thirds of the LDCs (Egypt, India and Turkey=5.2, Tanzania=5.5) and one third of the RDCs had mean self-esteem satisfaction scores above the world mean.

Exhibit 5.1 Participating countries' mean and standard deviation scores, and sample sizes for satisfaction with one's self-esteem

----

Country	Mean	SD	N
Austria	4.9	1.2	342
Bahrain	5.7	1.2	280
Bangladesh+	5.0	1.2	262
Belgium	5.0	0.9	143
Brazil	5.8	1.0	277
Cameroon	5.1	1.2	180
Canada	5.1	1.1	1631
Chile	5.2	1.1	262
Colombia	5.5	1.1	91
Egypt+	5.2	1.4	276
Finland	5.2	1.1	269
Germany	4.9	1.1	798
Greece	5.1	1.0	258
Hungary	4.6	0.9	228
India+	5.2	1.2	251
Israel	5.5	0.9	317
Japan	4.0	1.3	1199
Jordan	5.6	1.3	296
Kenya+	5.1	1.3	264
Korea	4.1	1.6	451
Mexico	5.3	0.9	233
Netherlands	5.0	1.1	354
New Zealand	4.9	1.0	322
Norway	5.0	1.1	233
Philippines	5.3	1.0	997
Portugal	5.1	1.0	383
Puerto Rico	5.4	1.1	299
Singapore	4.9	0.9	255
S. Africa	5.3	1.1	289
Spain	4.5	1.1	271
Sweden	4.8	1.1	266
Switzerland	4.9	1.0	340
Taiwan	4.5	1.2	2465
Tanzania+	5.5	1.2	223
Thailand	5.4	1.2	582
Turkey+	5.2	1.1	296

Exhibit 5.1 (continued)

Country	Mean	SD	N
U. Kingdom	4.8	1.0	224
USA	5.2	1.2	1345
Yugoslavia	5.0	1.3	323
Total Mean	5.1	1.2	456
Dev.C.Mean	5.1	1.1	491
L.D.C.Mean	5.2	1.2	262
World	5.1	1.2	8942

+ Below 142-country median on per capita GNP and literacy rate.

There were 3 countries clustered around the top 10% for mean self-esteem satisfaction scores, namely, Brazil=5.8, Bahrain=5.7 and Jordan=5.6. Following these countries, there was a cluster of 3 with mean scores of 5.5 consisting of Colombia, Israel and Tanzania. Brazil's self-esteem satisfaction score of 5.8 was 58% of one standard deviation above the world mean.

There were 4 countries in the bottom 10% for self-esteem satisfaction scores, namely, Japan=4.0, Korea=4.1, Spain and Taiwan=4.5. Japan's score of 4.0 was 92% of one standard deviation below the world mean.

Exhibit 5.2 lists the mean and standard deviation scores, and sample sizes for satisfaction with one's self-esteem for males and females in my 39 countries. The last row of the table indicates that the self-esteem satisfaction mean and standard deviation scores for the world balanced sample of males (N=4562) are 5.1 and 1.2, respectively, and for females (N=4380) the corresponding figures are 5.0 and 1.2. Thus, females seem to have slightly less self-esteem satisfaction than males.

The fourth row from the last in this exhibit (total mean) shows that the means of the mean self-esteem satisfaction scores for the 39 countries for males and females are exactly the same as the figures for the world balanced sample. However, the sample sizes for the fourth row from the last indirectly represent N=8937 males and N=8822 females.

For males, the mean of the self-esteem satisfaction scores of the LDCs (5.3) is higher than the means of the world, total sample and the LDCs (5.1). For females, the mean of the self-esteem for females.

Exhibit 5.2 Participating countries' mean and standard deviation scores, and sample sizes for satisfaction with one's self-esteem for males and females

----

Country	Males Mean	SD	N	Females Mean	SD	N
Austria	5.0	1.2	136	4.8	1.2	206
Bahrain	6.0	1.1	56	5.6	1.3	224
Bangladesh+	5.0	1.2	174	5.1	1.2	88
Belgium	4.9	1.0	80	5.0	0.9	63
Brazil	5.8	1.0	110	5.8	1.0	167
Cameroon	5.0	1.3	143	5.6	1.0	37
Canada	5.2	1.1	627	5.1	1.1	1000
Chile	5.3	1.0	141	5.0	1.1	121
Colombia	5.6	1.1	55	5.4	1.0	36
Egypt+	5.3	1.3	156	5.1	1.5	120
Finland	5.2	1.2	110	5.2	1.1	159
Germany	5.0	1.1	434	4.8	1.2	364
Greece	5.2	1.0	143	5.1	1.0	115
Hungary	4.5	1.0	59	4.6	0.8	169
India+	5.2	1.3	156	5.1	1.1	95
Israel	5.5	0.9	163	5.5	0.9	154
Japan	4.0	1.3	982	4.3	1.3	217
Jordan	5.5	1.3	236	5.7	1.4	60
Kenya+	5.2	1.2	149	4.9	1.4	115
Korea	4.2	1.6	355	3.7	1.5	96
Mexico	5.3	0.9	163	5.4	0.9	69
Netherlands	5.3	1.0	160	4.8	1.2	194
New Zealand	5.0	1.0	116	4.9	1.0	206
Norway	5.0	1.0	91	4.9	1.2	142
Philippines	5.3	1.0	317	5.3	0.9	680
Portugal	5.0	1.1	198	5.1	0.9	182
Puerto Rico	5.6	1.1	167	5.2	1.1	132
Singapore	5.2	0.9	42	4.8	0.9	213
S. Africa	5.3	1.1	127	5.4	1.1	162
Spain	4.7	1.1	132	4.4	1.1	139
Sweden	4.9	1.2	140	4.7	1.0	126
Switzerland	5.0	1.1	172	4.8	0.9	168
Taiwan	4.7	1.2	1278	4.4	1.1	1187
Tanzania+	5.6	1.2	153	5.4	1.2	70
Thailand	5.5	1.2	267	5.3	1.1	315

Exhibit 5.2 (continued)

Country	Males			Females		
	Mean	SD	N	Mean	SD	N
Turkey+	5.2	1.1	198	5.1	1.1	90
U. Kingdom	4.8	1.0	104	4.7	0.9	120
USA	5.3	1.1	472	5.1	1.2	873
Yugoslavia	5.0	1.3	175	4.9	1.3	148
Total Mean	5.1	1.1	229	5.0	1.1	226
Dev.C.Mean	5.1	1.1	241	5.0	1.1	250
L.D.C.Mean	5.3	1.2	164	5.1	1.3	96
World	5.1	1.2	4562	5.0	1.2	4380

+ Below 142-country median on per capita GNP and literacy rate.

satisfaction scores of the LDCs (5.1) is also higher than that of the other groups (5.0).

For males, 5 (83%) LDCs had self-esteem satisfaction scores above the world mean, while 17 (44%) RDCs had such scores. Among the LDCs, only Bangladesh=5.0 scored below the world mean. For females, 5 (83%) LDCs also had scores above the world mean, while 16 (41%) RDCs had such scores. Among the LDCs, only Kenya=4.9 scored below the world mean.

Generally speaking, then, on the basis of the figures in the previous two paragraphs, it seems fair to say that the self-esteem satisfaction of males and females in LDCs is probably higher than that of males and females in RDCs.

For males, the 5 countries clustered around the top 10% for self-esteem satisfaction scores were Bahrain=6.0, Brazil=5.8, and Colombia, Puerto Rico and Tanzania=5.6. For females, the 4 top countries were Brazil=5.8, Jordan=5.7, and Bahrain and Cameroon=5.6. For males, Bahrain's score was 75% of one standard deviation above the world mean, and for females Brazil's score was 67% of a standard deviation above the world mean.

For males, there were 3 countries clustered around the bottom 10% for self-esteem satisfaction scores, namely, Japan=4.0, Korea=4.2 and Hungary=4.5. For females, the 4 bottom countries were Korea=3.7, Japan=4.3, Spain and Taiwan=4.4. Japan's male score was 92% of one standard deviation below the world mean for males, while Korea's female score was 108% below the world mean

5.3 Satisfaction Explained by MDT for World Sample

Exhibit 5.3 is the correlation matrix for the variables employed in this chapter. There are 6 cases of moderate ($r > .50$) multicollinearity among the predictors.

Exhibit 5.4 gives the results of using MDT to explain satisfaction with one's own self-esteem in the world balanced sample. In the column under S (in this context, for "satisfaction with one's self-esteem") we find a total sample N of 7813 students, including 3978 males and 3835 females. MDT explained 52% of the variance in reported self-esteem satisfaction scores for the whole group, 49% for males and 56% for females.

Exhibit 5.3 Correlation matrix for satisfaction with one's self-esteem*

	SX	AG	WS	LD	B	SO	SD	SN	SP	SF	SB	SW
SX	-											
AG	9	-										
WS	ns	12	-									
LD	2	36	ns	-								
B	ns	4	14	5	-							
SO	6	ns	3	5	4	-						
SD	4	6	5	ns	ns	44	-					
SN	5	6	5	ns	ns	51	60	-				
SP	2	3	2	ns	ns	47	46	54	-			
SF	ns	3	4	5	5	21	28	31	32	-		
SB	ns	ns	5	ns	ns	44	37	43	55	31	-	
SW	ns	4	3	ns	ns	59	43	51	46	24	40	-
SE	5	2	ns	ns	4	61	40	47	44	21	41	65

* Decimal points omitted; underlined figures indicate negative correlations; P = .05 or better; N = 9092; ns = not significant.

All things considered, for the group as a whole, sex is the only demographic variable that has much of an impact on satisfaction with one's self-esteem. As one would expect after seeing the results in the previous section, it is negative (Sex=-.06, TES column). Although sex has a smaller negative direct effect on self-esteem satisfaction (Sex=-.03, S column), it also impacts negatively on the gaps regarding self/others and self/needs (Sex=-.06), and self/deserved (Sex=-.04). Being female apparently creates some liabilities that tend to increase discrepancies regarding one's self-esteem.

All things considered, with regard to self-esteem satisfaction for the whole group, the self/others gap (SO=.43) has the greatest impact, followed by self/wants (SW=.41). Self/needs (SN=.13) enters in a fairly distant third place, followed by self/best (SB=.11) and then self/progress (SP=.09). The gap concerning equity (SD=.05) is less than half as important as that concerning needs.

From the column under SW one finds that my set of predictors explains 44% of the variance in scores indicating the perceived gap between the sort of self-esteem students have and the sort they want. Returning to TESW, one finds again that it is social comparison scores (SO=.39) that dominate the lot of predictors. The next most influential predictor is self/needs (SN=.18), followed by self/progress (SP=.11), and then self/deserved (SD=.07) and self/best (SB=.06).

Exhibit 5.4 Satisfaction with one's self-esteem
(decimal points omitted)

World
Total Balanced Sample

	S	SW	SO	SD	SN	SP	SF	SB	TES	TESW
N	7813	7867	8618	8452	8588	0	8535	0	-	-
R^2	52	44	1	1	1	0	1	0	-	-
Pred										
Sex	-3	2	-6	-4	-6	0	0	0	-6	-2
Age	0	-2	0	-5	-7	0	0	0	-2	-4
WS	0	0	-3	-4	-4	0	4	0	-2	-2
LED	0	0	4	0	4	0	4	0	2	2
ETH	-2	2	-4	0	0	0	-4	0	-3	1
SO	27	39							43	39

Exhibit 5.4 (continued)

	S	SW	SO	SD	SN	SP	SF	SB	TES	TESW
SD	2	7							5	7
SN	6	18							13	18
SP	4	11							9	11
SF	0	-2							-1	-2
SB	8	6							11	6
SW	41								41	
Males										
N	3978	4011	0	4317	4379	0	4352	0	-	-
R^2	49	42	0	1	1	0	1	0	-	-
Age	0	-3	0	-7	-9	0	0	0	-3	-5
WS	0	0	0	-4	-4	0	3	0	-1	-1
LED	0	0	0	0	4	0	6	0	1	1
ETH	0	4	0	0	0	0	-7	0	2	4
SO	27	38							43	38
SD	0	9							4	9
SN	5	18							12	18
SP	4	11							9	11
SB	8	6							11	6
SW	41								41	
Females										
N	3835	3856	4221	4135	4209	0	0	0	-	-
R^2	56	47	1	1	1	0	0	0	-	-
Age	0	0	0	-3	-4	0	0	0	-1	-1
WS	3	0	-4	-5	-5	0	0	0	0	-3
LED	0	0	3	0	0	0	0	0	1	1
ETH	-3	0	-8	-5	-5	0	0	0	-8	-5
SO	26	41							43	41
SD	4	5							6	5
SN	8	19							16	19
SP	4	11							9	11
SF	0	-3							-1	-3
SB	8	6							11	6
SW	41								41	

5.4 Satisfaction Explained by MDT for Males and Females

With the exception of ethnicity for females, none of the demographic variables has an impact on satisfaction with one's self-esteem above .03 for males or females. For females, all things considered, living in a relatively advantaged country has a negative impact on satisfaction with one's own self-esteem (ETH=-.08). For males, living in such a country is positively, but modestly, related to self-esteem satisfaction (ETH=.02).

Considering perceived discrepancies relative to self-esteem satisfaction, the rank orderings of the three most influential predictors for males and females are exactly the same as the ordering for the group as a whole. For males and females, we have self/others (SO=.43) and self/wants (SW=.41). Self/needs is a bit more influential for females (SN=.16) than for males (SN=.12). After these triads, for males self/best (SB=.11) runs a close fourth place, followed by self/progress (SP=.09). For females, self/best (SB=.11) is not a particularly close fourth, and it is followed by self/progress (SP=.09).

In the context of all the predictors used here, for males and females considerations of needs are over twice as important as equity regarding satisfaction with one's self-esteem. So, the pattern here is similar to that for satisfaction with one's family and friends, and dissimilar to that for satisfaction with one's living partner.

Considering the relative impacts of my predictors on the gaps between what students have and want regarding self-esteem, the rank orderings of the three most influential predictors for males and females are the same. For males, the triad runs from self/others (SO=.38) to self/needs (SN=.18) to self/progress (SP=.11), and for females it runs SO=.41, SN=.19 and SP=.11. Considerations of equity (SD=.09) come in fourth for males, while self/best (SB=.06) is fourth for females.

5.5 Thirty-Seven Countries

Exhibit 5.5 shows the percent of variance explained by MDT in satisfaction with one's self-esteem scores for 37 countries, developed and less developed countries, and the world sample. The detailed regressions on which these figures are based are in Appendix 5. The means of the mean percents of variance explained in self-esteem satisfaction scores for 37 countries are one percentage point short of

Exhibit 5.5 Percent of variance explained by MDT in satisfaction
with one's self-esteem.

Country	Total	Males	Females
Austria	68	72	68
Bahrain	34	-	32
Bangladesh+	65	63	68
Belgium	-	-	-
Brazil	43	43	46
Cameroon	31	33	-
Canada	62	64	60
Chile	49	49	45
Colombia	-	-	-
Egypt+	46	37	-
Finland	76	73	80
Germany	62	60	64
Greece	43	37	52
Hungary	45	-	46
India+	38	36	-
Israel	40	35	48
Japan	50	47	62
Jordan	35	34	-
Kenya+	52	57	44
Korea	50	49	-
Mexico	42	38	-
Netherlands	57	40	63
New Zealand	55	54	56
Norway	73	-	78
Philippines	42	51	38
Portugal	38	43	-
Puerto Rico	50	52	43
Singapore	58	-	57
S. Africa	29	29	24
Spain	51	57	50
Sweden	72	72	72
Switzerland	66	74	56
Taiwan	46	44	46
Tanzania+	61	52	-
Thailand	37	38	35
Turkey+	39	39	-
U. Kingdom	53	57	51

Exhibit 5.5 (continued)

Country	Total	Males	Females
USA	63	56	66
Yugoslavia	51	49	51
Total Mean	51	50	54
Dev.C.Mean	51	50	53
L.D.C.Mean	50	47	56
World	52	49	54

+ Below 142-country median on per capita GNP and literacy rate.

the world percent for the whole group (51%), one above for males (50%), and exactly the same for females (54%).

For the group as a whole and males, MDT did a relatively better job accounting for self-esteem satisfaction in RDCs than in LDCs. Specifically, MDT accounted for an average of 51% of the variance in self-esteem satisfaction scores for the whole group in RDCs compared to 50% in LDCs, and 50% for males in RDCs compared to 47% in LDCs. For females, MDT accounted for an average of 53% of self-esteem satisfaction scores in RDCs compared to 56% in LDCs.

For the whole group, percents of variance explained in scores indicating satisfaction with one's self-esteem ranged from a high of 76% in Finland to a low of 29% in South Africa. There were 2 other country figures in the 70s (Norway=73% and Sweden=72%). Although there were no others in the 20s, there were 7 in the 30s.

For males, self-esteem satisfaction percents of variance explained ranged from a high of 74% for Switzerland to a low of 29% for South Africa. There were 3 other male figures in the 70s (Finland=73%, Austria and Sweden=72%), no other male figures in the 20s, but 9 in the 30s. Altogether there were 6 (18%) male figures above 60%.

For females, self-esteem satisfaction percents of variance explained ranged from a high of 80% for Finland to a low of 24% for South Africa. There were 2 female figures in the 70s (Norway=78% and Sweden=72%). Altogether there were 9 (32%) female figures above 60%.

Considering the results reviewed in this section, then, so far as explained variance in self-esteem satisfaction is concerned, on average MDT performed better for females than for males and there was a bigger share of female than male figures above 60%.

5.6 Prediction Success Ratios

Exhibit 5.6 lists the prediction success ratios for MDT in explanations of satisfaction with one's self-esteem for 37 countries, developed and less developed countries and the world balanced sample. The figure beginning the last row of the exhibit indicates that in accounting for self-esteem satisfaction in the balanced world sample MDT had a narrow prediction success ratio of 100% for the whole group. For males and females, MDT had a narrow ratio of 91%.

MDT had a broad prediction success ratio of 59% for the world sample explanation of satisfaction with one's self-esteem for the whole group, 44% for males and 51% for females.

Examination of the total mean prediction success ratios in Exhibit 5.6 again reveals a considerable drop in all figures compared to the world sample figures. For example, instead of a self-esteem satisfaction narrow ratio of 100% for the whole group, we have a total mean figure of 57%. The average total mean broad ratio is only 19%. The developed country mean prediction success ratios are all at least as high as those of the less developed country mean ratios.

Regarding notable successes explaining self-esteem satisfaction for the whole group, MDT had a narrow prediction success ratio of 92% for Taiwan, 83% for Japan and the United States, and 75% for Austria, Canada and Germany. Altogether, narrow ratios above 60% were obtained in 10 (27%) countries. For males, MDT achieved narrow ratios of 73% for Germany, Japan and Taiwan. For females, the figures reached 73% for Canada, Taiwan and the United States. Altogether, then, MDT obtained ratios above 60% for males in 7 (21%) countries, and for females in 4 (14%) countries.

MDT's lowest narrow ratio for the whole group was 25% for South Africa. For males, the lowest ratio was 18% for the Netherlands and South Africa, and for females it was again 18% for South Africa.

Exhibit 5.6 Prediction success ratios for MDT in explanations of
satisfaction with one's self-esteem*

Country	Total		Males		Females	
Austria	75	21	55	16	46	18
Bahrain	58	17	-	-	55	24
Bangladesh+	58	17	55	18	55	20
Belgium	-	-	-	-	-	-
Brazil	42	15	27	09	36	11
Cameroon	58	23	46	13	-	-
Canada	75	42	55	20	73	31
Chile	58	15	46	13	27	09
Colombia	-	-	-	-	-	-
Egypt+	33	11	27	11	-	-
Finland	50	19	64	20	36	16
Germany	75	34	73	27	64	27
Greece	42	17	27	18	36	11
Hungary	50	15	-	-	36	13
India+	42	15	27	13	-	-
Israel	50	15	64	20	46	18
Japan	83	47	73	49	46	22
Jordan	58	21	36	11	-	-
Kenya+	42	15	46	13	27	16
Korea	58	23	64	20	-	-
Mexico	67	21	27	16	-	-
Netherlands	42	17	18	07	36	11
New Zealand	50	21	55	18	46	18
Norway	58	26	-	-	36	16
Philippines	50	28	55	18	46	24
Portugal	50	17	55	18	-	-
Puerto Rico	67	17	46	13	36	11
Singapore	58	21	-	-	46	16
S. Africa	25	11	18	07	18	13
Spain	67	23	55	18	55	13
Sweden	58	17	36	11	46	13
Switzerland	67	19	55	18	46	13
Taiwan	92	40	73	27	73	27
Tanzania+	50	28	36	16	-	-
Thailand	50	23	55	24	36	20
Turkey+	42	15	46	13	-	-
U. Kingdom	58	15	64	22	46	18

Exhibit 5.6 (continued)

Country	Total		Males		Females	
USA	83	38	46	18	73	31
Yugoslavia	50	21	36	20	36	16
Total Mean	57	22	47	17	45	18
Dev.C.Mean	59	23	49	18	45	18
L.D.C.Mean	45	17	40	14	41	18
World	100	59	91	44	91	51

* The first figures in each column give the ratio of successful to total predicted total effects. The second figures give the ratio of successful to total predicted direct effects in the 8 regressions required for an application of MDT.
+ Below 142-country median on per capita GNP and literacy rate.

6

Married Compared to Unmarried Students

6.1   Introduction

In this chapter my marital status variable is dichotomized into two subsets consisting of only married students in one and all others (single, widowed, separated and divorced) in the other. In the next section (6.2) I provide a summary of the composition of the married sample and compare essential aspects of it to the unmarried residual. In Section 6.3, I employ the same simple linear model used in Volume One, Chapter 5 to explain life satisfaction and happiness on the basis of satisfaction in 12 domains and 8 demographic variables. Following that, I present an overview of the results of using MDT to explain happiness and satisfaction in all domains for married and unmarried students, males and females (6.4). Then the focus is sharpened and I review these results for each domain in comparison with the others for married and unmarried students, males and females (6.5). In the last section (6.6), the focus is sharpened again and I examine the results of using MDT to explain satisfaction with one's living partner when the latter is also one's marriage partner, for all married students, males and females.

6.2   Sample Composition

Exhibit 6.1 summarizes the sample composition of 803 married students, representing 8.9% of the world balanced sample (Volume One, Exhibit 3.5). Fifty-three percent of the students are male and 47% are female. Among unmarried students, 51% are male and 49% are female. About 61% of the married students are over 25 years of age, compared to only 10% of the unmarried students. Thirty-five percent of the married students work from 20 to 40 hours per week, compared to about 10% of the unmarried students. Seventy-four percent of the married students had at most 4 full years of university education, compared to 90% of the unmarried students. Ninety-six percent of married students were citizens of the country in which they were attending university, compared to 98% of the unmarried

Exhibit 6.1 Sample composition

Whole World
Married Students

Sex	N	%	Status in Country	N	%
Male	425	52.9	Citizen	763	96.0
Female	378	47.1	Landed Immig.	15	1.9
Total	803	100.0	Visa	17	2.1
			Total	795	100.0

Age	N	%	Country Distribution	N	%
16 or <	40	5.0			
17-19	10	1.2	Tanzania	103	12.8
20-22	123	15.3	Finland	68	8.5
23-25	138	17.2	Cameroon	42	5.2
26-30	249	31.0	Portugal	40	5.0
31-35	129	16.1	Germany	32	4.0
36+	114	14.2	Others	518	64.5
Total	803	100.0	Total	803	100.0

Formal Educat.	N	%	Major Studies	N	%
1 yr. u	137	17.1	General	66	8.2
2 years	149	18.5	Natural Sci.	60	7.5
3 years	179	22.2	Biolog. Sci.	39	4.9
4 years	133	16.6	Social Sci.	284	35.3
5 years	76	9.5	Humanities	115	14.3
Degree	76	9.5	Engineering	37	4.6
Other	53	6.6	Commerce	64	8.0
Total	803	100.0	Other	138	17.2
			Total	803	100.0

Work Status	N	%	Years in Country	N	%
Unempl.	333	41.5	1 or less*	115	14.3
E.5hpw	34	4.2	2 years	3	.4
E.10hpw	40	5.0	3 years	8	1.0
E.20hpw	63	7.8	4 years	5	.6
E.30hpw	73	9.1	5 years	2	.2
E.40hpw	146	18.2	6 to 10	5	.6
Other	114	14.2	11 to 15	4	.5
Total	803	100.0	16 to 20	39	4.9

Exhibit 6.1 (continued)

Years in Country	N	%
21 to 25	182	22.7
26 to 30	207	25.8
31 or more	233	29.0
Total	803	100.0

students. Five countries are over-represented in the sample. Nearly 13% of the married students are from Tanzania, 8.5% from Finland, 5.2% from Cameroon, 5% from Portugal and 4% from Germany. Each other country in the world is represented by 3% or less of this set of married students, and students from these countries constitute about 65% of the married student sample.

6.3 Life Satisfaction and Happiness Explained by Satisfaction in 12 Domains and 8 Demographic Variables for Married and Unmarried Students, Males and Females

In Volume One, Chapter 5, I reviewed some research literature and analyzed my own data based on the simple idea that life satisfaction and happiness are linear functions of the net satisfaction one gets from a dozen particular domains of life plus some background conditions. Exhibit 6.2 summarizes results of applying that simple model to married and unmarried male and female students. More precisely, this exhibit gives the results of regressing life satisfaction and happiness scores on satisfaction in 12 domains and 8 demographic or background variables. The 12 domain satisfaction scores cover satisfaction with health (HE), finances (FI), family relations (FA), paid employment (PE), friendships (FR), housing (HO), living partner (LP), recreation activity (RA), religion (RE), self-esteem (SE), transportation (TR) and education (ED). The 8 background variables cover sex, age, marital status (MS), work status (WS), years of university completed (LED), major course of study (COS), country of birth (B) and citizenship status (CIT). Details of the definitions of all these variables may be found in Appendix 1.

Columns one and four (under T for "total set") of the upper

Exhibit 6.2 Multiple regression of life satisfaction and happiness on satisfaction in 12 domains and 8 demographic variables for married and unmarried students, males and females (decimal points ommitted)

Married Students

	Satisfaction			Happiness		
	UT	MA	FE	UT	MA	FE
PVE	49	52	45	37	37	35
N	378	222	156	384	226	158
Pred						
FI	32	30	39	23	22	25
PE	0	0	0	-11	-14	0
HO	14	12	0	12	17	0
LP	18	18	20	38	42	35
RA	0	12	0	0	0	0
SE	14	11	20	10	0	16
ED	25	27	18	12	18	0
DEMO						
COS	0	0	0	0	0	-16

Unmarried Students

	Satisfaction			Happiness		
	UT	MA	FE	UT	MA	FE
PVE	47	48	45	24	25	23
N	2088	1141	947	2068	1126	942
Pred						
HE	13	12	16	9	9	11
FI	14	17	11	12	13	13
FA	7	0	10	0	0	0
FR	12	14	11	13	11	18
HO	12	12	13	7	8	0
LP	14	12	15	15	13	20
RA	10	12	8	8	9	0
RE	0	0	0	6	7	0
SE	17	20	15	12	13	13
TR	4	0	0	0	0	0
ED	20	21	20	7	9	7
DEMO						
AGE	-4	0	0	0	0	0
LED	-7	-8	-8	-8	-8	-7

half of Exhibit 6.2 show that a subset of the 20 predictors was able to explain 49% of the variance in life satisfaction scores and 37% of the variance in happiness scores for married students. The 8 demographic and 5 domain satisfaction predictors had no statistically significant direct effects on the dependent variables.

The top 3 predictors of life satisfaction scores for married students (column one) were satisfaction with one's finances (Beta=.32), university education (B=.25) and living partner (B=.18), while the top 4 predictors of happiness scores (column four) were satisfaction with one's living partner (B=.38), finances (B=.23), and housing and university education tied (B=.12). Satisfaction with one's housing and self-esteem (B=.14) were tied for fourth place in accounting for life satisfaction, while satisfaction with one's paid employment (B=-.11) was fourth in accounting for happiness, followed closely by satisfaction with one's self-esteem (B=.10). I have no idea why satisfaction with one's paid employment was negatively related to happiness or, for that matter, why it was unrelated to life satisfaction. Previous research reviewed in Volume One indicated that job satisfaction is usually positively related to life satisfaction and happiness, and a bit more to the former than the latter.

For male married students, the simple linear model was able to explain 52% of the variance in life satisfaction and 37% in happiness scores. The 3 top predictors of life satisfaction were satisfaction with one's finances (B=.30), university education (B=.27) and living partner (B=.18). For happiness, the top 3 predictors were satisfaction with one's living partner (B=.42), finances (B=.22) and university education (B=.18). Satisfaction with one's housing and recreation activity (B=.12) were tied for fourth place, with self-esteem (B=.11) close behind in accounting for life satisfaction, while satisfaction with one's paid employment (B=-.14) was alone in fourth place in accounting for happiness.

For female married students, the simple linear model was able to explain 45% of the variance in life satisfaction and 35% in happiness scores. The only successful predictors of life satisfaction were satisfaction with one's finances (B=.39), living partner and self-esteem (B=.20), and university education (B=.18). For happiness, the only successful predictors were satisfaction with one's living partner (B=.35), finances (B=.25), self-esteem (B=.16) and major course of study (B=-.16). The negative course of study figure seems to indicate that female students in engineering and commerce were likely to be less happy than students in general programs, natural and biological sciences.

Columns one and four of the lower half of Exhibit 6.2 show

that a subset of the 20 predictors was able to explain 47% of the variance in life satisfaction scores and only 24% of the variance in happiness scores for unmarried students. Six of the 8 demographic but only one of the domain satisfaction predictors had no statistically significant direct effects on the dependent variables.

The top 4 predictors of life satisfaction scores for unmarried students (column one) were satisfaction with one's university education (B=.20), self-esteem (B=.17), and finances and living partner (B=.14) tied, while the top 4 predictors of happiness scores (column four) were satisfaction with one's living partner (B=.15), friendships (B=.13), and finances and self-esteem (B=.12). Level of university education was negatively related to both life satisfaction (LED=-.07) and happiness (LED=-.08) scores. That is, considering only direct effects, as a student's level of education increased, his or her level of reported life satisfaction and happiness decreased. These relationships were very similar for unmarried males and females.

For male unmarried students, the simple linear model was able to explain 48% of the variance in life satisfaction and 25% in happiness scores. The 3 top predictors of life satisfaction were satisfaction with one's university education (B=.21), self-esteem (B=.20) and finances (B=.17). For happiness, there was a three way tie at the top consisting of satisfaction with one's finances, living partner and self-esteem (B=.13), followed by satisfaction with one's friendships (B=.11) and then another three way tie involving health, recreation and university education (B=.09).

For female unmarried students, the simple linear model was able to explain 45% of the variance in life satisfaction and only 23% in happiness scores. The top predictors of life satisfaction were satisfaction with one's university education (B=.20), health (B=.16), and living partner and self-esteem (B=.15). For happiness, the top predictors were satisfaction with one's living partner (B=.20), friendships (B=.18), and finances and self-esteem (B=.13).

Generally speaking, then, the most salient feature of these applications of the simple linear model concerns the relative impact of living partner satisfaction on happiness and life satisfaction. For married students as a whole, males and females, living partner satisfaction dominates the set of predictors of happiness. For unmarried students, living partner satisfaction still singularly tops the list of predictors of happiness for the whole group and females, while it shares first place with financial and self-esteem satisfaction for males. Living partner satisfaction is an important predictor of life satisfaction for married and unmarried students, but it is not the most influential predictor for either group. For married students as a whole, males and females, the most influential predictor of life satisfaction is satisfaction with one's finances, while for unmarried students, males and females, the most influential predictor of life satisfaction is satisfaction with one's university education.

6.4 Overview of Explanations by MDT of Happiness and Satisfaction in All Domains for Married and Unmarried Students, Males and Females

Exhibit 6.3 gives the averages of the means, standard deviations and sample sizes of my 14 dependent variables, as well the average percents of variance obtained when MDT was used to explain these variables for married and unmarried students, males and females. The 14 variables, again, are happiness and satisfaction with life as a whole, and satisfaction with one's health, finances, family relations, paid employment, friendships, housing, living partner, recreation activity, religion, self-esteem, transportation and university education.

Inspection of the figures in the first columns in the upper and lower parts of the exhibit reveals that on average all married students, males and females, had relatively higher levels of satisfaction and happiness than unmarried students. This is certainly consistent with the research reviewed in Chapter 1.2 showing that married people in the populations at large in virtually all countries report higher levels of life satisfaction and happiness than unmarried people. In the next section I will have more to say about both of these global indicators and my 12 domain satisfaction indicators as well.

Regarding married students as a whole, the average score of the 14 dependent variables is 5.0, compared to 4.7 for unmarried students. For married males, the average score is 4.9, compared to 4.7 for unmarried males. For married females, the average score is 5.0, compared to 4.8 for unmarried females. The average standard deviation score in all cases is 1.3. There is, then, a clear order of average reported satisfaction and happiness, or generally, of subjective well-being. Married females (5.0) are at the top, followed by married males (4.9), followed by unmarried females (4.8) and then unmarried males (4.7). The difference between the average scores for married males and females is not statistically significant, but those between married and unmarried students and between unmarried males and females are statistically significant. I suspect, but cannot

Exhibit 6.3 Average percents of variance explained, means,
standard deviations and sample sizes for married and unmarried
students, males and females

Married Students

Average for Dependent Variables	Variable Mean	St.Dev	N	N*	% of Variance Explained
Total	5.0	1.3	760	645	58
Males	4.9	1.3	405	340	59
Females	5.0	1.3	355	305	57

Unmarried Students

Average for Dependent Variables	Variable Mean	St.Dev	N	N*	% of Variance Explained
Total	4.7	1.3	7400	6500	54
Males	4.7	1.3	3781	3307	53
Females	4.8	1.3	3619	3193	55

* Number of cases used in the regression.

prove, that the small difference between the average scores for married male and female students would be sustained if the sample sizes were increased, and it would be statistically significant.

Inspection of the figures in the last columns in the upper and lower parts of Exhibit 6.3 reveals that on average MDT explained a greater percent of the variance in dependent variable scores for all married students, males and females, than for unmarried students. Regarding married students as a whole, the average percent of variance explained in the 14 dependent variable scores is 58%, compared to 54% for unmarried students. For married males, the average percent of variance explained is 59%, compared to 53% for unmarried males. For married females, the average percent of variance explained is 57%, compared to 55% for unmarried females.

Exhibit 6.4 gives the average sample sizes, squared multiple correlation coefficients, and total effects of every predictor on the 14

Exhibit 6.4 Mean sample sizes, R^2s, and total effects on 13
satisfaction variables and one happiness variable for married and
unmarried students, males and females

	Married Mean Score	Unmarried Mean Score
N	645	6500
R^2	58	54
Predictors		
Sex	5	2
Age	2	-2
Work Status	3	1
Education	0	-1
Ethnicity	-5	0
Self/Others	44	38
Self/Deserved	4	9
Self/Needs	15	13
Self/Progress	9	13
Self/Future	1	0
Self/Best	12	11
Self/Wants	41	38

	Males Married Mean	Unmarried Mean	Females Married Mean	Unmarried Mean
N	340	3307	305	3193
R^2	59	53	57	55
Predictors				
Age	1	-3	2	-2
Work Status	6	1	2	2
Education	2	1	1	-1
Ethnicity	-3	2	5	-2
Self/Others	46	39	43	37
Self/Deserved	5	10	4	8
Self/Needs	12	12	15	15
Self/Progress	8	12	10	14
Self/Future	-1	0	0	1
Self/Best	13	11	9	11
Self/Wants	41	37	41	38

dependent variables for married and unmarried male and female students. The first two rows of the upper and lower parts of the exhibit give the same information as the last two columns of the previous exhibit but in a different context. Reading down the first column we find that there is a fairly distinct rank ordering of predictors by their average total effects. For married students, the most influential predictor is the perceived self/others discrepancy (SO=.44), followed by self/wants (SW=.41), self/needs (SN=.15), self/best (SB=.12) and self/progress (SP=.09). For unmarried students, the total impacts of these same 5 predictors are not as distinct. Self/others and self/wants (SO=SW=.38) tie for first place, and self/needs and self/progress (SN=SP=.13) tie for second place. Self/best (SB=.11) stands alone, then, in third place.

For married students, two demographic variables have a greater average impact than considerations of equity. Sex has an average total effect of (Sex=.05) and ethnicity has an average impact of (ETH=-.05). That is, for married students, on average being female has a positive impact and being born in a country with a relatively superior per capita GNP and literacy rate has a negative impact on one's subjective well-being. The impact of the self/deserved gap (SD=.04) is slightly smaller than that of these two variables.

For unmarried students, equity considerations (SD=.09) occupy fourth place in importance, and they are considerably more important than any demographic variables. The average total effects score of the latter never rises above .02.

For married males, the top two predictors are self/others (SO=.46) and self/wants (SW=.41). Following these two at some distance, there is another pair, namely, self/best (SB=.13) and self/needs (SN=.12). Self/progress (SP=.08) occupies fifth place. The most influential demographic variable is work status (WS=.06), which means that on average the more hours per week a married male student works at paid employment, the higher is his level of subjective well-being.

For unmarried males, the top two predictors are again self/others (SO=.39) and self/wants (SW=.37). Following these two, again at some distance, there is a tied pair consisting of self/needs and self/progress (SN=SP=.12). Then self/best (SB=.11) and self/deserved (SD=.10) follow closely behind this pair. Unlike their married counterparts, work status (WS=.01) is relatively unimportant for unmarried males.

As in the cases of married and unmarried males, for married and unmarried females, the top two predictors are self/others and self/wants. However, for married females, self/others (SO=.43) is ranked above self/wants (SW=.41), while for unmarried females self/wants (SW=.38) is ranked above self/others (SO=.37). The rank ordering of the next 3 influential predictors is the same for married and unmarried females. For the former, we have self/needs (SN=.15) followed by self/progress (SP=.10) and self/best (SB=.09), while for the latter we have SN=.15, SP=.14 and SB=.11.

Although on average being born in a relatively advantaged country has a modest negative impact on the subjective well-being of married males (ETH=-.03), it has a positive impact on the subjective well-being of married females (ETH=.05). For unmarried males and females, the negative and positive impacts of ethnicity are reversed. For the unmarried males, on average being born in a relatively advantaged country has a small positive impact on subjective well-being (ETH=.02), while for the unmarried females the impact is negative (ETH=-.02).

Exhibit 6.5 gives the average sample sizes, squared multiple correlation coefficients, and total effects of every predictor on the 13 self/wants variables corresponding to the 14 dependent variables for married and unmarried male and female students. (Recall that a single self/wants variable is used for the two global indicators of happiness and satisfaction with life as a whole.) Reading down the first column we find that on average MDT explains 49% of the variance in the perceived gap between what married students (N=652) have and want regarding my 14 dependent variables. The perceived self/others discrepancy (SO=.43) is by far the most influential predictor in the set, followed by self/needs (SN=.17) and self/progress (SP=.12).

For unmarried students, on average MDT explains 48% of the variance in the perceived gap between what such students (N=6562) have and want regarding my 14 dependent variables. The perceived self/others discrepancy (SO=.34) is again the most influential predictor in the set, followed by self/needs (SN=.19) and then self/deserved (SD=.12) and self/progress (SP=.11). In the given set of predictors, considerations of equity are three times as important for unmarried (SD=.12) as for married (SD=.04) students.

For married males (N=343), on average MDT explained 48% of the variance in self/wants gap scores, compared to 47% for unmarried males (N=3345). On average the top predictor of self/wants gap scores for married males is self/others (SO=.45), and that is followed by self/needs (SN=.17). Following these two, there is a triad in close succession consisting of self/progress (SP=.09), self/best (SB=.08) and work status (WS=.07).

For unmarried males, the top predictor is again self/others

Exhibit 6.5 Mean sample sizes, R^2s, and total effects on 13 self/wants variables for married and unmarried students, males and females

	Married Mean Score	Unmarried Mean Score
N	652	6562
R^2	49	48
Predictors		
Sex	5	3
Age	2	0
Work Status	3	-1
Education	0	0
Ethnicity	0	3
Self/Others	43	34
Self/Deserved	4	12
Self/Needs	17	19
Self/Progress	12	11
Self/Future	-1	-3
Self/Best	7	9

	Males Married Mean	Unmarried Mean	Females Married Mean	Unmarried Mean
N	343	3345	309	3318
R^2	48	47	49	48
Predictors				
Age	2	-2	1	1
Work Status	7	-1	0	-2
Education	2	1	1	0
Ethnicity	1	6	-1	0
Self/Others	45	36	44	32
Self/Deserved	3	13	4	11
Self/Needs	17	18	16	21
Self/Progress	9	10	11	12
Self/Future	-2	-3	-2	-2
Self/Best	8	8	6	9

(SO=.36), followed by self/needs (SN=.18), self/deserved (SD=.13) and self/progress (SP=.10). Again, unlike their married counterparts, work status (WS=-.01) is relatively unimportant for unmarried males. Considerations of equity are 4 times as important for unmarried (SD=.13) as for married (SD=.03) male students.

As in the cases of married and unmarried males, on average the top predictor of self/wants gap scores is self/others for married (SO=.44) and unmarried (SO=.32) females. The rank ordering of the next 2 influential predictors is the same for married and unmarried females. For the former, we have self/needs (SN=.16) followed by self/progress (SP=.11), while for the latter we have SN=.21 and SP=.12.

6.5 Domain Specific Explanations by MDT of Happiness and Satisfaction in All Domains for Married and Unmarried Students, Males and Females

Exhibit 6.6 gives the means, standard deviations and sample sizes of my 14 dependent variables, as well the percents of variance obtained when MDT was used to explain these variables for married students, males and females. Exhibit 6.7 gives the same information for unmarried students, males and females.

We have already established that, considering all 14 dependent variables, on average married students have higher levels of subjective well-being than unmarried students. Comparing the last six rows of Exhibits 6.6 and 6.7, it is clear that married students as a whole, and married males and females have higher levels of life satisfaction and happiness than their unmarried counterparts. For life satisfaction, the mean score of married students (N=776) is 5.0, compared to 4.7 for unmarried students (N=7986). For married male students (N=411), the mean life satisfaction score is 4.9, compared to 4.7 for unmarried students (N=4060). For married female students (N=365), the mean life satisfaction score is 5.1, compared to 4.8 for unmarried students (N=3926). For happiness, the mean score of married students (N=767) is 5.0, compared to 4.7 for unmarried students (N=7767). For married male students (N=409), the mean happiness score is 4.9, compared to 4.6 for unmarried students (N=3914). For married female students (N=358), the mean happiness score is 5.1, compared to 4.7 for unmarried students (N=3853).

If one regards these global indicator results as summary measures of the subjective well-being or quality of life of my sampled

Exhibit 6.6 Percents of variance explained, means, standard deviations and sample sizes for married students, males and females

----

Dependent
Variables:

Satisfaction with		Variable Mean	St.Dev	N	N*	% of Variance Explained
Health	T	5.4	1.1	798	681	52
	M	5.4	1.0	423	354	50
	F	5.3	1.1	375	327	55
Finances	T	4.2	1.3	790	693	63
	M	4.1	1.4	421	365	61
	F	4.4	1.2	369	328	64
Family	T	5.5	1.2	794	672	53
	M	5.4	1.2	421	349	48
	F	5.5	1.2	373	323	58
Job	T	4.3	1.5	524	435	63
	M	4.3	1.4	315	261	60
	F	4.3	1.6	209	174	67
Friends	T	5.2	1.1	797	694	53
	M	5.1	1.1	422	364	57
	F	5.2	1.1	375	330	49
Housing	T	4.8	1.4	794	694	65
	M	4.6	1.4	419	365	68
	F	5.0	1.3	375	329	62
Partner	T	5.9	1.2	773	642	57
	M	5.9	1.2	407	336	52
	F	5.9	1.2	366	306	66
Recreation	T	4.7	1.3	781	672	56
	M	4.6	1.3	411	348	59
	F	4.7	1.2	370	324	53
Religion	T	5.0	1.4	674	529	63
	M	5.0	1.5	355	273	68
	F	5.0	1.3	319	256	60
Self-esteem	T	5.3	1.1	782	665	56
	M	5.3	1.2	412	350	56
	F	5.3	1.5	370	315	55
Transport.	T	4.3	1.5	792	684	68
	M	4.2	1.5	421	355	67
	F	4.4	1.5	371	329	70

Exhibit 6.6 (continued)

Satisfaction with		Variable Mean	St.Dev	N	N*	% of Variance Explained
Education	T	5.0	1.2	794	670	51
	M	4.9	1.3	420	354	58
	F	5.0	1.1	374	316	42
Life	T	5.0	1.1	776	652	57
	M	4.9	1.2	411	342	62
	F	5.1	1.1	365	310	52
Happiness	T	5.0	1.3	767	646	55
	M	4.9	1.3	409	341	59
	F	5.1	1.3	358	305	50

* Number of cases used in the regression.

undergraduates, then one may say that there is a clear rank ordering among the various groups. Indeed, the ordering is precisely the same as the one described in the previous section. Married female students have the highest levels of subjective well-being, followed by married males, and then unmarried females and finally unmarried males. Unlike some of the figures in the previous section, all of the differences between the means of the four groups compared here are statistically significant at the .05 level.

If one counts the relative frequency with which mean scores are higher for married than for unmarried students, males and females, one can get another kind of rough summary measure of the subjective well-being of the four groups. Using this technique, married students (10/14) rank well above unmarried students (1/14), and married females (12/14) rank higher than married males (10/14), but unmarried males (3/14) rank higher than unmarried females (2/14).

All things considered regarding the three ways of summarizing my results concerning the subjective well-being of married versus unmarried students, the way used in the paragraph before the previous one appears to be the most rigorous way from a statistical point of view. However, it must be remembered that in order to apply that technique, one has to assume that the global measures of life satisfaction and happiness are good summary measures of subjective well-being or quality of life. Because I think that is a fair assumption given the evidence reviewed in Volume One, I am glad to accept as fact the rank ordering resulting from applying that technique. Fortunately, regarding the rank ordering of married versus unmarried students, the three techniques yield the same results. It is only in the ordering of unmarried males and females where one of the three techniques yields results that differ from those of the other two.

In Chapter 1.2 it was noted that Exhibit 7.1 of Volume One shows that for my global sample of undergraduates, satisfaction with one's family life has the highest average ratings for all 12 domains and life as a whole. Inspection of the average ratings for the 12 domains for married students in Exhibit 6.6 shows that satisfaction with one's living partner dominates the set. The ratings for the whole group, males and females are exactly the same, namely, 5.9. So, (recalling the results in Exhibit 6.2) for married students, the life domain that yields the highest level of net satisfaction independently of all other domains is precisely the domain that has the greatest positive impact on happiness with life as a whole.

The average ratings for family satisfaction are the second highest in the set. For the whole group of married students and for married females, the mean family satisfaction score is 5.5. For married males, the mean score is 5.4. There is only one other domain in which levels of satisfaction reach a score of 5.4. For the whole group of married students and for males, the mean score for satisfaction with one's health is 5.4, while for married females it is 5.3. Thus, average ratings for health satisfaction are the third highest in the set of scores for 14 domains.

As one might expect, given the sample size of unmarried students compared to that of the whole world balanced sample, the rank orderings of average domain satisfaction scores are very similar. In the case of the top three domains, the orderings are exactly the same. Average family satisfaction scores dominate the set, followed by friendship satisfaction and then health.

The domain yielding the lowest average satisfaction ratings for married students is that concerning finances. For the group as a whole, the mean score is 4.2, for married males it is 4.1 and for married females it is 4.4. In fact, there are no other mean scores as low as 4.1 in the total set of 42 scores listed in Exhibit 6.6. So, (recalling the results in Exhibit 6.2) for married students, the life domain that yields the lowest level of net satisfaction independently of all other domains is, unfortunately for them, the domain that has the greatest positive impact on satisfaction with life as a whole.

Exhibit 6.7 Percents of variance explained, means, standard deviations and sample sizes for unmarried students, males and females

----

Dependent
Variables:

Satisfaction with		Variable Mean	St.Dev	N	N*	% of Variance Explained
Health	T	5.1	1.1	8185	7339	51
	M	5.1	1.1	4178	3732	52
	F	5.2	1.1	4007	3607	50
Finances	T	4.2	1.3	7963	7163	53
	M	4.1	1.3	4083	3680	51
	F	4.2	1.3	3880	3483	55
Family	T	5.3	1.2	8130	7204	55
	M	5.3	1.2	4138	3615	54
	F	5.4	1.2	3992	3589	55
Job	T	3.9	1.6	3937	3245	65
	M	3.8	1.6	2052	1690	64
	F	4.0	1.5	1885	1550	66
Friends	T	5.3	1.2	8109	7338	50
	M	5.2	1.2	4136	3710	48
	F	5.3	1.2	3973	3628	51
Housing	T	4.8	1.3	8124	7203	54
	M	4.7	1.4	4150	3674	54
	F	4.9	1.3	3974	3529	52
Partner	T	5.0	1.5	4867	4039	67
	M	5.0	1.5	2584	2133	64
	F	5.1	1.5	2283	1906	70
Recreation	T	4.7	1.3	8062	7210	51
	M	4.7	1.4	4125	3679	52
	F	4.8	1.3	3937	3531	51
Religion	T	4.8	1.5	6265	5038	63
	M	4.8	1.5	3155	2508	61
	F	4.9	1.4	3110	2530	66
Self-esteem	T	5.0	1.2	8088	7096	52
	M	5.1	1.2	4115	3600	48
	F	5.0	1.2	3973	3496	56
Transport.	T	4.1	1.5	7981	7105	60
	M	4.1	1.6	4084	3641	59
	F	4.1	1.4	3897	3464	61

Exhibit 6.7 (continued)

Satisfaction with		Mean	Variable St.Dev	N	N*	% of Variance Explained
Education	T	4.6	1.3	8141	7231	49
	M	4.6	1.3	4159	3687	51
	F	4.7	1.2	3982	3544	47
Life	T	4.7	1.1	7986	6995	44
	M	4.7	1.1	4060	3543	45
	F	4.8	1.1	3926	3452	43
Happiness	T	4.7	1.3	7767	6800	41
	M	4.6	1.3	3914	3402	39
	F	4.7	1.3	3853	3398	43

* Number of cases used in the regression.

For unmarried students, the lowest average satisfaction ratings belong to the transportation domain. The ratings for the whole group, males and females are the same, namely, 4.1. In the total set of 42 scores in Exhibit 6.7 those are the only three scores as low as 4.1.

Reading down the last column in Exhibit 6.6, one finds that for married students, MDT was most successful in explaining the variance in the domains of transportation, housing and religion. For all married students, MDT accounted for 68% of the variance in scores indicating satisfaction with one's transportation. For married males, it accounted for 67% and for married females it accounted for 70% of the variance in such scores. MDT explained 65% of the variance in housing satisfaction scores for all married students, 68% for married males and 62% for married females. For the whole group of married students, MDT explained 63% of the variance in scores indicating satisfaction with one's religion. For married males, it explained 68% and for married females it explained 60% of such scores.

Considering all 14 dependent variables listed in the column, my theory was least successful in accounting for satisfaction with one's university education. For the whole group of married students, it explained 51% of the variance in education satisfaction scores, while for married males it explained 58% and for married females it explained 42%. There is no other figure as low as 42% in the column.

Reading down the last column in Exhibit 6.7, one finds that for unmarried students, MDT was most successful in explaining the variance in the domains of living partner, paid employment and religion. For all unmarried students, MDT accounted for 67% of the variance in scores indicating satisfaction with one's living partner. For unmarried males, it accounted for 64% and for unmarried females it accounted for 70% of the variance in such scores. MDT explained 65% of the variance in job satisfaction scores for all unmarried students, 64% for unmarried males and 66% for unmarried females. For the whole group of unmarried students, MDT explained 63% of the variance in scores indicating satisfaction with one's religion. For unmarried males, it explained 61% and for unmarried females it explained 66% of such scores.

Among the 12 domains, the theory was again least successful in accounting for satisfaction with one's university education. For the whole group of unmarried students, it explained 49% of the variance in education satisfaction scores, while for unmarried males it explained 51% and for unmarried females it explained 47%. Considering all 14 dependent variables listed in the column, MDT was least successful in accounting for happiness and then life satisfaction.

6.6 Satisfaction With One's Living Partner Explained by MDT for Married and Unmarried Students, Males and Females

Exhibit 6.8 gives the detailed results of using MDT to explain satisfaction with one's living partner for married students. An exhibit giving the detailed results of using MDT to explain satisfaction with one's living partner for unmarried students may be found in Appendix 7. As one would expect, the latter results are very similar to those for the whole world balanced sample in Exhibit 4.4. In the column under S in Exhibit 6.8, we find a total sample N of 642 students, including 336 males and 306 females. MDT explained 57% of the variance in reported living partner satisfaction scores for the whole group, 52% for males and 66% for females.

All things considered, for the group of married students as a whole, being female has a positive impact on satisfaction with one's living partner (Sex=.06, TES column) and on the gap between what one has and wants regarding one's partner (Sex=.07, TESW column). Age has a small negative effect on living partner satisfaction and on

Exhibit 6.8 Satisfaction with one's living partner
(decimal points omitted)

Whole World
Married Students

	S	SW	SO	SD	SN	SP	SF	SB	TES	TESW
N	642	646	746	724	733	745	710	727	-	-
R^2	57	57	3	1	1	2	1	1	-	-
Pred										
Sex	0	0	8	0	0	10	0	8	6	7
Age	0	0	0	0	0	-9	0	-8	-2	-2
WS	0	0	0	0	0	0	11	0	0	0
LED	0	0	0	0	-7	0	0	0	0	0
ETH	0	0	-14	-9	-10	0	0	0	-8	-9
SO	22	57							47	57
SD	7	8							11	8
SP	0	14							6	14
SB	15	8							19	8
SW	44								44	

Males

	S	SW	SO	SD	SN	SP	SF	SB	TES	TESW
N	336	338	388	377	385	0	370	0	-	-
R^2	52	60	2	1	1	0	1	0	-	-
Age	0	8	0	0	0	0	0	0	3	8
WS	0	0	0	0	0	0	12	0	0	0
LED	0	0	0	0	-10	0	0	0	-1	-1
ETH	0	0	-16	-10	0	0	0	0	-8	-10
SO	16	62							43	62
SD	13	0							13	0
SN	0	11							5	11
SB	14	16							21	16
SW	43								43	

Females

	S	SW	SO	SD	SN	SP	SF	SB	TES	TESW
N	306	308	358	0	348	355	340	0	-	-
R^2	66	53	2	0	1	2	1	0	-	-
Age	0	0	-10	0	0	-13	0	0	-7	-9
WS	0	0	0	0	0	0	12	0	0	0
ETH	-8	0	-12	0	-12	0	0	0	-15	-7
SO	28	56							55	56
SP	0	24							12	24
SB	18	0							18	0
SW	48								48	

the gap regarding self/wants (Age=-.02). Being born in a relatively advantaged country also has a negative impact on living partner satisfaction (ETH=-.08) and its corresponding self/wants gap (ETH=-.09).

Reading down the TES column in Exhibit 6.8, one finds that, all things considered, with regard to living partner satisfaction for the whole group of married students, the self/others gap (SO=.47) has the greatest impact, followed by self/wants (SW=.44). Following these predictors at some distance, self/best (SP=.19) enters in a fairly distant third place, followed by self/deserved (SD=.11) and then self/progress (SP=.06). In the context of the given set of predictors, the gaps concerning needs and future expectations have no role to play at all.

From the column under SW one finds that my set of predictors explains 57% of the variance in scores indicating the perceived gap between the sort of living partner married students have and the sort they want. Returning to TESW, one finds again that it is social comparison scores (SO=.57) that dominate the lot of predictors. Coming far behind self/others, the next most influential predictor is self/progress (SP=.14). Self/deserved and self/best (SD=SB=.08) are equally important, and somewhat less so than ethnicity (ETH=-.09).

Of all the demographic variables, ethnicity has the greatest impact on satisfaction with one's living partner for married males (ETH=-.08)) and married females (ETH=-.15). For married males, age has a small positive effect (Age=.03), while for married females it has a negative effect (Age=-.07).

Considering perceived discrepancies relative to living partner satisfaction, the rank ordering of the three most influential predictors for married females is exactly the same as the ordering for the whole group of married students. For married females, we have self/others (SO=.55), self/wants (SW=.48) and self/best (SB=.18). For married males, we have a tie between self/others and self/wants (SO=SW=.43), and then self/best (SB=.21). After this triad, for married males self/deserved (SD=.13) occupies third place. For married females, self/progress (SB=.12) occupies fourth place among discrepancy predictors but fifth place in the total set of predictors. In the given context, considerations of progress and the future have no role to play for married males, while considerations of equity, needs and the future have no role to play for married females.

Considering the relative impacts of my predictors on the gaps between what students have and want regarding living partners, the self/others gap is almost four times as influential as its next rival for married males (SO=.62) and over twice as influential as its next rival for married females (SO=.56). For married males, self/best (SB=.16) is the second most important predictor, followed by self/needs (SN=.11). For married females, second place is occupied by the self/progress gap (SP=.24), which is followed by the two demographic predictors with negative impacts, namely, ethnicity (ETH=-.07) and age (AGE=-.09).

7

Concluding Remarks

I began this volume with some remarks from Nye's (1988) excellent review of the past 50 years of research on marriage and the family, and especially marital success. Throwing modesty to the winds, I expressed some gratification in the fact that MDT can explain substantially more of the variance in the relevant dependent variables concerning satisfaction with one's family and living partner than Nye indicated typical theories can explain. I hope and believe the preceding chapters have provided an adequate justification for my biased view. If so, I suppose one would have to regard this as the most important contribution in this volume. Apart from this, however, I think the following results are worth remembering.

Just as national probability samples from several countries have shown that people tend to report higher levels of satisfaction from their family relations than from any other domain of life, so does my sample of university students. However, for married students, the highest levels of satisfaction are reported for their living partners. Again, just as previous research in many countries has shown that married people tend to report higher levels of subjective well-being than unmarried people, so does my sample of married university students. Indeed, if one regards the global measures of life satisfaction and happiness as summary indicators of the subjective well-being of my sampled undergraduates, then one finds a clear rank ordering among the various groups. Married female students have the highest levels of subjective well-being, followed by married males, and then unmarried females and finally unmarried males.

For three of the four domains examined here, females report higher satisfaction ratings than males, i.e., for family relations, friendships and living partners. For the fourth domain, self-esteem, males report higher satisfaction levels.

For all four domains, MDT explains a greater percent of the variance in the dependent variable for females than for males.

Considering the total effects of my seven discrepancy predictors, social comparisons and aspiration/achievement gaps are generally the two most influential contributors to satisfaction in all four domains. Indeed, with one exception, in every case the self/others gap dominates the set. The single exception involves the explanation of satisfaction with one's self-esteem for males, in which case the order of importance of these two predictors is reversed.

While perceived equity was a bit more important than need fulfillment for the life satisfaction and happiness of males (Volume One, Chapter 6.2) and the reverse was true for females, for all four domains examined here, with one exception, the self/needs variable is more influential than the self/deserved variable for males and females. The single exception involves the explanation of satisfaction with one's living partner for males, in which case the order of importance of these two predictors is reversed.

Regarding applications of the simple linear model, for married students as a whole, males and females, living partner satisfaction dominates the set of predictors of happiness. For unmarried students, living partner satisfaction leads the list of predictors of happiness for the whole group and females, and it shares first place with financial and self-esteem satisfaction for males. For married students as a whole, males and females, the most influential predictor of life satisfaction is satisfaction with one's finances, while for unmarried students, males and females, the most influential predictor of life satisfaction is satisfaction with one's university education.

Regarding applications of MDT, on average it explained a greater percent of the variance in dependent variable scores for all married students, males and females, than for unmarried students. Considering all 14 dependent variables, on average the two most influential predictors for married and unmarried males and females are the same, namely, self/others and self/wants. However, for married and unmarried males and for married females, self/others is ranked above self/wants, while for unmarried females self/wants is ranked above self/others. For married and unmarried males and females, on average self/needs is ranked above self/deserved.

Regarding living partner satisfaction, for married males social comparison and aspiration/achievement gap scores are equally influential predictors, while for married females the former are more influential than the latter. In the context of the given set of discrepancy predictors, living partner satisfaction is influenced more by equity than by need fulfillment scores for married males, but neither of these variables has any impact for married females.

References

Allred, K.D. and T.W. Smith: 1989, "The hardy personality: cognitive and physiological responses to evaluative threat", *Journal of Personality and Social Psychology*, 56, pp.257-266.

Andrews, F.M. and S.B. Withey: 1976, *Social Indicators of Well-Being* (Plenum Press, New York).

Anson, O.: 1989, "Marital status and women's health revisited: the importance of a proximate adult", *Journal of Marriage and the Family*, 51, pp.185-194.

Ball, R.E. and L. Robbins: 1986, "Black husbands' satisfaction with their family life", *Journal of Marriage and the Family*, 48, pp.849-855.

Berry, R.E. and F.L. Williams: 1987, "Assessing the relationship between quality of life and marital and income satisfaction: a path analytic approach", *Journal of Marriage and the Family*, 49, pp.107 116.

Broman, C.L.: 1988, "Satisfaction among Blacks: the significance of marriage and parenthood", *Journal of Marriage and the Family*, 50, pp.45-51.

Broderick, J.E. and K.D. O'Leary: 1986, "Contributions of affect, attitudes, and behavior to marital satisfaction", *Journal of Consulting and Clinical Psychology*, 54, pp.514-517.

Burgess, E. and L. Cottrell: 1939, *Predicting Success or Failure in Marriage* (Prentice-Hall, Inc., New York).

Callan, V.J.: 1987, "The personal and marital adjustment of mothers and of voluntarily and involuntarily childless wives", *Journal of Marriage and the Family*, 49, pp.847-856.

Campbell, A.: 1981, *The Sense of Well-Being in America* (McGraw-Hill, New York).

Campbell, A.P., P.E. Converse and W.L. Rodgers: 1976, *The Quality of American Life* (Russell Sage Foundation, New York).

Campbell, J.D.: 1990, "Self-esteem and clarity of the self-concept", *Journal of Personality and Social Psychology*, 59, pp.538-549.

Campbell, J.D., P.J. Fairey and B. Fehr: 1986, "Better than me or better than thee? Reactions to intrapersonal and interpersonal performance feedback", *Journal of Personality*, 54, pp.479-493.

Cassidy, M.L.: 1985, "Role conflict in the post parental period", *Research on Aging*, 7, pp.433-454.

Cate, R.M., S.A. Lloyd and E. Long: 1988, "The role of rewards and fairness in developing premarital relationships", *Journal of Marriage and the Family*, 50, pp.443-452.

Chassin, L., A. Zeiss, K. Cooper and J. Reaven: 1985, "Role perceptions, self-role congruence and marital satisfaction in dual-worker couples with preschool children", *Social Psychology Quarterly*, 48, pp.301-311.

Clark, M.S. and H.T. Reis: 1988, "Interpersonal processes in close relationships", *Annual Review of Psychology*, 39, pp.609-672

Cooper, K., L. Chassin and A. Zeiss: 1985, "The relation of sex-role self-concept and sex-role attitudes to the marital satisfaction and personal adjustment of dual-worker couples with preschool children", *Sex Roles*, 12, pp.227-241.

Eichler, M.: 1983, *Families in Canada Today: Recent Changes and Their Policy Consequences* (Gage Publishing Ltd, Toronto).

Essex, M.J. and S. Nam: 1987, "Marital status and loneliness among older women: the differential importance of close family and friends", *Journal of Marriage and the Family*, 49, pp.93-106.

Farrell, J. and K.S. Markides: 1985, "Marriage and health: a three-generation study of Mexican Americans", *Journal of Marriage and the Family*, 47, pp.1029-1036.

Feingold, A.: 1990, "Gender differences in effects of physical attractiveness on romantic attraction: a comparison across five research paradigms", *Journal of Personality and Social Psychology*, 59, pp.981-993.

Franzoi, S.L., M.H. Davis and R.D. Young: 1985, "The effects of private self-consciousness and perspective taking on satisfaction in close relationships", *Journal of Personality and Social Psychology*, 48, pp.1584-1594.

Glenn, N.D.: 1990, "Quantitative research on marital quality in the 1980s: A critical review", *Journal of Marriage and the Family*, 52, pp.818-831.

Glenn, N.D. and S. McLanahan: 1982, "Children and marital happiness: A further specification of the relationship", *Journal of Marriage and the Family*, 44, pp.63-72.

Glenn, N.D. and C. Weaver: 1979, "A note on family situation and global happiness", *Social Forces*, 57, pp.960-967.

Halford, W.K., K. Hahlweg and M. Dunne: 1990, "The cross-cultural consistency of marital communication associated with marital distress", *Journal of Marriage and the Family*, 52, pp.487-500.

Haring-Hidore, M.J., W.A. Stock, M.A. Okun and R.A. Witter: 1985, "Marital status and subjective well-being: a research synthesis", *Journal of Marriage and the Family*, 47, pp.947-953.

Hendrick, S.S., C. Hendrick and N.L. Adler: 1988, "Romantic relationships: love, satisfaction, and staying together", *Journal of Personality and Social Psychology*, 54, pp.980-988.

Holman, T.B. and M. Jacquart: 1988, "Leisure-activity patterns and marital satisfaction: a further test", *Journal of Marriage and the Family*, 50, pp.69-77.

Jacobson, N.S.: 1983, "Expanding the range and applicability of behavioral marital therapy", *Behavior Therapist*, 6, pp.189-191.

Jones, C., L. Marsden and L. Tepperman: 1990, *Lives of Their Own: The Individualization of Women's Lives* (Oxford University Press, Toronto).

Jones, E. and C. Gallois: 1989, "Spouses' impressions of rules for communication in public and private marital conflicts", *Journal of Marriage and the Family*, 51, pp.957-967.

Kernis, M.H., J. Brockner and B.S. Frankel: 1989, "Self-esteem and reactions to failure: the mediating role of overgeneralization", *Journal of Personality and Social Psychology*, 57, pp.707-714.

Kurdek, L.A. and J.P. Schmitt: 1987, "Partner homogamy in married, heterosexual cohabiting, gay, and lesbian couples", *The Journal of Sex Research*, 23, pp.212-232.

Lavee, Y., H.I. McCubbin and D.H. Olson: 1987, "The effect of stressful life events and transitions on family functioning and well-being", *Journal of Marriage and the Family*, 49, pp.857-873.

Lazarus, R.S. and S. Folkman: 1984, *Stress, Appraisal and Coping* (Springer, New York).

Long, E.C.J. and D.W. Andrews: 1990, "Perspective taking as a predictor of marital adjustment", *Journal of Personality and Social Psychology*, 59, pp.126-131.

Major, B. *et al.*: 1990, "Perceived social support, self-efficacy, and adjustment to abortion", *Journal of Personality and Social Psychology*, 59, pp.452-463.

Margolin, L. and L. White: 1987, "The continuing role of physical attractiveness in marriage", *Journal of Marriage and the Family*, 49, pp.21-27.

Markides, K.S. and J. Farrell: 1985, "Marital status and depression among Mexican Americans", *Social Psychiatry*, 20, pp.86-91.

Mashal, M.M.S.: 1985, "Marital power, role expectations and marital satisfaction", *International Journal of Women's Studies*, 8, pp.40-46.

Mastekaasa, A.: 1990, "Marital status, distress, and well-being: an international comparison". Paper presented at the XII World Congress of Sociology, Madrid 9-13 July 1990.

Michalos, A.C.: 1982, *North American Social Report*, Vol. 5: *Economics, Religion and Morality* (D. Reidel Pub. Co., Dordrecht).

Michalos, A.C.: 1982a, "The satisfaction and happiness of some senior citizens in rural Ontario", *Social Indicators Research*, 11, pp. 1-30.

Michalos, A.C.: 1983, "Satisfaction and happiness in a rural northern resource community", *Social Indicators Research*, 13, pp. 225-252.

Michalos, A.C.: 1985, "Multiple discrepancies theory (MDT)", *Social Indicators Research*, 16, pp. 347-413.

Michalos, A.C.: 1986, "Job satisfaction, marital satisfaction and the quality of life: a review and a preview", *Research on the Quality of Life*, ed. by F.M. Andrews (University of Michigan Press, Ann Arbor) pp.57-83.

Michalos, A.C.: 1987, "What makes people happy?". *Levekarsforskning Konferanserapport* (Proceedings of the Seminar on Welfare Research), (Norwegian Research Council for Science and the Humanities, Oslo, Norway) pp.12-93.

Michalos, A.C.: 1988, "Integrated development planning using socio-economic and quality-of-life indicators", *Innovative Approaches to Development Planning* (Unesco, Paris) pp.113-216.

Miller, S.M. and N. Kirsch: 1987, "Sex differences in cognitive coping with stress", *Gender and Stress*, ed. by R.C. Barnett, L. Biener and G.K. Baruch (Free Press, New York) pp.278-307.

Moffitt, P.F., N.D. Spence and R.D. Goldney: 1986, "Mental health in marriage: the roles of need for affiliation, sensitivity to rejection, and other factors", *Journal of Clinical Psychology*, 42, pp.68-76.

Nye, F.I.: 1988, "Fifty years of family research, 1937-1987", *Journal of Marriage and the Family*, 50, pp.305-316.

Oppong, J.R., R.G. Ironside and L.W. Kennedy: 1988, "Perceived quality of life in a centre-periphery framework", *Social Indicators Research*, 20, pp.605-620.

Pedhazur, E.J.: 1982, *Multiple Regression in Behavioral Research* (Holt, Rinehart and Winston, New York).

Pelham, B.W. and W.B. Swann, Jr.: 1989: "From self-conceptions to self-worth: on the sources and structure of global self-esteem", *Journal of Personality and Social Psychology*, 57, pp.672-680.

Pittman, J.F. and S.A. Lloyd: 1988, "Quality of family life, social support, and stress", *Journal of Marriage and the Family*, 50, pp.53-67.

Rhodewalt, F. and J.B. Zone: 1989, "Appraisal of life change, depression, and illness in hardy and nonhardy women", *Journal of Personality and Social Psychology*, 56, pp.81-88.

Robertson, J.F. and R.L. Simons: 1989, "Family factors, self-esteem, and adolescent depression", *Journal of Marriage and the Family*, 51, pp.125-138.

Sabatelli, R.M.: 1988, "Exploring relationship satisfaction: a social exchange perspective on the interdependence between theory, research, and practice", *Family Relations*, 37, pp.217-222.

Sabatelli, R.M. and J. Pearce: 1986, "Exploring marital expectations", *Journal of Social and Personal Relationships*, 3, pp.307-321.

Schmitt, J.P. and L.A. Kurdek: 1985, "Age and gender differences in and personality correlates of loneliness in different relationships", *Journal of Personality Assessment*, 49, pp.485-496.

Snowden, L.R., T.L. Schott, S.J. Awalt and J. Gillis-Knox: 1988, "Marital satisfaction in pregnancy: stability and change", *Journal of Marriage and the Family*, 50, pp.325-333.

Spanier, G.B. and R. Lewis: 1980, "Marital quality: a review of the seventies", *Journal of Marriage and the Family*, 42, pp.825-839.

Spitze, G.: 1988, "Women's employment and family relations: a review", *Journal of Marriage and the Family*, 50, pp.595-618.

Swann, W.B., B.W. Pelham and D.S. Krull: 1989, "Agreeable fancy or disagreeable truth? Reconciling self-enhancement and self-verification", *Journal of Personality and Social Psychology* 57, pp.782-791.

Tanfer, K.: 1987, "Patterns of premarital cohabitation among never-married women in the United States", *Journal of Marriage and the Family*, 49, pp.483-497.

Thompson, L. and A.J. Walker: 1989, "Gender in families: women and men in marriage, work, and parenthood", *Journal of Marriage and the Family*, 51, pp.845-871).

Thornton, A.: 1989, "Changing attitudes toward family issues in the United States", *Journal of Marriage and the Family*, 51, pp.873-893.

Trovato, F. and G. Lauris: 1989, "Marital status and mortality in Canada: 1951-1981', *Journal of Marriage and the Family*, 51, pp.907-922.

Veenhoven, R.: 1983, "The growing impact of marriage", *Social Indicators Research*, 12, pp.49-63.

Veevers, J.E.: 1979, "Voluntary childlessness: a review of issues and evidence", *Marriage and Family Review*, 2, pp.2-26.

Veevers, J.E.: 1988, "The 'real' marriage squeeze", *Sociological Perspectives*, 31, pp.169-189.

Wright, L.S., K. Springs Matlock and D.T. Matlock: 1985, "Parents of handicapped children: their self-ratings, life satisfaction and parental adequacy", *The Exceptional Child*, 32, pp.37-40.

Zapf, W., *et al.* : 1987, "German social report: living conditions and subjective well-being, 1978-1984", *Social Indicators Research*, 19, pp.1-173.

Appendix 1 Abbreviations and definitions

The following abbreviations and definitions apply to all exhibits in this book.

a: Not in equation: This occurs in columns to indicate that a particular predictor or explanatory variable was not used in some regression.

B: Country of birth.

CIT: Citizenship status: Following Canadian usage, there were typically 3 options, namely, citizen of the country in which the survey was taken, landed immigrant or visa student.

COS: Major course of study: General studies, natural sciences, biological sciences, social sciences, humanities, engineering, commerce or others.

DEMO: Demographic variables: sex, age, marital status, work status, level of education, major course of study, country of birth, citizenship status, length of time one has been in the country in which one is attending university.

ED: Education: One's formal education as provided in the university (or college) one is presently attending.

ETH: Ethnicity: Denotes either of two demographic variables indicating (1) the length of time one has been in the country in which one is currently attending university or (2) one's country of birth. Ethnicity is operationalized by the former variable in the analysis of individual countries and by the latter variable in analyses involving groups of countries. See also TIC and B.

FA: Family relations: Kind of contact and frequency of contact one has with one's family members. This includes personal contact, phone calls, and letters.

FI: Finances: One's income and assets (including investments, property, etc.).

FR: Friendships: Kind of contact and frequency of contact one has with one's friends. This includes personal contact, phone calls, and letters.

H: Happiness: The reference is always to one's happiness with life as a whole; one's happiness, all things considered; or global happiness. The term itself is left undefined on the questionnaire.

HE: Health: The present state of one's general, overall health (relatively free of common and chronic illnesses).

HO: Housing: The present type, atmosphere and state of one's home (apartment, house, farm, room, etc.).

LDC: Less Developed Country.

LED: Level of education: Denotes a demographic variable indicating the highest level of formal education completed.

LP: Living partner: Includes marriage partner; partner sharing intimate relations.

M: Mean: The arithmetic mean of a row or column of scores. Global scores are never averaged in with domain scores.

MDT: Multiple Discrepancies Theory.

MS: Marital status: single, married, widowed, separated, divorced.

N: Number of valid cases in the sample.

PE: Paid employment: Any work for wages, salaries or fees.

Pred: Predictors: Predictor or explanatory variables in a regression equation.

PVE: Percent of variance explained: The reference is always to the variance of the dependent variable named at the top of a column of figures. In some tables % is used.

R^2: The multiple correlation coefficient squared.

RA: Recreation activity: Personal recreation activities one engages in for pure pleasure, when one is not doing normal daily chores or some type of work.   This includes relaxing, reading, television viewing, regular get-togethers, church activities, arts and crafts, exercises, trips, etc.

RDC: Relatively Developed Country.

RE: Religion: One's spiritual fulfillment.

S: Satisfaction: The reference is either to particular domains of life (e.g., satisfaction with one's own health, satisfaction with one's housing, etc.) or to satisfaction with life as a whole (global satisfaction). The context indicates whether domain or global satisfaction is being considered. The term 'satisfaction' itself is left undefined.

SB: Self/best: The perceived discrepancy between what one has now and the best one has ever had before.

SD: Self/deserved: The perceived discrepancy between what one has now and deserves or merits.

SE: Self/esteem: How one feels about oneself; one's sense of self-respect.

SF: Self/future: The perceived discrepancy between what one has now and what one expects to have five years from now.

SN: Self/needs: The perceived discrepancy between what one has now and needs.

SO: Self/others: The perceived discrepancy between what one has now and others have, when the others are specified as living in the same area, having the same sex and being roughly the same age as the respondent.

SP: Self/progress: The perceived discrepancy between what one has now and what, three years ago, one expected to have at this point in life.

SS: Social support: Frequency with which one receives information, encouragement, indications of appreciation, respect or care.

SW: Self/wants: The perceived discrepancy between what one has now and wants.

TEH: Total effects on happiness: See TES and substitute 'happiness' for 'satisfaction'.

TES: Total effects on satisfaction: The direct effects of predictor variables on satisfaction are indicated by the path coefficients or beta values of those variables when satisfaction is regressed on those variables. The indirect effects are indicated by the joint product of the path coefficients connecting the predictor variables to satisfaction via mediating variables. The total effects of the predictor variables on satisfaction are given by the sum of direct and indirect effects.

TESW: Total effects on a self/wants variable: See TES and substitute 'self/wants' for 'satisfaction'.

TIC: Length of time one has been in the country in which one is attending university.

TR: Transportation: Public and private transportation (e.g., including convenience and expense.

WS: Work status: Denotes a demographic variable indicating one's paid employment status, e.g., unemployed, typically employed about 10 hours per week, etc.

Appendix 2 Results of regressions using MDT to explain satisfaction with one's family relations, alphabetically by country and university (decimal points omitted)

Austria, University of Vienna

	S	SW	SO	SD	SN	SP	SF	SB	TES	TESW
N	317	317	344	323	340	0	343	344	-	-
R^2	72	60	1	1	2	0	2	1	-	-
Pred										
Age	0	0	-13	0	0	0	0	0	-6	-6
LED	-7	0	0	-13	-15	0	0	0	-11	-5
ETH	0	0	0	0	0	0	13	-12	-3	-1
SO	19	44							43	44
SD	11	15							19	15
SN	0	17							9	17
SP	0	11							6	11
SB	14	12							21	12
SW	55								55	

Males

	S	SW	SO	SD	SN	SP	SF	SB	TES	TESW
N	128	128	0	0	0	0	137	0	-	-
R^2	72	64	0	0	0	0	5	0	-	-
ETH	0	0	0	0	0	0	23	0	0	0
SO	15	53							51	53
SD	0	17							11	17
SP	12	0							12	0
SF	0	-11							-7	-11
SB	0	25							17	25
SW	67								67	

Females

	S	SW	SO	SD	SN	SP	SF	SB	TES	TESW
N	189	189	0	192	205	206	0	0	-	-
R^2	71	58	0	6	3	2	0	0	-	-
LED	0	0	0	-25	-17	0	0	0	-7	-8
ETH	0	0	0	0	0	-15	0	0	-1	-2
SO	21	41							42	41
SD	13	13							20	13
SN	0	27							14	27
SP	0	16							8	16
SB	15	0							15	0
SW	52								52	

Bahrain, University College of Arts, Science and Education

	S	SW	SO	SD	SN	SP	SF	SB	TES	TESW
N	213	216	0	253	257	0	0	249	-	-
R^2	44	46	0	2	3	0	0	3	-	-
Pred										
Age	0	0	0	14	20	0	0	17	1	3
SO	26	59							44	59
SN	0	14							4	14
SP	21	0							21	0
SW	31								31	
Females										
N	175	178	0	205	0	0	206	204	-	-
R^2	46	46	0	3	0	0	2	2	-	-
Age	0	0	0	18	0	0	0	15	0	0
WS	0	0	0	0	0	0	14	0	0	0
SO	26	59							44	59
SN	0	14							4	14
SP	23	0							23	0
SW	31								31	

Bangladesh, Dhaka University

	S	SW	SO	SD	SN	SP	SF	SB	TES	TESW
N	294	294	311	310	307	0	311	0	-	-
R^2	63	61	1	2	2	0	2	0	-	-
Pred										
LED	0	0	0	-13	-14	0	15	0	-4	-7
ETH	0	0	-13	0	0	0	0	0	-6	-4
SO	26	33							46	33
SD	0	12							7	12
SN	0	37							22	37
SP	0	10							6	10
SW	59								59	
Males										
N	123	123	0	128	0	0	0	0	-	-
R^2	59	53	0	3	0	0	0	0	-	-
LED	0	0	0	-19	0	0	0	0	-3	-4
SO	0	21							16	21
SD	0	23							18	23
SN	0	30							23	30
SP	0	19							15	19
SW	77								77	

Bangladesh, Dhaka University (continued)

	S	SW	SO	SD	SN	SP	SF	SB	TES	TESW
Females										
N	171	171	182	182	180	0	181	0	-	-
R^2	69	68	2	3	2	0	2	0	-	-
WS	0	0	0	18	0	0	0	0	0	0
LED	0	0	-17	0	0	0	15	0	-11	-8
ETH	0	0	0	0	-16	0	0	0	-3	-7
SO	47	46							66	46
SN	0	42							17	42
SW	41								41	

Belgium, Catholic University of Louvain

	S	SW	SO	SD	SN	SP	SF	SB	TES	TESW
N	110	110	0	120	0	126	127	129	-	-
R^2	67	49	0	5	0	10	4	5	-	-
Pred										
Sex	0	0	0	0	0	32	-21	24	6	0
Age	0	0	0	-24	0	0	0	0	-2	-5
SO	40	57							61	57
SD	0	21							8	21
SP	19	0							19	0
SW	37								37	

Brazil, Pontifical Catholic University of Minas Gerais

	S	SW	SO	SD	SN	SP	SF	SB	TES	TESW
N	253	253	0	0	0	273	275	275	-	-
R^2	58	54	0	0	0	3	1	2	-	-
Pred										
Sex	0	0	0	0	0	17	0	16	2	3
LED	0	0	0	0	0	0	13	0	0	0
SO	24	36							41	36
SD	0	15							7	15
SN	14	17							22	17
SP	0	20							9	20
SW	47								47	
Males										
N	98	98	0	0	0	0	0	0	-	-
R^2	59	42	0	0	0	0	0	0	-	-
SO	23	37							41	37
SD	19	22							30	22
SP	0	21							10	21
SW	48								48	

Brazil, Pontifical Catholic U. of Minas Gerais (continued)

	S	SW	SO	SD	SN	SP	SF	SB	TES	TESW
Females										
N	155	155	0	0	0	0	0	0	-	-
R^2	56	61	0	0	0	0	0	0	-	-
SO	31	40							51	40
SD	0	14							7	14
SN	0	20							10	20
SP	0	21							11	21
SW	50								50	

Cameroon, Yaounde University

	S	SW	SO	SD	SN	SP	SF	SB	TES	TESW
N	140	143	0	177	0	0	0	0	-	-
R^2	50	37	0	2	0	0	0	0	-	-
Pred										
Sex	0	0	0	15	0	0	0	0	2	4
SO	26	40							40	40
SD	0	29							10	29
SP	25	0							25	0
SW	36								36	
Males										
N	111	113	0	0	0	0	0	0	-	-
R^2	57	32	0	0	0	0	0	0	-	-
SO	25	41							39	41
SD	0	24							8	24
SP	21	0							21	0
SB	18	0							18	0
SW	33								33	

Canada

	S	SW	SO	SD	SN	SP	SF	SB	TES	TESW
N	1502	1506	0	1561	0	1576	1578	1574	-	-
R^2	64	53	0	1	0	1	3	1	-	-
Pred										
Sex	0	5	0	0	0	6	0	8	4	6
ETH	0	5	0	-5	0	0	16	0	1	3
SO	27	42							46	42
SD	4	12							10	12
SN	5	16							12	16
SF	-4	-7							-7	-7
SB	12	17							20	17
SW	46								46	

Canada (continued)

	S	SW	SO	SD	SN	SP	SF	SB	TES	TESW
Males										
N	579	580	609	0	0	0	609	0	-	-
R^2	62	46	1	0	0	0	2	0	-	-
LED	0	0	10	0	0	0	0	0	5	4
ETH	0	0	0	0	0	0	16	0	1	3
SO	28	39							46	39
SD	0	14							6	14
SN	0	14							6	14
SF	0	-9							-4	-9
SB	20	14							26	14
SW	46								46	
Females										
N	922	925	0	0	0	0	968	0	-	-
R^2	65	58	0	0	0	0	3	0	-	-
ETH	0	6	0	0	0	0	16	0	2	5
SO	28	45							50	45
SD	7	10							12	10
SN	0	18							9	18
SF	-6	-5							-8	-5
SB	8	19							17	19
SW	48								48	

Canada, Dalhousie University

	S	SW	SO	SD	SN	SP	SF	SB	TES	TESW
N	251	260	0	0	0	0	270	0	-	-
R^2	63	49	0	0	0	0	5	0	-	-
Pred										
Age	-10	0	0	0	0	0	0	0	-10	0
LED	0	0	0	0	0	0	-15	0	0	0
ETH	0	0	0	0	0	0	23	0	0	0
SO	30	37							49	37
SD	0	18							9	18
SN	0	13							7	13
SB	13	19							23	19
SW	50								50	
Females										
N	168	169	0	0	0	0	0	180	-	-
R^2	60	49	0	0	0	0	0	2	-	-
Age	0	0	0	0	0	0	0	15	4	3
LED	-11	0	0	0	0	0	0	0	-11	0
SO	34	38							52	38

Canada, Dalhousie University (continued)

	S	SW	SO	SD	SN	SP	SF	SB	TES	TESW
SD	0	16							7	16
SN	0	15							7	15
SB	13	22							23	22
SW	46								46	

Canada, University of Guelph

	S	SW	SO	SD	SN	SP	SF	SB	TES	TESW
N	307	307	0	0	0	327	330	330	-	-
R^2	66	54	0	0	0	1	9	1	-	-
Pred										
Sex	0	0	0	0	0	11	0	0	0	0
Age	0	0	0	0	0	0	0	-11	-2	-1
ETH	0	0	0	0	0	0	31	0	0	0
SO	29	45							52	45
SD	0	21							11	21
SN	0	13							7	13
SB	14	12							20	12
SW	50								50	
Males										
N	171	171	0	0	0	0	187	0	-	-
R^2	57	44	0	0	0	0	2	0	-	-
ETH	0	0	0	0	0	0	16	0	0	0
SO	25	42							45	42
SD	0	27							13	27
SB	18	16							26	16
SW	48								48	
Females										
N	134	134	0	0	140	139	141	0	-	-
R^2	78	66	0	0	3	3	24	0	-	-
ETH	0	0	0	0	-18	-20	50	0	-3	-5
SO	38	63							73	63
SN	0	25							14	25
SW	55								55	

Canada, Mount Saint Vincent University

	S	SW	SO	SD	SN	SP	SF	SB	TES	TESW
N	268	268	0	0	0	279	0	279	-	-
R^2	55	57	0	0	0	1	0	1	-	-
Pred										
WS	0	0	0	0	0	-13	0	-12	-1	-2
SO	15	48							38	48

Canada, Mount Saint Vincent University (continued)

	S	SW	SO	SD	SN	SP	SF	SB	TES	TESW
SD	16	0							16	0
SN	0	19							9	19
SF	-15	-10							-20	-10
SB	0	19							9	19
SW	47								47	

Females

	S	SW	SO	SD	SN	SP	SF	SB	TES	TESW
N	248	248	0	0	0	0	260	0	-	-
R^2	54	58	0	0	0	0	1	0	-	-
ETH	0	0	0	0	0	0	13	0	-3	-1
SO	15	48							37	48
SD	17	0							17	0
SN	0	19							9	19
SF	-16	-11							-21	-11
SB	0	21							10	21
SW	45								45	

Canada, Saint Mary's University

	S	SW	SO	SD	SN	SP	SF	SB	TES	TESW
N	299	300	316	0	0	315	313	0	-	-
R^2	61	49	5	0	0	1	3	0	-	-
Pred										
Sex	0	0	0	0	0	0	12	0	-	-
Age	0	0	0	0	0	0	14	0	0	0
LED	0	0	19	0	0	0	0	0	9	9
ETH	0	0	-17	0	0	-11	0	0	-8	-8
SO	32	46							48	46
SN	13	22							21	22
SB	17	17							23	17
SW	34								34	

Males

	S	SW	SO	SD	SN	SP	SF	SB	TES	TESW
N	161	161	169	0	0	168	168	0	-	-
R^2	60	41	8	0	0	3	2	0	-	-
LED	0	0	25	0	0	0	0	0	13	11
ETH	0	0	-22	0	0	-19	-17	0	-13	-13
SO	40	44							53	44
SN	0	15							4	15
SP	0	19							6	19
SB	27	0							27	0
SW	29								29	

Canada, Saint Mary's University (continued)

	S	SW	SO	SD	SN	SP	SF	SB	TES	TESW
Females										
N	137	138	0	0	0	0	144	146	-	-
R^2	64	57	0	0	0	0	4	2	-	-
Age	0	0	0	0	0	0	20	-17	-1	-3
ETH	-11	0	0	0	0	0	0	0	-11	0
SO	18	50							45	50
SN	0	27							15	27
SP	18	0							18	0
SB	0	15							8	15
SW	54								54	

Canada, Simon Fraser University

	S	SW	SO	SD	SN	SP	SF	SB	TES	TESW
N	280	281	0	0	0	0	0	0	-	-
R^2	73	58	0	0	0	0	0	0	-	-
Pred										
Sex	0	9	0	0	0	0	0	0	4	9
SO	36	46							57	46
SN	0	21							10	21
SF	0	-11							-5	-11
SB	16	17							24	17
SW	46								46	
Males										
N	104	105	0	0	0	0	0	0	-	-
R^2	64	48	0	0	0	0	0	0	-	-
SO	22	42							43	42
SN	0	27							13	27
SF	0	-21							-10	-21
SB	23	0							23	0
SW	49								49	
Females										
N	176	176	0	0	0	0	0	0	-	-
R^2	79	64	0	0	0	0	0	0	-	-
SO	43	49							64	49
SN	0	22							9	22
SB	14	23							24	23
SW	42								42	

Chile, Austral University of Chile

	S	SW	SO	SD	SN	SP	SF	SB	TES	TESW
N	231	232	0	0	0	0	251	0	-	-

Chile, Austral University of Chile (continued)

	S	SW	SO	SD	SN	SP	SF	SB	TES	TESW
R^2	49	39	0	0	0	0	3	0	-	-
Pred										
Sex	0	0	0	0	0	0	-17	0	0	0
SO	31	43							48	43
SD	0	18							7	18
SN	12	0							12	0
SB	0	15							6	15
SW	40								40	
Males										
N	118	118	0	0	0	0	0	0	-	-
R^2	50	43	0	0	0	0	0	0	-	-
SO	30	35							47	35
SN	0	21							10	21
SB	0	25							12	25
SW	49								49	
Females										
N	113	114	0	0	0	0	0	0	-	-
R^2	49	42	0	0	0	0	0	0	-	-
WS	-14	0	0	0	0	0	0	0	-14	0
ETH	0	18	0	0	0	0	0	0	5	18
SO	33	41							45	41
SD	19	29							28	29
SW	30								30	

Egypt, Ain Shams University

	S	SW	SO	SD	SN	SP	SF	SB	TES	TESW
N	221	223	0	0	0	263	0	0	-	-
R^2	47	52	0	0	0	1	0	0	-	-
Pred										
Sex	0	0	0	0	0	12	0	0	2	2
SO	34	62							48	62
SD	15	0							15	0
SP	13	18							17	18
SW	23								23	
Males										
N	121	123	0	0	0	0	0	0	-	-
R^2	39	67	0	0	0	0	0	0	-	-
SO	48	73							48	73
SD	26	0							26	0
SP	0	16							0	16

Egypt, Ain Shams University (continued)

	S	SW	SO	SD	SN	SP	SF	SB	TES	TESW
Females										
N	100	100	0	0	0	0	0	117	-	-
R^2	53	36	0	0	0	0	0	3	-	-
WS	0	0	0	0	0	0	0	19	0	0
LED	-14	0	0	0	0	0	0	0	-14	0
SO	45	51							63	51
SP	0	18							6	18
SW	35								35	

Finland, University of Helsinki

	S	SW	SO	SD	SN	SP	SF	SB	TES	TESW
N	254	257	269	0	0	0	0	271	-	-
R^2	63	57	3	0	0	0	0	6	-	-
Pred										
Sex	0	0	17	0	0	0	0	22	11	12
Age	0	0	0	0	0	0	0	18	3	4
SO	14	47							46	47
SD	0	11							8	11
SN	0	21							15	21
SB	0	20							14	20
SW	69								69	
Males										
N	99	102	110	0	0	0	0	0	-	-
R^2	61	53	3	0	0	0	0	0	-	-
WS	0	0	20	0	0	0	0	0	7	9
SO	0	47							37	47
SN	0	23							18	23
SB	0	21							17	21
SW	79								79	
Females										
N	155	155	0	0	0	0	0	161	-	-
R^2	62	55	0	0	0	0	0	5	-	-
Age	0	0	0	0	0	0	0	23	3	5
SO	14	49							48	49
SN	0	27							19	27
SB	0	20							14	20
SW	69								69	

Federal Republic of Germany

	S	SW	SO	SD	SN	SP	SF	SB	TES	TESW
N	686	688	0	0	757	761	744	757	-	-

Federal Republic of Germany (continued)

	S	SW	SO	SD	SN	SP	SF	SB	TES	TESW
R^2	64	58	0	0	1	1	1	1	-	-
Pred										
WS	0	0	0	0	0	0	-7	0	0	0
LED	0	0	0	0	8	9	0	8	3	3
SO	24	38							42	38
SD	0	13							6	13
SN	13	19							22	19
SB	8	24							20	24
SW	48								48	

Males

	S	SW	SO	SD	SN	SP	SF	SB	TES	TESW
N	371	373	0	397	417	0	404	413	-	-
R^2	63	61	0	1	1	0	1	1	-	-
Age	7	0	0	0	0	0	0	0	7	0
WS	0	0	0	10	0	0	-10	0	2	1
LED	0	-10	0	0	10	0	0	13	-2	-6
SO	24	47							47	47
SD	9	14							16	14
SN	8	19							17	19
SB	0	16							8	16
SW	49								49	

Females

	S	SW	SO	SD	SN	SP	SF	SB	TES	TESW
N	315	315	0	0	0	344	0	0	-	-
R^2	64	57	0	0	0	2	0	0	-	-
Age	0	10	0	0	0	0	0	0	5	10
WS	0	0	0	0	0	-14	0	0	0	0
SO	23	28							36	28
SD	0	11							5	11
SN	16	24							27	24
SB	8	31							23	31
SW	47								47	

Germany, Federal College of Public Administration

	S	SW	SO	SD	SN	SP	SF	SB	TES	TESW
N	232	234	0	0	0	0	0	0	-	-
R^2	64	62	0	0	0	0	0	0	-	-
Pred										
Age	0	10	0	0	0	0	0	0	5	10
SO	22	36							38	36
SD	0	12							5	12
SN	25	15							32	15
SB	0	31							14	31

Germany, Federal College of Public Admin. (continued)

	S	SW	SO	SD	SN	SP	SF	SB	TES	TESW
SW	45								45	
Males										
N	135	137	0	0	0	0	0	0	-	-
R^2	64	64	0	0	0	0	0	0	-	-
Age	0	10	0	0	0	0	0	0	4	10
SO	29	42							45	42
SD	0	21							8	21
SN	25	0							25	0
SB	0	32							12	32
SW	38								38	
Females										
N	97	97	0	0	0	0	0	0	-	-
R^2	66	57	0	0	0	0	0	0	-	-
SO	0	32							17	32
SN	19	23							31	23
SP	20	0							20	0
SF	14	0							14	0
SB	0	37							20	37
SW	53								53	

Germany, University of Frankfurt

	S	SW	SO	SD	SN	SP	SF	SB	TES	TESW
N	229	229	0	0	0	270	0	268	-	-
R^2	60	56	0	0	0	2	0	2	-	-
Pred										
Age	10	0	0	0	0	0	0	0	10	0
LED	0	0	0	0	0	14	0	14	2	3
SO	27	40							50	40
SD	0	17							10	17
SN	0	19							11	19
SB	0	23							13	23
SW	57								57	
Males										
N	139	139	0	0	0	163	0	159	-	-
R^2	64	61	0	0	0	2	0	2	-	-
LED	11	0	0	0	0	17	0	17	12	2
SO	21	48							44	48
SD	20	18							29	18
SN	0	19							9	19
SB	0	13							6	13
SW	48								48	

Germany, University of Frankfurt (continued)

	S	SW	SO	SD	SN	SP	SF	SB	TES	TESW
Females										
N	90	90	0	0	0	0	0	109	-	-
R^2	53	49	0	0	0	0	0	6	-	-
WS	0	0	0	0	0	0	0	26	6	9
SO	23	24							37	24
SN	0	36							22	36
SB	0	36							22	36
SW	60								60	

Germany, University of Mannheim

	S	SW	SO	SD	SN	SP	SF	SB	TES	TESW
N	224	224	0	0	0	0	0	0	-	-
R^2	66	59	0	0	0	0	0	0	-	-
Pred										
SO	29	40							50	40
SN	0	31							16	31
SB	11	21							22	21
SW	52								52	
Males										
N	96	96	0	0	0	0	0	106	-	-
R^2	65	62	0	0	0	0	0	5	-	-
LED	13	0	0	0	0	0	0	0	13	0
SO	0	50							41	50
SN	0	37							30	37
SW	81								81	
Females										
N	127	127	0	0	0	133	0	0	-	-
R^2	67	58	0	0	0	5	0	0	-	-
WS	0	0	0	0	0	-24	0	0	0	0
SO	36	36							53	36
SN	0	29							13	29
SB	13	28							26	28
SW	46								46	

Greece, Aristotelian University of Thessaloniki

	S	SW	SO	SD	SN	SP	SF	SB	TES	TESW
N	223	229	253	258	0	0	0	0	-	-
R^2	48	38	2	3	0	0	0	0	-	-
Pred										
Sex	0	-11	0	13	0	0	0	0	-3	-11
Age	0	0	15	0	0	0	0	0	8	4

Greece, Aristotelian U. of Thessaloniki (continued)

	S	SW	SO	SD	SN	SP	SF	SB	TES	TESW
ETH	0	0	0	-16	0	0	0	0	0	0
SO	44	29							51	29
SN	0	41							10	41
SP	18	0							18	0
SW	24								24	

Males

	S	SW	SO	SD	SN	SP	SF	SB	TES	TESW
N	122	126	142	144	0	143	0	0	-	-
R^2	46	41	3	5	0	3	0	0	-	-
LED	0	0	0	0	0	-19	0	0	-3	0
ETH	0	0	-18	-23	0	0	0	0	-9	-7
SO	42	36							51	36
SN	0	38							10	38
SP	18	0							18	0
SW	25								25	

Females

	S	SW	SO	SD	SN	SP	SF	SB	TES	TESW
N	101	103	111	0	0	0	0	0	-	-
R^2	50	35	5	0	0	0	0	0	-	-
WS	0	17	0	0	0	0	0	0	4	17
ETH	0	0	24	0	0	0	0	0	11	0
SO	46	0							46	0
SN	0	41							10	41
SP	19	26							25	26
SW	24								24	

Hungary, University of Economics

	S	SW	SO	SD	SN	SP	SF	SB	TES	TESW
N	211	211	0	0	0	221	0	219	-	-
R^2	61	44	0	0	0	1	0	5	-	-
Pred										
Sex	15	0	0	0	0	13	0	0	18	3
WS	0	0	0	0	0	0	0	23	0	0
SO	21	33							39	33
SD	0	19							10	19
SN	0	16							9	16
SP	12	20							23	20
SF	-14	0							-14	0
SW	53								53	

Females

	S	SW	SO	SD	SN	SP	SF	SB	TES	TESW
N	155	155	0	0	0	0	0	160	-	-
R^2	61	47	0	0	0	0	0	4	-	-
WS	0	0	0	0	0	0	0	21	0	0

Hungary, University of Economics (continued)

	S	SW	SO	SD	SN	SP	SF	SB	TES	TESW
SO	22	32							38	32
SD	0	18							9	18
SN	15	22							26	22
SP	0	15							7	15
SF	-14	0							-14	0
SW	49								49	

India, University of Delhi

	S	SW	SO	SD	SN	SP	SF	SB	TES	TESW
N	204	208	0	246	248	242	0	242	-	-
R^2	37	30	0	5	2	4	0	1	-	-
Pred										
Age	0	0	0	-28	-15	-25	0	0	-9	-4
LED	0	0	0	20	0	18	0	0	4	0
ETH	0	0	0	0	0	0	0	-14	-1	-4
SO	23	23							31	23
SN	0	23							8	23
SP	22	0							22	0
SB	0	22							7	22
SW	33								33	
Males										
N	121	124	0	155	159	151	0	0	-	-
R^2	40	37	0	5	3	2	0	0	-	-
Age	0	0	0	-28	-18	-16	0	0	-6	-7
LED	0	0	0	22	0	0	0	0	2	6
SO	25	29							35	29
SD	0	25							9	25
SP	22	0							22	0
SB	0	21							7	21
SW	35								35	

Israel, Hebrew University of Jerusalem

	S	SW	SO	SD	SN	SP	SF	SB	TES	TESW
N	306	306	309	309	0	0	0	0	-	-
R^2	61	58	3	6	0	0	0	0	-	-
Pred										
Age	0	0	0	-22	0	0	0	0	-3	0
ETH	0	0	-17	-13	0	0	0	0	-11	-8
SO	37	49							57	49
SD	12	0							12	0
SN	0	24							10	24

Israel, Hebrew University of Jerusalem (continued)

	S	SW	SO	SD	SN	SP	SF	SB	TES	TESW
SP	0	17							7	17
SW	41								41	
Males										
N	157	157	158	158	0	158	0	0	-	-
R^2	54	50	2	2	0	4	0	0	-	-
Age	0	0	0	-16	0	0	0	0	0	0
LED	0	0	0	0	0	20	0	0	0	0
ETH	0	0	-16	0	0	0	0	0	-10	-8
SO	46	48							63	48
SN	0	26							9	26
SF	0	-21							-7	-21
SW	35								35	
Females										
N	149	149	151	151	151	0	149	0	-	-
R^2	71	69	3	7	2	0	4	0	-	-
Age	-17	10	0	-28	0	0	21	0	-11	10
ETH	0	0	-18	0	-18	0	0	0	-13	-14
SO	28	50							58	50
SN	0	28							17	28
SP	0	18							11	18
SW	60								60	

Japan

	S	SW	SO	SD	SN	SP	SF	SB	TES	TESW
N	1122	1131	1198	1187	1187	1178	1192	0	-	-
R^2	55	52	3	7	1	1	1	0	-	-
Pred										
Sex	0	0	10	7	6	0	-7	0	6	6
Age	0	9	0	0	0	0	0	0	4	9
LED	0	-10	12	0	0	0	0	0	1	-6
ETH	10	0	0	6	0	6	0	0	11	1
SO	28	31							41	31
SD	9	12							14	12
SN	0	31							13	31
SB	6	9							10	9
SW	42								42	
Males										
N	919	927	980	972	0	0	0	0	-	-
R^2	56	52	1	1	0	0	0	0	-	-
Age	0	9	10	0	0	0	0	0	7	12
LED	7	-11	0	0	0	0	0	0	2	-11

Japan (continued)

	S	SW	SO	SD	SN	SP	SF	SB	TES	TESW
ETH	7	0	0	6	0	0	0	0	8	1
SO	23	31							36	31
SD	13	12							18	12
SN	0	34							14	34
SF	0	6							3	6
SB	8	9							12	9
SW	42								42	

Females

	S	SW	SO	SD	SN	SP	SF	SB	TES	TESW
N	203	204	218	215	0	211	0	0	-	-
R^2	54	50	3	4	0	2	0	0	-	-
Age	0	0	0	0	0	16	0	0	0	0
LED	0	0	19	21	0	0	0	0	10	7
SO	39	36							54	36
SN	0	27							11	27
SB	0	17							7	17
SW	42								42	

Japan, Sophia University

	S	SW	SO	SD	SN	SP	SF	SB	TES	TESW
N	238	239	260	259	258	254	258	257	-	-
R^2	36	49	1	3	1	3	3	4	-	-
Pred										
Sex	0	0	0	19	13	17	0	0	2	6
Age	0	0	-12	0	0	0	18	-22	-6	-6
WS	0	-10	0	0	0	0	0	0	-3	-10
SO	40	22							46	22
SN	0	23							6	23
SP	0	19							5	19
SB	0	15							4	15
SW	27								27	

Males

	S	SW	SO	SD	SN	SP	SF	SB	TES	TESW
N	159	159	0	0	0	0	172	171	-	-
R^2	44	53	0	0	0	0	2	5	-	-
Age	0	0	0	0	0	0	0	-23	0	0
WS	0	-13	0	0	0	0	0	0	-3	-13
LED	0	0	0	0	0	0	17	0	0	0
SO	37	25							42	25
SN	0	30							6	30
SP	20	23							24	23
SW	19								19	

Japan, University of Tokai

	S	SW	SO	SD	SN	SP	SF	SB	TES	TESW
N	285	286	0	0	0	0	0	0	-	-
R^2	70	57	0	0	0	0	0	0	-	-
Pred										
SO	22	30							35	30
SD	14	0							14	0
SN	12	46							33	46
SP	8	11							13	11
SW	42								42	

Males

	S	SW	SO	SD	SN	SP	SF	SB	TES	TESW
N	202	203	0	0	0	0	0	0	-	-
R^2	70	57	0	0	0	0	0	0	-	-
Age	0	19	0	0	0	0	0	0	7	19
LED	0	-15	0	0	0	0	0	0	-6	-15
SO	20	23							29	23
SD	15	0							15	0
SN	17	48							36	48
SB	9	15							15	15
SW	39								39	

Japan, Tokai and Denkitsushin Universities

	S	SW	SO	SD	SN	SP	SF	SB	TES	TESW
N	599	606	0	0	0	628	0	0	-	-
R^2	57	51	0	0	0	1	0	0	-	-
Pred										
Age	0	6	0	0	0	9	0	0	3	6
SO	15	36							32	36
SD	13	16							21	16
SN	10	29							24	29
SW	48								48	

Males

	S	SW	SO	SD	SN	SP	SF	SB	TES	TESW
N	558	565	0	0	0	583	0	0	-	-
R^2	56	50	0	0	0	1	0	0	-	-
Age	0	0	0	0	0	9	0	0	0	0
SO	14	36							32	36
SD	20	15							28	15
SN	0	31							16	31
SW	51								51	

Jordan, Yarmouk University

	S	SW	SO	SD	SN	SP	SF	SB	TES	TESW
N	262	264	0	0	294	0	0	0	-	-

132

Jordan, Yarmouk University (continued)

	S	SW	SO	SD	SN	SP	SF	SB	TES	TESW
Pred										
WS	0	0	0	0	-12	0	0	0	-3	-3
LED	0	14	0	0	0	0	0	0	3	14
SO	33	46							44	46
SN	21	23							27	23
SW	24								24	
Males										
N	209	210	0	0	0	233	0	0	-	-
R^2	43	46	0	0	0	4	0	0	-	-
WS	0	0	0	0	0	-14	0	0	0	0
LED	0	11	0	0	0	18	0	0	3	11
SO	33	49							45	49
SN	21	26							27	26
SW	24								24	

Kenya, University of Nairobi

	S	SW	SO	SD	SN	SP	SF	SB	TES	TESW
N	242	246	0	0	0	0	0	0	-	-
R^2	58	54	0	0	0	0	0	0	-	-
Pred										
Sex	0	-12	0	0	0	0	0	0	-7	-12
SO	0	48							27	48
SD	0	13							7	13
SN	28	0							28	0
SP	0	14							8	14
SB	0	11							6	11
SW	57								57	
Males										
N	136	139	0	0	0	0	0	0	-	-
R^2	44	44	0	0	0	0	0	0	-	-
SO	0	57							27	57
SN	29	0							29	0
SF	0	-22							-11	-22
SW	48								48	
Females										
N	106	107	115	0	0	117	0	0	-	-
R^2	70	65	3	0	0	3	0	0	-	-
WS	0	0	19	0	0	20	0	0	8	15
SO	0	46							29	46
SN	30	17							41	17
SP	0	28							17	28

Kenya, University of Nairobi (continued)

	S	SW	SO	SD	SN	SP	SF	SB	TES	TESW
SW	62								62	

Korea, Korea University

	S	SW	SO	SD	SN	SP	SF	SB	TES	TESW
N	429	430	0	440	443	0	438	0	-	-
R^2	59	59	0	1	2	0	2	0	-	-
Pred										
Sex	0	0	0	0	-10	0	0	0	-2	-1
WS	0	0	0	0	0	0	13	0	-1	-2
LED	0	0	0	-11	-11	0	0	0	-2	-3
SO	21	53							50	53
SD	0	14							8	14
SN	9	10							15	10
SF	0	-12							-7	-12
SW	55								55	
Males										
N	345	346	0	0	0	0	349	0	-	-
R^2	56	59	0	0	0	0	1	0	-	-
WS	0	0	0	0	0	0	13	0	-1	-2
SO	19	57							50	57
SD	0	20							11	20
SP	11	0							11	0
SF	0	-12							-7	-12
SW	54								54	

Mexico, University of Baja California Sur

	S	SW	SO	SD	SN	SP	SF	SB	TES	TESW
N	206	208	0	0	0	0	0	242	-	-
R^2	44	31	0	0	0	0	0	1	-	-
Pred										
Sex	0	0	0	0	0	0	0	13	3	3
SO	24	24							32	24
SN	19	0							19	0
SP	0	23							8	23
SB	12	22							20	22
SW	34								34	
Males										
N	146	148	0	0	169	0	0	0	-	-
R^2	49	25	0	0	2	0	0	0	-	-
Age	-15	0	0	0	-16	0	0	0	-15	0
SO	29	24							38	24

Mexico, University of Baja California Sur (continued)

	S	SW	SO	SD	SN	SP	SF	SB	TES	TESW
SP	0	20							7	20
SB	22	22							30	22
SW	37								37	

Netherlands, Erasmus University

	S	SW	SO	SD	SN	SP	SF	SB	TES	TESW
N	502	503	520	521	523	513	520	521	-	-
R^2	63	53	2	3	1	4	2	4	-	-
Pred										
Sex	0	0	15	16	10	21	-14	21	9	14
SO	31	32							46	32
SD	11	22							22	22
SN	0	25							12	25
SP	0	11							5	11
SF	7	9							11	9
SW	48								48	
Males										
N	290	291	0	0	0	0	0	0	-	-
R^2	62	54	0	0	0	0	0	0	-	-
SO	37	36							52	36
SD	0	18							8	18
SN	11	25							22	25
SP	0	16							7	16
SF	9	0							9	0
SW	42								42	
Females										
N	209	209	0	0	0	0	0	0	-	-
R^2	65	57	0	0	0	0	0	0	-	-
SO	30	25							45	25
SD	0	28							16	28
SN	0	32							19	32
SW	58								58	

Netherlands, University of Leiden

	S	SW	SO	SD	SN	SP	SF	SB	TES	TESW
N	313	316	352	0	354	0	0	0	-	-
R^2	67	50	2	0	2	0	0	0	-	-
Pred										
Sex	0	0	0	0	-15	0	0	0	-4	-6
Age	0	0	-15	0	0	0	0	0	-6	-5
SO	22	32							41	32

Netherlands, University of Leiden (continued)

	S	SW	SO	SD	SN	SP	SF	SB	TES	TESW
SD	0	10							6	10
SN	0	39							23	39
SP	17	0							17	0
SF	9	0							9	0
SB	0	15							9	15
SW	60								60	

Males

	S	SW	SO	SD	SN	SP	SF	SB	TES	TESW
N	137	138	0	150	160	0	157	156	-	-
R^2	58	31	0	6	9	0	2	2	-	-
LED	0	0	0	26	-16	0	0	17	0	0
ETH	0	0	0	0	-30	0	17	0	-5	-8
SO	26	28							41	28
SN	0	28							15	28
SP	21	0							21	0
SB	0	26							14	26
SW	53								53	

Females

	S	SW	SO	SD	SN	SP	SF	SB	TES	TESW
N	176	178	196	0	194	0	193	0	-	-
R^2	71	63	2	0	4	0	2	0	-	-
Age	0	0	-17	0	0	0	0	0	-7	-5
WS	0	0	0	0	21	0	0	0	7	10
LED	0	0	0	0	0	0	15	0	2	0
SO	20	32							41	32
SN	0	49							33	49
SP	11	13							20	13
SF	12	0							12	0
SW	67								67	

New Zealand, Massey University

	S	SW	SO	SD	SN	SP	SF	SB	TES	TESW
N	313	314	0	0	0	319	0	320	-	-
R^2	68	59	0	0	0	1	0	1	-	-
Pred										
Sex	-7	0	0	0	0	0	0	0	-7	0
Age	0	0	0	0	0	-12	0	-13	-2	-2
SO	22	45							50	45
SD	0	10							6	10
SN	0	20							12	20
SP	0	17							10	17
SB	8	0							8	0
SW	61								61	

New Zealand, Massey University (continued)

Males

	S	SW	SO	SD	SN	SP	SF	SB	TES	TESW
N	111	112	0	0	115	0	0	0	-	-
R^2	62	66	0	0	3	0	0	0	-	-
WS	0	0	0	0	-21	0	0	0	-3	-5
SO	18	49							50	49
SN	0	24							16	24
SF	0	-19							-12	-19
SB	0	17							11	17
SW	65								65	

Females

	S	SW	SO	SD	SN	SP	SF	SB	TES	TESW
N	202	202	0	0	0	205	0	206	-	-
R^2	72	57	0	0	0	2	0	2	-	-
Age	0	0	0	0	0	-17	0	-15	-4	-4
SO	24	46							51	46
SN	0	24							14	24
SP	0	19							11	19
SB	13	0							13	0
SW	58								58	

Norway

	S	SW	SO	SD	SN	SP	SF	SB	TES	TESW
N	201	203	228	0	0	0	227	228	-	-
R^2	59	38	1	0	0	0	1	2	-	-
Pred										
Sex	0	0	0	0	0	0	13	0	-1	-2
Age	0	0	13	0	0	0	0	14	4	5
WS	-12	0	0	0	0	0	0	0	-12	0
SO	18	35							30	35
SD	16	0							16	0
SN	17	29							27	29
SP	17	0							17	0
SF	0	-14							-5	-14
SW	33								33	

Females

	S	SW	SO	SD	SN	SP	SF	SB	TES	TESW
N	128	128	0	0	0	0	0	141	-	-
R^2	62	42	0	0	0	0	0	3	-	-
Age	0	0	0	0	0	0	0	19	4	0
WS	-12	0	0	0	0	0	0	0	-12	0
ETH	0	14	0	0	0	0	0	0	6	14
SO	16	34							29	34
SD	27	0							27	0

Norway (continued)

	S	SW	SO	SD	SN	SP	SF	SB	TES	TESW
SN	0	30							12	30
SF	0	-15							-6	-15
SB	19	0							19	0
SW	39								39	

Norway, University of Oslo

	S	SW	SO	SD	SN	SP	SF	SB	TES	TESW
N	115	117	0	0	136	133	0	0	-	-
R^2	65	53	0	0	4	5	0	0	-	-
Pred										
Sex	0	0	0	0	-21	0	0	0	-4	-8
ETH	0	15	0	0	0	24	0	0	7	15
SO	0	41							20	41
SD	30	0							30	0
SN	0	39							19	39
SB	24	0							24	0
SW	48								48	

Philippines

	S	SW	SO	SD	SN	SP	SF	SB	TES	TESW
N	931	933	969	967	967	970	968	963	-	-
R^2	57	46	1	1	1	2	2	1	-	-
Pred										
Sex	0	0	-8	0	0	0	-7	0	-4	-3
LED	-6	0	0	11	12	13	-13	11	-2	5
SO	28	43							46	43
SN	7	17							14	17
SP	0	7							3	7
SB	13	15							19	15
SW	41								41	
Males										
N	301	301	0	0	0	0	0	0	-	-
R^2	62	56	0	0	0	0	0	0	-	-
SO	26	48							50	48
SD	0	14							7	14
SN	0	22							11	22
SB	14	0							14	0
SW	49								49	
Females										
N	630	632	0	654	655	654	653	652	-	-
R^2	54	42	0	2	2	2	3	2	-	-

Philippines (continued)

	S	SW	SO	SD	SN	SP	SF	SB	TES	TESW
LED	-6	0	0	13	15	16	-18	14	-2	5
SO	31	40							47	40
SN	0	16							6	16
SB	16	21							24	21
SW	40								40	

Philippines, De La Salle University

	S	SW	SO	SD	SN	SP	SF	SB	TES	TESW
N	292	293	0	0	0	0	0	0	-	-
R^2	68	58	0	0	0	0	0	0	-	-
Pred										
SO	30	49							48	49
SN	15	34							27	34
SB	15	0							15	0
SW	36								36	
Males										
N	139	139	0	0	0	0	0	0	-	-
R^2	70	56	0	0	0	0	0	0	-	-
ETH	11	0							11	0
SO	26	52							52	52
SN	0	29							14	29
SB	20	0							20	0
SW	49								49	
Females										
N	152	153	0	0	0	0	0	0	-	-
R^2	65	57	0	0	0	0	0	0	-	-
SO	41	47							55	47
SN	21	37							32	37
SW	30								30	

Philippines, Philippine Normal College

	S	SW	SO	SD	SN	SP	SF	SB	TES	TESW
N	291	292	0	0	305	307	305	0	-	-
R^2	40	26	0	0	2	1	3	0	-	-
Pred										
Sex	0	0	0	0	0	0	-18	0	0	0
Age	0	0	0	0	0	0	13	0	0	0
WS	0	0	0	0	-15	-12	0	0	-1	0
SO	26	32							35	32
SP	11	0							11	0
SB	15	27							23	27

Philippines, Philippine Normal College (continued)

	S	SW	SO	SD	SN	SP	SF	SB	TES	TESW
SW	29								29	
Females										
N	263	264	0	0	275	277	275	274	-	-
R^2	37	22	0	0	2	1	1	1	-	-
Age	0	0	0	0	0	0	13	0	0	0
WS	0	0	0	0	-14	-12	0	-13	-3	-3
SO	31	30							40	30
SP	18	0							18	0
SB	0	26							8	26
SW	30								30	

Philippines, University of the Philippines

	S	SW	SO	SD	SN	SP	SF	SB	TES	TESW
N	351	351	360	362	360	0	0	361	-	-
R^2	61	55	1	2	1	0	0	2	-	-
Pred										
Sex	0	0	-12	-14	-12	0	0	-16	-9	-11
WS	0	8	0	0	0	0	0	0	4	8
SO	24	44							48	44
SN	0	22							12	22
SP	8	0							8	0
SB	0	21							12	21
SW	55								55	
Males										
N	136	136	0	140	0	0	0	0	-	-
R^2	55	57	0	5	0	0	0	0	-	-
WS	0	14	0	0	0	0	0	0	8	14
LED	0	0	0	24	0	0	0	0	0	0
SO	26	46							51	46
SN	0	26							14	26
SB	0	16							9	16
SW	54								54	
Females										
N	215	215	0	0	0	0	0	0	-	-
R^2	64	54	0	0	0	0	0	0	-	-
SO	26	44							50	44
SN	0	18							10	18
SB	11	25							25	25
SW	54								54	

Portugal, Technical University of Lisbon

	S	SW	SO	SD	SN	SP	SF	SB	TES	TESW
N	203	203	0	0	218	217	0	218	-	-
R^2	52	54	0	0	2	2	0	3	-	-
Pred										
Sex	0	0	0	0	0	0	0	19	2	3
Age	-14	0	0	0	0	0	0	0	-14	0
WS	0	0	0	0	15	-15	0	0	3	5
SO	24	40							46	40
SN	0	30							17	30
SF	0	-16							-9	-16
SB	0	15							8	15
SW	55								55	
Males										
N	116	116	97	0	98	97	106	98	-	-
R^2	57	55	4	0	9	7	4	4	-	-
Age	-16	0	0	0	0	0	0	0	-16	0
WS	0	0	23	0	32	28	-22	22	21	26
SO	21	32							41	32
SN	0	31							19	31
SF	0	-21							-13	-21
SB	0	19							12	19
SW	61								61	

Puerto Rico, University of Puerto Rico

	S	SW	SO	SD	SN	SP	SF	SB	TES	TESW
N	277	277	0	0	0	0	0	0	-	-
R^2	61	44	0	0	0	0	0	0	-	-
Pred										
SO	36	53							57	53
SD	15	20							23	20
SW	40								40	
Males										
N	150	150	0	0	0	0	169	0	-	-
R^2	59	42	0	0	0	0	2	0	-	-
ETH	0	0	0	0	0	0	-16	0	0	0
SO	28	56							55	56
SD	13	16							21	16
SW	49								49	
Females										
N	127	127	0	0	0	0	0	0	-	-
R^2	63	47	0	0	0	0	0	0	-	-
SO	43	42							56	42

Puerto Rico, University of Puerto Rico (continued)

	S	SW	SO	SD	SN	SP	SF	SB	TES	TESW
SD	17	20							23	20
SP	0	17							5	17
SW	30								30	

Singapore, National University of Singapore

	S	SW	SO	SD	SN	SP	SF	SB	TES	TESW
N	246	246	256	251	255	253	0	255	-	-
R^2	72	63	1	2	2	3	0	3	-	-
Pred										
Sex	0	0	13	14	14	18	0	17	13	13
SO	24	51							51	51
SN	0	20							11	20
SP	17	0							17	0
SB	0	20							11	20
SW	53								53	

Females

	S	SW	SO	SD	SN	SP	SF	SB	TES	TESW
N	206	206	0	0	0	0	0	0	-	-
R^2	70	60	0	0	0	0	0	0	-	-
SO	19	50							44	50
SD	14	0							14	0
SN	0	22							11	22
SP	12	0							12	0
SB	0	17							9	17
SW	50								50	

Republic of South Africa, University of Zululand

	S	SW	SO	SD	SN	SP	SF	SB	TES	TESW
N	220	231	287	0	286	286	282	0	-	-
R^2	34	36	3	0	2	2	2	0	-	-
Pred										
LED	0	0	18	0	16	16	13	0	8	6
SO	30	33							43	33
SD	0	29							11	29
SB	0	14							5	14
SW	38								38	

Males

	S	SW	SO	SD	SN	SP	SF	SB	TES	TESW
N	106	110	129	0	0	127	0	0	-	-
R^2	33	25	6	0	0	3	0	0	-	-
LED	0	0	26	0	0	3	0	0	11	9
SO	27	35							41	35
SD	0	24							10	24

Republic of South Africa, U. of Zululand (continued)

	S	SW	SO	SD	SN	SP	SF	SB	TES	TESW
SF	-16	0							-16	0
SW	40								40	
Females										
N	114	121	0	0	159	0	0	0	-	-
R^2	37	49	0	0	3	0	0	0	-	-
LED	0	0	0	0	19	0	0	0	2	6
SO	32	27							42	27
SD	0	33							13	33
SN	0	29							11	29
SW	38								38	

Spain, University of Madrid

	S	SW	SO	SD	SN	SP	SF	SB	TES	TESW
N	253	254	0	0	0	266	0	0	-	-
R^2	55	36	0	0	0	3	0	0	-	-
Pred										
Sex	11	0	0	0	0	19	0	0	11	0
LED	-10	0	0	0	0	0	0	0	-10	0
SO	29	46							45	46
SD	18	16							24	16
SN	0	11							4	11
SB	10	0							10	0
SW	35								35	
Males										
N	127	127	0	0	0	0	0	0	-	-
R^2	58	38	0	0	0	0	0	0	-	-
LED	-13	0	0	0	0	0	0	0	-13	0
SO	39	55							54	55
SD	24	0							24	0
SB	0	15							4	15
SW	27								27	
Females										
N	126	127	0	0	0	0	131	0	-	-
R^2	51	36	0	0	0	0	3	0	-	-
LED	0	0	0	0	0	0	-18	0	0	0
SO	23	35							40	35
SD	0	22							11	22
SN	0	20							10	20
SP	21	0							21	0
SW	49								49	

Sweden, University of Uppsala

	S	SW	SO	SD	SN	SP	SF	SB	TES	TESW
N	211	211	0	0	0	0	0	260	-	-
R^2	69	56	0	0	0	0	0	2	-	-
Pred										
Sex	0	0	0	0	0	0	0	14	0	0
SO	33	45							55	45
SN	0	32							15	32
SP	13	14							20	14
SF	-13	0							-13	0
SW	48								48	

Males

	S	SW	SO	SD	SN	SP	SF	SB	TES	TESW
N	105	105	129	126	0	0	0	0	-	-
R^2	67	48	3	4	0	0	0	0	-	-
Age	0	0	0	21	0	0	0	0	0	0
ETH	0	0	-20	0	0	0	0	0	-12	-8
SO	44	38							57	38
SN	0	25							9	25
SP	15	20							22	20
SF	-17	0							-17	0
SW	35								35	

Females

	S	SW	SO	SD	SN	SP	SF	SB	TES	TESW
N	106	106	0	124	0	124	0	125	-	-
R^2	72	62	0	4	0	3	0	8	-	-
Age	-11	0	0	0	0	-19	0	-36	-15	-6
LED	0	0	0	0	0	0	0	22	2	4
SO	21	52							54	52
SN	0	32							21	32
SF	-12	0							-12	0
SB	0	17							11	17
SW	64								64	

Switzerland, University of Freiburg

	S	SW	SO	SD	SN	SP	SF	SB	TES	TESW
N	306	307	0	0	0	334	0	335	-	-
R^2	71	53	0	0	0	2	0	2	-	-
Pred										
Sex	0	0	0	0	0	14	0	15	1	1
LED	0	10	0	0	0	0	0	0	6	10
SO	28	40							50	40
SD	12	19							23	19
SN	0	17							9	17
SP	0	9							5	9

Switzerland, University of Freiburg (continued)

	S	SW	SO	SD	SN	SP	SF	SB	TES	TESW
SF	0	11							6	11
SW	55								55	
Males										
N	158	158	0	0	0	0	0	0	-	-
R^2	69	50	0	0	0	0	0	0	-	-
ETH	0	13	0	0	0	0	0	0	7	13
SO	23	45							47	45
SD	18	25							31	25
SB	0	16							9	16
SW	53								53	
Females										
N	148	149	0	0	165	0	0	0	-	-
R^2	74	55	0	0	3	0	0	0	-	-
LED	0	0	0	0	20	0	0	0	5	6
SO	32	45							56	45
SN	11	28							26	28
SF	0	22							12	22
SW	54								54	

Taiwan

	S	SW	SO	SD	SN	SP	SF	SB	TES	TESW
N	2314	2317	0	2457	2465	2452	2439	2470	-	-
R^2	41	37	0	1	1	1	1	1	-	-
Pred										
Sex	-3	0	0	6	0	5	-7	8	-1	2
Age	0	0	0	0	0	0	-7	0	0	0
WS	0	-5	0	0	0	0	5	0	-2	-5
LED	0	0	0	0	0	-5	0	0	-1	-1
ETH	0	0	0	0	4	0	0	0	0	1
SO	26	32							36	32
SD	6	15							11	15
SN	6	17							11	17
SP	8	10							11	10
SF	-6	0							-6	0
SB	0	6							2	6
SW	32								32	
Males										
N	1180	1182	0	0	0	1266	1262	0	-	-
R^2	38	37	0	0	0	1	1	0	-	-
Age	0	0	0	0	0	0	-8	0	1	0
WS	0	-5	0	0	0	0	0	0	-2	-5

Taiwan (continued)

	S	SW	SO	SD	SN	SP	SF	SB	TES	TESW
LED	0	0	0	0	0	-7	0	0	0	-1
SO	26	35							37	35
SD	6	17							11	17
SN	6	14							10	14
SP	6	10							9	10
SF	-6	0							-6	0
SB	0	7							2	7
SW	31								31	

Females

	S	SW	SO	SD	SN	SP	SF	SB	TES	TESW
N	1134	1135	0	0	0	1186	0	0	-	-
R^2	44	36	0	0	0	1	0	0	-	-
WS	0	-5	0	0	0	-8	0	0	-3	-6
SO	25	30							35	30
SD	8	15							13	15
SN	0	20							7	20
SP	9	11							13	11
SF	-7	0							-7	0
SB	7	0							7	0
SW	33								33	

Tanzania, University of Dar Es Salaam

	S	SW	SO	SD	SN	SP	SF	SB	TES	TESW
N	178	180	0	213	216	0	216	0	-	-
R^2	42	38	0	3	4	0	6	0	-	-
Pred										
WS	0	0	0	0	0	0	17	0	0	0
LED	0	0	0	-18	-20	0	15	0	0	0
SO	21	50							39	50
SP	22	20							29	20
SW	36								36	

Males

	S	SW	SO	SD	SN	SP	SF	SB	TES	TESW
N	118	119	0	145	145	0	148	0	-	-
R^2	46	31	0	2	3	0	6	0	-	-
WS	0	0	0	0	0	0	17	0	0	0
LED	0	0	0	-17	-20	0	17	0	0	0
SO	25	56							44	56
SP	26	0							26	0
SW	33								33	

Thailand

	S	SW	SO	SD	SN	SP	SF	SB	TES	TESW
N	544	546	0	0	575	577	577	576	-	-
R^2	47	40	0	0	1	1	21	6	-	-
Pred										
Sex	0	9	0	0	0	8	0	0	6	10
Age	0	0	0	0	0	0	-44	0	0	0
WS	0	0	0	0	-10	0	-44	0	-1	-1
LED	0	-11	0	0	0	-10	13	0	-8	-13
SO	18	46							42	46
SN	0	12							6	12
SP	12	15							20	15
SW	51								51	

Males

	S	SW	SO	SD	SN	SP	SF	SB	TES	TESW
N	244	246	0	0	0	0	262	262	-	-
R^2	38	41	0	0	0	0	15	6	-	-
Age	0	0	0	0	0	0	-24	14	0	0
WS	0	0	0	0	0	0	17	-18	0	0
ETH	0	0	0	0	0	0	14	0	0	0
SO	13	42							33	42
SN	0	18							9	18
SP	13	20							22	20
SW	47								47	

Females

	S	SW	SO	SD	SN	SP	SF	SB	TES	TESW
N	300	300	0	0	0	0	315	314	-	-
R^2	52	40	0	0	0	0	31	8	-	-
Age	0	0	0	0	0	0	-57	28	0	0
LED	0	-15	0	0	0	0	13	0	-8	-15
SO	22	44							45	44
SD	0	18							10	18
SP	12	11							18	11
SW	53								53	

Thailand, Chiang Mai University

	S	SW	SO	SD	SN	SP	SF	SB	TES	TESW
N	278	278	0	0	0	0	0	288	-	-
R^2	50	41	0	0	0	0	0	2	-	-
Pred										
ETH	0	0	0	0	0	0	0	-17	0	0
SO	17	44							43	44
SD	0	15							9	15
SP	0	23							14	23
SW	59								59	

Thailand, Chiang Mai University (continued)

	S	SW	SO	SD	SN	SP	SF	SB	TES	TESW
Males										
N	121	121	0	0	0	0	0	126	-	-
R^2	45	46	0	0	0	0	0	3	-	-
Age	0	0	0	0	0	0	0	-19	0	0
SO	0	45							30	45
SN	0	19							13	19
SP	0	20							13	20
SW	67								67	
Females										
N	157	157	0	0	0	163	0	162	-	-
R^2	55	42	0	0	0	2	0	6	-	-
Age	0	0	0	0	0	0	0	27	4	0
LED	0	-16	0	0	0	0	0	0	-9	-16
ETH	0	0	0	0	o	-17	0	-35	-7	-4
SO	21	38							42	38
SD	0	21							11	21
SP	0	21							11	21
SB	15	0							15	0
SW	54								54	

Thailand, University of Srinakharinwirot

	S	SW	SO	SD	SN	SP	SF	SB	TES	TESW
N	266	268	0	0	286	289	0	0	-	-
R^2	44	37	0	0	2	2	0	0	-	-
Pred										
Sex	0	12	0	0	0	0	0	0	6	12
WS	0	0	0	0	-16	0	0	0	0	0
LED	0	0	0	0	0	-15	0	0	-3	-2
SO	19	52							43	52
SP	15	15							22	15
SW	46								46	
Males										
N	123	125	0	0	0	136	0	0	-	-
R^2	35	36	0	0	0	3	0	0	-	-
LED	0	0	0	0	0	-19	0	0	-7	-5
SO	0	44							19	44
SP	27	28							39	28
SW	42								42	
Females										
N	143	143	0	0	0	0	0	0	-	-
R^2	51	37	0	0	0	0	0	0	-	-

Thailand, University of Srinakharinwirot (continued)

	S	SW	SO	SD	SN	SP	SF	SB	TES	TESW
WS	-13	0	0	0	0	0	0	0	-13	0
SO	25	50							50	50
SD	0	18							9	18
SW	50								50	

Turkey, University of Uludag

	S	SW	SO	SD	SN	SP	SF	SB	TES	TESW
N	284	284	288	288	289	289	286	289	-	-
R^2	46	47	3	3	2	2	4	1	-	-
Pred										
Sex	0	0	-12	0	0	0	0	0	-6	-4
Age	0	0	0	16	0	0	-13	12	2	7
WS	0	0	-17	0	0	0	0	0	-8	-6
LED	0	0	0	-18	-14	-14	21	0	0	0
SO	37	35							46	35
SD	0	37							9	37
SP	18	0							18	0
SF	0	-11							-3	-11
SW	25								25	
Males										
N	194	194	197	197	198	198	196	0	-	-
R^2	63	50	4	4	5	4	6	0	-	-
Age	0	0	0	19	18	0	-18	0	9	10
WS	0	0	-21	0	0	0	0	0	-10	-7
LED	0	0	0	-20	-24	-20	24	0	-11	-11
SO	35	35							47	35
SD	0	35							12	35
SN	18	0							18	0
SF	-11	-16							-16	-16
SW	34								34	

United Kingdom, University of York

	S	SW	SO	SD	SN	SP	SF	SB	TES	TESW
N	205	206	220	217	0	221	0	221	-	-
R^2	58	46	4	4	0	2	0	4	-	-
Pred										
Sex	0	0	18	14	0	17	0	20	13	12
Age	0	-11	-17	0	0	0	0	0	-15	-19
ETH	0	0	0	-17	0	0	0	0	0	0
SO	45	47							64	47
SN	0	16							6	16

United Kingdom, University of York (continued)

	S	SW	SO	SD	SN	SP	SF	SB	TES	TESW
SB	0	17							7	17
SW	40								40	
Males										
N	96	96	104	101	101	104	103	0	-	-
R^2	66	45	5	7	4	6	4	0	-	-
Age	0	0	0	0	0	-26	0	0	0	0
WS	0	0	0	0	-22	0	0	0	0	0
LED	0	0	-24	-29	0	0	23	0	-20	-19
SO	57	58							76	58
SF	0	-24							-8	-24
SW	32								32	
Females										
N	109	110	116	116	0	0	117	0	-	-
R^2	50	44	7	6	0	0	4	0	-	-
Age	0	-18	-28	0	0	0	0	0	-21	-32
LED	0	0	0	0	0	0	-21	0	0	0
ETH	0	0	0	-26	0	0	0	0	0	0
SO	27	51							49	51
SB	15	20							24	20
SW	43								43	

United States of America

	S	SW	SO	SD	SN	SP	SF	SB	TES	TESW
N	1245	1253	1324	0	1322	1321	0	1310	-	-
R^2	65	58	1	0	1	1	0	1	-	-
Pred										
Sex	0	4	9	0	0	6	0	8	8	10
Age	0	0	0	0	0	-10	0	0	-1	-1
WS	0	0	-8	0	0	0	0	0	-6	-4
LED	0	0	6	0	0	0	0	0	3	3
ETH	0	0	0	0	-7	0	0	0	-1	-1
SO	36	50							56	50
SD	7	7							10	7
SN	0	16							6	16
SP	0	9							4	9
SF	5	0							5	0
SB	12	11							16	11
SW	40								40	
Males										
N	431	436	0	0	0	0	0	0	-	-
R^2	64	53	0	0	0	0	0	0	-	-

United States of America (continued)

	S	SW	SO	SD	SN	SP	SF	SB	TES	TESW
Age	6	0	0	0	0	0	0	0	6	0
SO	39	53							56	53
SN	10	16							15	16
SP	12	0							12	0
SB	0	17							5	17
SW	32								32	

Females

	S	SW	SO	SD	SN	SP	SF	SB	TES	TESW
N	814	817	859	0	857	857	0	853	-	-
R^2	65	61	1	0	1	1	0	1	-	-
Age	0	0	0	0	0	-12	0	-9	-2	-2
WS	0	0	-9	0	0	0	0	0	-5	-4
ETH	0	0	0	0	-10	0	0	0	-1	-2
SO	34	49							55	49
SD	7	8							10	8
SN	0	17							7	17
SP	0	9							4	9
SF	5	-5							3	-5
SB	12	10							16	10
SW	43								43	

USA, Arizona State University

	S	SW	SO	SD	SN	SP	SF	SB	TES	TESW
N	200	200	0	212	0	0	213	0	-	-
R^2	70	59	0	3	0	0	2	0	-	-
Pred										
Sex	0	0	0	-19	0	0	14	0	-2	-4
SO	27	45							54	45
SD	0	19							11	19
SN	-16	0							-16	0
SP	18	0							18	0
SB	0	31							19	31
SW	60								60	

Females

	S	SW	SO	SD	SN	SP	SF	SB	TES	TESW
N	146	146	0	0	0	0	0	0	-	-
R^2	70	59	0	0	0	0	0	0	-	-
SO	26	42							20	29
SD	0	29							20	29
SN	-23	0							-23	0
SP	15	0							15	0
SB	0	24							16	24
SW	68								68	

USA, Cornell University

	S	SW	SO	SD	SN	SP	SF	SB	TES	TESW
N	102	102	0	0	0	111	0	109	-	-
R^2	72	72	0	0	0	5	0	7	-	-
Pred										
Sex	0	0	0	0	0	0	0	27	7	4
LED	0	0	0	0	0	-25	0	0	-2	-5
ETH	11	0	0	0	0	0	0	0	11	0
SO	34	51							56	51
SN	0	23							10	23
SP	0	20							9	20
SB	21	14							27	14
SW	43								43	

USA, Edison Community College

	S	SW	SO	SD	SN	SP	SF	SB	TES	TESW
N	140	141	0	0	145	145	0	0	-	-
R^2	63	46	0	0	8	2	0	0	-	-
Pred										
WS	0	0	0	0	-23	0	0	0	-1	-4
ETH	0	0	0	0	-16	-17	0	0	-1	-3
SO	57	50							67	50
SD	14	0							14	0
SN	0	17							3	17
SF	0	-20							-4	-20
SW	20								20	
Females										
N	97	97	0	0	99	0	0	0	-	-
R^2	61	49	0	0	3	0	0	0	-	-
WS	0	0	0	0	-21	0	0	0	0	0
SO	52	41							61	41
SD	17	17							21	17
SP	0	19							4	19
SB	0	-21							5	21
SW	22								22	

USA, University of Illinois

	S	SW	SO	SD	SN	SP	SF	SB	TES	TESW
N	259	261	278	0	0	276	273	271	-	-
R^2	60	51	2	0	0	4	1	2	-	-
Pred										
Sex	0	0	15	0	0	17	0	16	12	9
LED	0	0	0	0	0	-17	0	0	0	0

USA, University of Illinois (continued)

	S	SW	SO	SD	SN	SP	SF	SB	TES	TESW
ETH	0	0	0	0	0	0	12	0	0	0
SO	40	62							62	62
SN	0	16							6	16
SB	15	0							15	0
SW	35								35	

Males

	S	SW	SO	SD	SN	SP	SF	SB	TES	TESW
N	119	120	0	0	0	0	0	0	-	-
R^2	52	49	0	0	0	0	0	0	-	-
SO	38	63							56	63
SD	20	0							20	0
SB	0	15							4	15
SW	29								29	

Females

	S	SW	SO	SD	SN	SP	SF	SB	TES	TESW
N	141	141	0	0	148	0	148	148	-	-
R^2	64	54	0	0	4	0	3	2	-	-
WS	0	0	0	0	0	0	0	-17	-3	0
ETH	0	-12	0	0	-22	0	18	0	-7	-17
SO	39	56							61	56
SN	0	23							9	23
SB	15	0							15	0
SW	40								40	

USA, Ohio State University, Newark

	S	SW	SO	SD	SN	SP	SF	SB	TES	TESW
N	253	256	268	0	266	0	0	0	-	-
R^2	63	59	2	0	4	0	0	0	-	-

Pred

	S	SW	SO	SD	SN	SP	SF	SB	TES	TESW
Age	9	0	14	0	0	0	0	0	17	7
WS	0	0	0	0	15	0	0	0	3	3
ETH	0	0	0	0	-17	0	0	0	-4	-3
SO	35	50							54	50
SN	14	19							21	19
SP	0	18							7	18
SW	38								38	

Males

	S	SW	SO	SD	SN	SP	SF	SB	TES	TESW
N	119	121	0	0	127	0	128	0	-	-
R^2	62	53	0	0	3	0	2	0	-	-
LED	0	0	0	0	20	0	0	0	5	6
ETH	0	0	0	0	0	0	18	0	0	0
SO	39	36							52	36
SN	16	29							26	29

USA, Ohio State University, Newark (continued)

	S	SW	SO	SD	SN	SP	SF	SB	TES	TESW
SP	0	21							8	21
SW	36								36	

Females

	S	SW	SO	SD	SN	SP	SF	SB	TES	TESW
N	134	135	0	0	139	0	0	0	-	-
R^2	64	66	0	0	3	0	0	0	-	-
ETH	0	0	0	0	-18	0	0	0	0	0
SO	40	65							71	65
SF	13	0							13	0
SB	0	25							12	25
SW	47								47	

USA, Sangamon State University

	S	SW	SO	SD	SN	SP	SF	SB	TES	TESW
N	137	140	0	0	0	150	0	0	-	-
R^2	72	64	0	0	0	3	0	0	-	-
Pred										
Age	0	0	0	0	0	-18	0	0	0	0
SO	27	54							56	54
SN	15	25							29	25
SB	0	15							8	15
SW	54								54	

USA, Smith College (Females)

	S	SW	SO	SD	SN	SP	SF	SB	TES	TESW
N	153	153	160	162	160	158	0	0	-	-
R^2	70	71	7	5	6	4	0	0	-	-
Pred										
Age	0	0	-28	-24	-26	0	0	0	-21	-23
LED	-12	0	0	0	0	-22	0	0	-14	-3
SO	27	61							63	61
SN	0	22							13	22
SP	0	15							9	15
SW	59								59	

Yugoslavia, University of Zagreb

	S	SW	SO	SD	SN	SP	SF	SB	TES	TESW
N	289	290	325	324	317	0	317	321	-	-
R^2	54	43	1	2	1	0	1	2	-	-
Pred										
Sex	0	-10	0	0	12	0	-12	0	1	-6
Age	-12	0	0	0	0	0	0	-14	-12	0

Yugoslavia, University of Zagreb (continued)

	S	SW	SO	SD	SN	SP	SF	SB	TES	TESW
WS	0	0	-12	-14	0	0	0	0	-7	-5
SO	32	42							43	42
SD	15	0							15	0
SN	13	31							21	31
SF	-12	0							-12	0
SW	25								25	
Males										
N	155	155	0	170	0	0	0	170	-	-
R^2	59	43	0	2	0	0	0	3	-	-
Age	-18	0	0	0	0	0	0	-19	-17	-4
WS	0	0	0	-16	0	0	0	0	-2	0
SO	18	47							35	47
SD	12	0							12	0
SN	28	22							36	22
SP	0	-16							-6	-16
SF	-24	0							-24	0
SB	-15	23							23	23
SW	36								36	
Females										
N	134	135	0	0	0	0	0	151	-	-
R^2	58	48	0	0	0	0	0	3	-	-
WS	-14	0	0	0	0	0	0	-19	-18	0
SO	48	24							52	24
SN	0	36							6	36
SP	0	18							3	18
SB	21	0							21	0
SW	17								17	

Appendix 3 Results of regressions using MDT to explain satisfaction with one's friendships, alphabetically by country and university (decimal points omitted)

Austria, University of Vienna

	S	SW	SO	SD	SN	SP	SF	SB	TES	TESW
N	315	315	0	0	0	343	0	343	-	-
R²	60	61	0	0	0	1	0	1	-	-
Pred										
Sex	9	0	0	0	0	0	0	0	9	0
Age	0	-8	0	0	0	0	0	0	-4	-8
WS	0	7	0	0	0	11	0	13	4	9
SO	19	47							43	47
SN	17	28							31	28
SF	0	-8							-4	-8
SB	0	13							7	13
SW	50								50	

Males

	S	SW	SO	SD	SN	SP	SF	SB		
N	123	123	0	0	0	0	0	0	-	-
R²	65	63	0	0	0	0	0	0	-	-
ETH	0	-16	0	0	0	0	0	0	-8	-16
SO	0	43							21	43
SN	29	29							43	29
SP	0	19							9	19
SB	14	0							14	0
SW	49								49	

Females

	S	SW	SO	SD	SN	SP	SF	SB		
N	192	192	0	0	0	206	0	0	-	-
R²	57	60	0	0	0	3	0	0	-	-
Age	0	-9	0	0	0	-22	0	0	-5	-9
LED	0	0	0	0	0	16	0	0	0	0
SO	27	49							54	49
SN	0	26							14	26
SB	0	15							8	15
SW	54								54	

Bahrain, University College of Arts, Science and Education

	S	SW	SO	SD	SN	SP	SF	SB	TES	TESW
N	22	224	0	0	0	0	250	0	-	-
R²	37	38	0	0	0	0	1	0	-	-
Pred										
Sex	0	0	0	0	0	0	-13	0	0	0
Age	-12	0	0	0	0	0	0	0	-12	0

Bahrain, U. C. of Arts, Science and Education (continued)

	S	SW	SO	SD	SN	SP	SF	SB	TES	TESW
SO	18	50							38	50
SD	0	21							8	21
SB	16	0							16	0
SW	39								39	
Females										
N	180	182	0	0	0	0	0	0	-	-
R^2	38	39	0	0	0	0	0	0	-	-
Age	-20	0	0	0	0	0	0	0	-20	0
ETH	0	-14	0	0	0	0	0	0	-6	-14
SO	0	46							18	46
SD	17	26							27	26
SB	20	0							20	0
SW	40								40	

Bangladesh, Dhaka University

	S	SW	SO	SD	SN	SP	SF	SB	TES	TESW
N	307	307	314	313	312	0	0	0	-	-
R^2	53	52	2	3	4	0	0	0	-	-
Pred										
Sex	0	10	14	17	14	0	0	0	12	19
ETH	0	0	0	0	-16	0	0	0	-2	-5
SO	18	30							29	30
SD	13	0							13	0
SN	0	34							13	34
SP	19	0							19	0
SF	0	-11							-4	-11
SB	0	13							5	13
SW	38								38	
Males										
N	130	130	0	0	132	0	0	0	-	-
R^2	53	55	0	0	3	0	0	0	-	-
Age	0	14	0	0	0	0	0	0	5	14
ETH	0	0	0	0	-19	0	0	0	-2	-6
SO	24	42							40	42
SN	0	33							13	33
SP	23	0							23	0
SF	0	-15							-6	-15
SW	38								38	
Females										
N	177	177	0	0	180	0	0	0	-	-
R^2	53	47	0	0	2	0	0	0	-	-

Canada, Mount Saint Vincent University (continued)

	S	SW	SO	SD	SN	SP	SF	SB	TES	TESW
R^2	53	54	0	2	0	0	0	0	-	-
Pred										
WS	0	0	0	-14	0	0	0	0	0	0
SO	0	43							21	43
SN	0	27							13	27
SP	14	0							14	0
SF	-18	0							-18	0
SB	13	14							20	14
SW	49								49	
Females										
N	256	256	0	0	0	0	0	0	-	-
R^2	54	53	0	0	0	0	0	0	-	-
SO	0	41							20	41
SN	0	29							14	29
SP	15	0							15	0
SF	-21	0							-21	0
SB	13	14							20	14
SW	48								48	

Canada, Saint Mary's University

	S	SW	SO	SD	SN	SP	SF	SB	TES	TESW
N	311	312	316	0	0	315	0	0	-	-
R^2	58	52	3	0	0	1	0	0	-	-
Pred										
Sex	0	0	0	0	0	12	0	0	1	1
Age	0	0	-14	0	0	0	0	0	-7	-7
LED	0	0	22	0	0	0	0	0	11	11
ETH	10	0	0	0	0	0	0	0	10	0
SO	30	51							52	51
SD	11	0							11	0
SN	0	11							5	11
SP	0	11							5	11
SB	0	11							5	11
SW	44								44	
Males										
N	167	168	169	0	0	0	0	0	-	-
R^2	46	43	6	0	0	0	0	0	-	-
LED	0	0	25	0	0	0	0	0	12	12
ETH	13	0	0	0	0	0	0	0	13	0
SO	31	47							47	47
SD	16	0							16	0

Canada, Saint Mary's University (continued)

	S	SW	SO	SD	SN	SP	SF	SB	TES	TESW
SP	0	27							9	27
SW	34								34	
Females										
N	143	143	0	0	146	0	145	0	-	-
R^2	70	59	0	0	2	0	3	0	-	-
Age	0	0	0	0	-16	0	0	0	-1	-2
LED	0	0	0	0	0	0	20	0	0	0
SO	30	68							70	68
SN	0	15							9	15
SW	59								59	

Canada, Simon Fraser University

	S	SW	SO	SD	SN	SP	SF	SB	TES	TESW
N	289	289	0	296	0	299	0	301	-	-
R^2	62	53	0	2	0	1	0	3	-	-
Pred										
Sex	0	16	0	0	0	0	0	12	9	18
Age	-10	0	0	0	0	-13	0	0	-10	0
LED	0	0	0	0	0	0	0	-14	-1	-2
ETH	0	0	0	-14	0	0	0	0	1	-2
SO	27	38							47	38
SD	-10	12							-4	12
SN	16	21							27	21
SB	0	16							8	16
SW	52								52	
Males										
N	111	111	0	0	0	113	0	115	-	-
R^2	66	48	0	0	0	6	0	6	-	-
Age	0	0	0	0	0	-25	0	0	0	0
WS	0	0	0	0	0	20	0	0	0	0
LED	0	0	0	0	0	0	0	-19	0	0
ETH	0	0	0	0	0	0	0	21	0	0
SO	41	44							63	44
SN	0	31							15	31
SW	49								49	
Females										
N	178	178	185	181	0	186	0	186	-	-
R^2	54	53	3	4	0	2	0	2	-	-
Age	-11	0	0	0	0	0	0	-15	-13	-3
LED	0	0	0	0	0	-15	0	0	0	0
ETH	0	0	-18	-21	0	0	0	0	-9	-10

Canada, Simon Fraser University (continued)

	S	SW	SO	SD	SN	SP	SF	SB	TES	TESW
SO	21	38							43	38
SD	0	13							7	13
SN	0	18							10	18
SF	0	-12							-7	-12
SB	0	17							10	17
SW	57								57	

Chile, Austral University of Chile

	S	SW	SO	SD	SN	SP	SF	SB	TES	TESW
N	231	233	0	0	0	0	251	0	-	-
R^2	39	36	0	0	0	0	1	0	-	-
Pred										
Sex	0	14	0	0	0	0	-13	0	5	16
SO	42	47							56	47
SN	0	20							6	20
SF	0	-14							-4	-14
SW	30								30	
Males										
N	122	123	0	0	0	0	0	132	-	-
R^2	35	34	0	0	0	0	0	3	-	-
Age	0	0	0	0	0	0	0	-18	0	0
SO	39	50							54	50
SF	0	-24							-7	-24
SW	29								29	
Females										
N	109	110	0	0	0	117	0	0	-	-
R^2	48	43	0	0	0	3	0	0	-	-
WS	0	-18	0	0	0	18	0	0	-5	-18
LED	16	0	0	0	0	0	0	0	16	0
SO	48	44							60	44
SN	0	32							9	32
SW	28								28	

Egypt, Ain Shams University

	S	SW	SO	SD	SN	SP	SF	SB	TES	TESW
N	238	240	0	0	0	0	0	0	-	-
R^2	46	47	0	0	0	0	0	0	-	-
Pred										
SO	30	62							53	62
SN	0	14							5	14
SP	15	0							15	0

Egypt, Ain Shams University (continued)

	S	SW	SO	SD	SN	SP	SF	SB	TES	TESW
SW	37								37	
Males										
N	133	134	0	0	153	0	150	0	-	-
R^2	32	34	0	0	3	0	2	0	-	-
Age	0	16	0	0	0	0	0	0	6	16
LED	0	0	0	0	19	0	-16	0	0	0
SO	28	51							47	51
SP	0	16							6	16
SW	37								37	
Females										
N	105	106	0	0	0	0	0	0	-	-
R^2	60	60	0	0	0	0	0	0	-	-
LED	-14	0	0	0	0	0	0	0	-14	0
SO	32	78							59	78
SP	24	0							24	0
SW	35								35	

Finland, University of Helsinki

	S	SW	SO	SD	SN	SP	SF	SB	TES	TESW
N	257	259	271	0	272	269	0	271	-	-
R^2	70	55	2	0	4	4	0	3	-	-
Pred										
Sex	0	0	0	0	14	15	0	19	5	5
Age	-9	0	-15	0	-14	-12	0	0	-23	-12
WS	-9	0	0	0	0	0	0	0	-9	0
SO	24	46							49	46
SN	0	36							19	36
SP	12	0							12	0
SW	54								54	
Males										
N	101	103	0	0	0	0	0	0	-	-
R^2	71	56	0	0	0	0	0	0	-	-
LED	-14	0	0	0	0	0	0	0	-14	0
SO	23	58							57	58
SN	0	26							15	26
SF	-12	0							-12	0
SW	58								58	
Females										
N	156	156	0	0	0	160	0	0	-	-
R^2	67	53	0	0	0	2	0	0	-	-
Age	-16	0	0	0	0	-17	0	0	-16	0

Finland, University of Helsinki (continued)

	S	SW	SO	SD	SN	SP	SF	SB	TES	TESW
SO	31	38							52	38
SN	0	42							23	42
SW	55								55	

Federal Republic of Germany

	S	SW	SO	SD	SN	SP	SF	SB	TES	TESW
N	701	702	761	726	761	763	751	761	-	-
R^2	62	55	1	1	1	1	2	2	-	-
Pred										
Sex	0	0	9	0	8	11	-10	14	8	9
Age	0	0	0	-8	0	0	0	0	-1	0
WS	0	0	0	0	0	0	-12	0	0	0
SO	15	40							37	40
SD	7	0							7	0
SN	9	29							25	29
SB	7	22							19	22
SW	54								54	
Males										
N	377	378	0	0	0	0	408	0	-	-
R^2	65	56	0	0	0	0	1	0	-	-
WS	8	0	0	0	0	0	-11	0	8	0
SO	29	39							50	39
SN	0	33							18	33
SB	8	21							19	21
SW	54								54	
Females										
N	324	324	0	332	0	0	343	0	-	-
R^2	61	54	0	3	0	0	2	0	-	-
Age	0	0	0	-18	0	0	0	0	-2	0
WS	0	0	0	0	0	0	-14	0	0	0
SO	0	38							22	38
SD	13	0							13	0
SN	18	21							30	21
SP	0	13							8	13
SB	0	16							9	16
SW	58								58	

Germany, Federal College of Public Administration

	S	SW	SO	SD	SN	SP	SF	SB	TES	TESW
N	236	236	251	242	249	251	246	250	-	-
R^2	59	59	3	1	3	4	2	3	-	-

Germany, Federal College of Public Admin. (continued)

	S	SW	SO	SD	SN	SP	SF	SB	TES	TESW
Pred										
Sex	0	0	18	14	18	20	-15	19	15	17
SO	14	46							36	46
SN	27	34							43	34
SB	0	13							6	13
SW	47								47	
Males										
N	138	138	0	0	0	0	0	0	-	-
R^2	64	58	0	0	0	0	0	0	-	-
SO	23	38							40	38
SD	0	19							9	19
SN	24	36							40	36
SW	45								45	
Females										
N	98	98	103	0	0	0	102	0	-	-
R^2	51	60	6	0	0	0	4	0	-	-
Age	0	0	27	0	0	0	0	0	7	14
ETH	0	0	0	0	0	0	-23	0	0	0
SO	0	53							26	53
SN	32	22							43	22
SB	0	18							9	18
SW	49								49	

Germany, University of Frankfurt

	S	SW	SO	SD	SN	SP	SF	SB	TES	TESW
N	238	238	0	0	0	0	268	271	-	-
R^2	64	51	0	0	0	0	1	2	-	-
Pred										
Sex	0	0	0	0	0	0	0	15	3	5
ETH	0	0	0	0	0	0	12	0	0	0
SO	25	31							42	31
SD	12	0							12	0
SN	0	27							15	27
SB	0	32							18	32
SW	56								56	
Males										
N	142	142	108	0	0	0	160	0	-	-
R^2	64	54	4	0	0	0	3	0	-	-
WS	11	0	21	0	0	0	0	0	22	7
ETH	0	0	0	0	0	0	19	0	0	0
SO	32	34							51	34

Germany, University of Frankfurt (continued)

	S	SW	SO	SD	SN	SP	SF	SB	TES	TESW
SN	0	28							16	28
SB	0	32							18	32
SW	56								56	
Females										
N	96	96	0	0	0	0	108	0	-	-
R^2	67	45	0	0	0	0	4	0	-	-
WS	0	0	0	0	0	0	-23	0	0	0
SO	18	25							32	25
SD	25	0							25	0
SN	0	28							16	28
SB	0	32							18	32
SW	56								56	

Germany, University of Mannheim

	S	SW	SO	SD	SN	SP	SF	SB	TES	TESW
N	226	227	0	0	0	239	0	0	-	-
R^2	65	56	0	0	0	2	0	0	-	-
Pred										
LED	0	0	0	0	0	-14	0	0	0	0
SO	0	44							29	44
SN	14	25							30	25
SB	11	19							23	19
SW	65								65	
Males										
N	96	97	0	0	0	0	0	0	-	-
R^2	69	60	0	0	0	0	0	0	-	-
SO	34	42							58	42
SN	0	31							18	31
SB	0	19							11	19
SW	57								57	
Females										
N	129	129	0	132	0	0	0	0	-	-
R^2	66	55	0	8	0	0	0	0	-	-
Age	0	0	0	-30	0	0	0	0	-3	-5
SO	0	45							27	45
SD	0	15							9	15
SN	21	0							21	0
SP	0	28							17	28
SB	13	0							13	0
SW	59								59	

Greece, Aristotelian University of Thessaloniki

	S	SW	SO	SD	SN	SP	SF	SB	TES	TESW
N	244	244	0	257	0	0	259	259	-	-
R^2	45	31	0	3	0	0	2	1	-	-
Pred										
Sex	0	0	0	17	0	0	15	0	-2	0
ETH	0	0	0	0	0	0	0	-13	0	0
SO	37	39							46	39
SD	-13	0							-13	0
SP	26	27							32	27
SW	22								22	

Males

	S	SW	SO	SD	SN	SP	SF	SB	TES	TESW
N	137	137	147	0	146	147	0	0	-	-
R^2	38	36	2	0	4	3	0	0	-	-
Age	0	0	0	0	0	-20	0	0	-7	0
WS	0	0	-17	0	0	0	0	0	-6	0
LED	0	-21	0	0	0	0	0	0	0	-21
ETH	0	0	0	0	-22	0	0	0	0	0
SO	40	48							40	48
SD	-18	0							-18	0
SP	36	0							36	0
SB	0	22							0	22

Females

	S	SW	SO	SD	SN	SP	SF	SB	TES	TESW
N	107	107	0	114	0	115	115	0	-	-
R^2	57	31	0	5	0	4	4	0	-	-
WS	0	0	0	0	0	23	-23	0	2	6
LED	0	0	0	-24	0	0	0	0	0	0
SO	40	22							48	22
SN	20	24							28	24
SP	0	27							10	27
SW	35								35	

Hungary, University of Economics

	S	SW	SO	SD	SN	SP	SF	SB	TES	TESW
N	215	215	0	0	0	0	0	0	-	-
R^2	60	60	0	0	0	0	0	0	-	-
Pred										
Sex	13	0	0	0	0	0	0	0	13	0
SO	28	33							42	33
SD	0	13							6	13
SN	16	33							30	33
SP	0	17							7	17
SW	43								43	

Hungary, University of Economics (continued)

	S	SW	SO	SD	SN	SP	SF	SB	TES	TESW
Females										
N	157	157	0	0	0	0	0	0	-	-
R^2	58	61	0	0	0	0	0	0	-	-
SO	26	33							41	33
SN	16	37							32	37
SP	0	22							10	22
SW	44								44	

India, University of Delhi

	S	SW	SO	SD	SN	SP	SF	SB	TES	TESW
N	220	224	0	0	0	0	0	0	-	-
R^2	52	29	0	0	0	0	0	0	-	-
Pred										
Sex	0	20	0	0	0	0	0	0	6	20
Age	-12	0	0	0	0	0	0	0	-12	0
WS	9	0	0	0	0	0	0	0	9	0
ETH	14	0	0	0	0	0	0	0	14	0
SO	40	38							51	38
SD	19	19							25	19
SW	29								29	
Males										
N	136	139	0	0	0	0	0	0	-	-
R^2	55	26	0	0	0	0	0	0	-	-
ETH	14	0	0	0	0	0	0	0	14	0
SO	39	40							48	40
SP	31	19							35	19
SW	23								23	

Israel, Hebrew University of Jerusalem

	S	SW	SO	SD	SN	SP	SF	SB	TES	TESW
N	307	307	0	0	309	0	0	0	-	-
R^2	56	46	0	0	1	0	0	0	-	-
Pred										
Sex	0	13	0	0	0	0	0	0	5	13
ETH	0	0	0	0	12	0	0	0	3	2
SO	23	26							34	26
SD	0	18							7	18
SN	13	18							20	18
SP	15	23							24	23
SW	41								41	

Israel, Hebrew University of Jerusalem (continued)

	S	SW	SO	SD	SN	SP	SF	SB	TES	TESW
Males										
N	157	157	0	0	0	0	157	0	-	-
R²	57	42	0	0	0	0	3	0	-	-
ETH	0	0	0	0	0	0	-20	0	0	0
SO	31	29							43	29
SD	0	22							9	22
SN	20	0							20	0
SP	0	31							13	31
SW	42								42	
Females										
N	150	150	0	0	0	0	0	0	-	-
R²	54	48	0	0	0	0	0	0	-	-
SO	18	25							30	25
SD	0	14							7	14
SN	0	45							21	45
SP	22	0							22	0
SW	47								47	

Japan

	S	SW	SO	SD	SN	SP	SF	SB	TES	TESW
N	1146	1152	1200	1195	1199	1195	1197	1191	-	-
R²	53	52	3	1	1	1	1	3	-	-
Pred										
Sex	0	0	12	10	9	7	0	14	8	9
Age	6	0	0	0	0	0	12	0	6	0
WS	0	0	0	0	6	0	0	0	1	1
LED	0	-5	11	0	0	0	0	6	2	-2
SO	22	25							32	25
SD	12	15							18	15
SN	0	22							9	22
SP	10	17							17	17
SB	0	7							3	7
SW	41								41	
Males										
N	942	968	983	979	984	0	982	0	-	-
R²	54	52	1	1	1	0	2	0	-	-
Age	5	0	0	0	-9	0	13	0	4	-2
WS	0	0	0	7	0	0	-7	0	1	1
LED	0	-5	0	0	0	0	0	0	-2	-5
ETH	0	0	11	0	0	0	0	0	3	3
SO	20	25							31	25

Japan (continued)

	S	SW	SO	SD	SN	SP	SF	SB	TES	TESW
SD	10	15							17	15
SN	0	24							11	24
SP	11	15							18	15
SB	0	6							3	6
SW	44								44	
Females										
N	204	204	217	216	215	213	0	0	-	-
R^2	50	48	3	2	2	2	0	0	-	-
Age	14	0	0	0	0	16	0	0	15	5
LED	0	0	20	0	16	0	0	0	9	9
ETH	0	0	0	14	0	0	0	0	3	0
SO	29	27							37	27
SD	22	0							22	0
SN	0	25							7	25
SP	0	28							8	28
SW	29								29	

Japan, Sophia University

	S	SW	SO	SD	SN	SP	SF	SB	TES	TESW
N	237	242	260	260	260	259	259	252	-	-
R^2	40	52	2	4	5	2	5	3	-	-
Pred										
Sex	0	0	15	22	24	15	-23	19	13	14
WS	0	-14	0	0	0	0	0	0	-5	-14
SO	20	29							30	29
SD	17	30							28	30
SP	0	22							8	22
SW	36								36	
Males										
N	158	164	0	0	0	175	0	0	-	-
R^2	37	53	0	0	0	3	0	0	-	-
Age	0	0	0	0	0	-18	0	0	-1	-3
WS	0	-18	0	0	0	0	0	0	-8	-18
SO	25	28							37	28
SD	0	34							15	34
SP	0	18							8	18
SW	43								43	

Japan, Tokai University

	S	SW	SO	SD	SN	SP	SF	SB	TES	TESW
N	299	289	301	0	300	0	0	298	-	-

Japan, Tokai University (continued)

	S	SW	SO	SD	SN	SP	SF	SB	TES	TESW
R²	60	60	4	0	2	0	0	4	-	-
Pred										
Sex	0	0	17	0	0	0	0	16	5	7
Age	10	0	0	0	0	0	0	13	11	2
WS	0	0	15	0	13	0	0	0	8	9
SO	13	31							27	31
SD	16	0							16	0
SN	14	31							28	31
SP	0	19							8	19
SB	0	12							5	12
SW	44								44	
Males										
N	208	208	217	215	217	0	0	214	-	-
R²	60	57	2	1	2	0	0	2	-	-
Age	0	0	0	0	0	0	0	15	0	0
WS	0	0	0	0	14	0	0	0	5	5
ETH	0	0	16	14	0	0	0	0	5	5
SO	19	29							33	29
SN	21	36							38	36
SP	0	23							11	23
SW	48								48	

Japan, Tokai and Denkitsushin Universities

	S	SW	SO	SD	SN	SP	SF	SB	TES	TESW
N	620	621	0	0	0	636	638	641	-	-
R²	56	49	0	0	0	1	1	1	-	-
Pred										
Age	0	0	0	0	0	0	0	-8	0	0
ETH	0	0	0	0	0	-10	9	0	-2	-2
SO	22	25							33	25
SD	11	16							18	16
SN	0	23							11	23
SP	11	18							19	18
SW	45								45	
Males										
N	575	576	0	0	0	590	592	0	-	-
R²	58	50	0	0	0	1	1	0	-	-
ETH	0	0	0	0	0	-10	9	0	-2	-2
SO	20	27							33	27
SD	10	14							17	14
SN	0	26							12	26

Japan, Tokai and Denkitsushin Universities (continued)

	S	SW	SO	SD	SN	SP	SF	SB	TES	TESW
SP	11	16							19	1 6
SW	47								47	

Jordan, Yarmouk University

	S	SW	SO	SD	SN	SP	SF	SB	TES	TESW
N	273	274	0	296	297	296	293	0	-	-
R^2	41	35	0	2	2	1	4	0	-	-
Pred										
Age	0	0	0	0	0	0	-21	0	-1	-3
ETH	0	0	0	16	14	12	18	0	2	5
SO	34	42							48	42
SN	0	19							6	19
SF	0	12							4	12
SB	11	14							16	14
SW	33								33	
Males										
N	220	221	238	237	239	236	234	0	-	-
R^2	41	40	1	2	2	4	3	0	-	-
Age	0	0	0	0	0	0	-22	0	0	0
WS	0	0	0	0	0	-15	0	0	0	0
ETH	0	0	13	15	15	20	15	0	7	8
SO	26	45							43	45
SD	0	15							6	15
SB	14	18							21	18
SW	38								38	

Kenya, University of Nairobi

	S	SW	SO	SD	SN	SP	SF	SB	TES	TESW
N	254	257	0	0	0	0	0	269	-	-
R^2	44	45	0	0	0	0	0	1	-	-
Pred										
LED	0	12	0	0	0	0	0	0	-4	-12
ETH	0	0	0	0	0	0	0	12	2	0
SO	35	35							45	35
SD	0	18							5	18
SN	0	17							5	17
SF	0	-15							-4	-15
SB	16	0							16	0
SW	29								29	
Males										
N	138	141	0	0	0	0	0	0	-	-

Kenya, University of Nairobi (continued)

	S	SW	SO	SD	SN	SP	SF	SB	TES	TESW
R^2	33	48	0	0	0	0	0	0	-	-
LED	0	-13	0	0	0	0	0	0	0	-13
SO	42	22							42	22
SD	0	22							0	22
SN	0	19							0	19
SB	23	24							23	24

Females

	S	SW	SO	SD	SN	SP	SF	SB	TES	TESW
N	116	116	0	0	0	0	0	0	-	-
R^2	60	43	0	0	0	0	0	0	-	-
WS	-13	0	0	0	0	0	0	0	-13	0
SO	32	41							48	41
SN	0	24							10	24
SP	23	0							23	0
SF	0	-18							-7	-18
SW	40								40	

Korea, Korea University

	S	SW	SO	SD	SN	SP	SF	SB	TES	TESW
N	434	435	442	439	0	441	0	0	-	-
R^2	62	58	2	1	0	1	0	0	-	-
Pred										
Sex	-10	0	0	-9	0	-12	0	0	-12	-3
LED	0	0	14	0	0	0	0	0	7	7
SO	17	52							48	52
SD	0	14							8	14
SP	0	13							8	13
SF	0	-13							8	13
SB	9	0							9	0
SW	60								60	

Males

	S	SW	SO	SD	SN	SP	SF	SB	TES	TESW
N	347	347	352	0	350	351	0	351	-	-
R^2	60	57	3	0	1	1	0	2	-	-
WS	0	0	0	0	12	11	0	14	3	3
LED	0	0	17	0	0	0	0	0	9	9
SO	21	55							52	55
SN	0	12							7	12
SP	0	12							7	12
SF	0	-11							-6	-11
SB	10	0							10	0
SW	56								56	

Mexico, University of Baja California Sur

	S	SW	SO	SD	SN	SP	SF	SB	TES	TESW
N	217	219	0	240	240	0	0	243	-	-
R^2	29	31	0	1	4	0	0	2	-	-
Pred										
Sex	0	0	0	13	14	0	0	0	1	2
Age	0	0	0	0	-17	0	0	0	0	0
WS	-12	0	0	0	0	0	0	14	-13	2
LED	0	18	0	0	0	0	0	0	6	18
ETH	0	-16	0	0	0	0	0	0	-6	-16
SO	28	23							36	23
SD	0	16							6	16
SP	0	18							6	18
SB	0	16							6	16
SW	35								35	
Males										
N	149	151	0	0	169	0	0	172	-	-
R^2	29	21	0	0	3	0	0	3	-	-
Age	0	0	0	0	-19	0	0	0	0	0
WS	-21	0	0	0	0	0	0	20	-21	0
SO	28	17							34	17
SD	0	24							9	24
SP	0	20							7	20
SW	36								36	

Netherlands, Erasmus University

	S	SW	SO	SD	SN	SP	SF	SB	TES	TESW
N	509	510	523	524	0	518	0	522	-	-
R^2	45	45	1	1	0	2	0	1	-	-
Pred										
Sex	0	0	0	11	0	14	0	12	3	5
WS	0	-9	-10	0	0	0	0	0	-7	-11
SO	18	20							27	20
SD	0	25							11	25
SN	12	24							23	24
SP	0	12							5	12
SB	9	0							9	0
SW	44								44	
Males										
N	297	297	305	304	0	0	0	0	-	-
R^2	51	45	2	1	0	0	0	0	-	-
WS	0	0	-15	-12	0	0	0	0	-6	-6
SO	24	20							31	20

Netherlands, Erasmus University (continued)

	S	SW	SO	SD	SN	SP	SF	SB	TES	TESW
SD	0	28							10	28
SN	16	24							25	24
SP	14	13							19	13
SW	37								37	
Females										
N	209	210	0	0	0	0	0	0	-	-
R^2	38	47	0	0	0	0	0	0	-	-
SO	0	28							15	28
SD	0	20							11	20
SN	0	24							13	24
SP	0	13							7	13
SB	16	0							16	0
SW	54								54	

Netherlands, University of Leiden

	S	SW	SO	SD	SN	SP	SF	SB	TES	TESW
N	317	317	0	0	0	0	350	0	-	-
R^2	59	50	0	0	0	0	1	0	-	-
Pred										
Age	-9	0	0	0	0	0	-11	0	-9	0
LED	0	11	0	0	0	0	0	0	6	11
SO	19	42							42	42
SN	0	29							16	29
SP	13	11							19	11
SB	0	12							7	12
SW	55								55	
Males										
N	140	140	0	150	161	0	156	0	-	-
R^2	60	40	0	2	5	0	4	0	-	-
Age	0	0	0	0	0	0	-22	0	0	0
WS	0	0	0	16	0	0	0	0	0	0
LED	0	0	0	0	-16	0	0	0	-2	-4
ETH	0	0	0	0	-24	0	0	0	-3	-5
SO	19	53							54	53
SN	0	22							14	22
SW	65								65	
Females										
N	177	177	0	0	0	0	0	0	-	-
R^2	59	59	0	0	0	0	0	0	-	-
Age	-11	0	0	0	0	0	0	0	-11	0
WS	0	-10	0	0	0	0	0	0	-5	-10

Netherlands, University of Leiden (continued)

	S	SW	SO	SD	SN	SP	SF	SB	TES	TESW
LED	0	19	0	0	0	0	0	0	9	19
SO	20	37							37	37
SN	0	42							20	42
SP	23	0							23	0
SB	0	18							9	18
SW	47								47	

New Zealand, Massey University

	S	SW	SO	SD	SN	SP	SF	SB	TES	TESW
N	314	315	320	321	0	319	319	320	-	-
R^2	55	54	3	2	0	6	3	4	-	-
Pred										
Sex	0	10	15	0	0	17	-13	12	14	19
Age	-9	0	0	-14	0	-18	0	-18	-14	-5
WS	0	0	-11	0	0	0	14	0	-4	-3
ETH	0	0	0	0	0	11	0	0	1	2
SO	27	30							40	30
SN	0	27							11	27
SP	0	17							7	17
SB	15	13							21	13
SW	42								42	
Males										
N	113	113	115	115	115	114	0	114	-	-
R^2	60	64	5	4	5	5	0	8	-	-
Age	0	0	0	0	-23	0	0	0	-6	-9
LED	0	0	0	-22	0	-23	0	-29	-8	-7
ETH	0	19	25	0	0	0	0	0	12	25
SO	28	25							33	25
SN	18	40							26	40
SP	28	0							28	0
SB	0	25							5	25
SW	20								20	
Females										
N	201	202	205	206	0	205	204	206	-	-
R^2	53	46	2	2	0	3	3	2	-	-
Age	-12	0	0	0	0	0	0	0	-12	0
WS	0	0	-17	-17	0	-18	18	-16	-11	-10
SO	21	34							36	34
SN	0	22							10	22
SP	0	25							11	25
SB	16	0							16	0

New Zealand, Massey University (continued)

	S	SW	SO	SD	SN	SP	SF	SB	TES	TESW
SW	45								45	

Norway

	S	SW	SO	SD	SN	SP	SF	SB	TES	TESW
N	201	202	0	0	0	0	229	228	-	-
R^2	56	40	0	0	0	0	2	4	-	-
Pred										
Sex	0	12	0	0	0	0	0	15	6	14
Age	-13	-17	0	0	0	0	0	-15	-21	-19
WS	0	13	0	0	0	0	0	0	5	13
ETH	0	18	0	0	0	0	15	0	7	16
SO	15	28							26	28
SN	15	22							24	22
SP	24	0							24	0
SF	0	-12							-5	-12
SB	0	14							6	14
SW	40								40	
Females										
N	126	127	0	0	0	0	0	0	-	-
R^2	43	35	0	0	0	0	0	0	-	-
ETH	0	15	0	0	0	0	0	0	5	15
SO	19	23							27	23
SN	0	29							10	29
SP	31	0							31	0
SB	0	19							7	19
SW	36								36	

Norway, University of Oslo

	S	SW	SO	SD	SN	SP	SF	SB	TES	TESW
N	117	118	0	0	135	0	0	137	-	-
R^2	56	38	0	0	2	0	0	4	-	-
Pred										
Sex	0	0	0	0	-17	0	0	0	-2	-4
LED	0	-15	0	0	0	0	0	-21	-7	-15
SO	17	31							31	31
SN	0	21							9	21
SP	33	0							33	0
SB	0	22							10	22
SW	44								44	

Philippines

	S	SW	SO	SD	SN	SP	SF	SB	TES	TESW
N	939	943	972	0	970	0	971	0	-	-
R^2	38	33	1	0	1	0	1	0	-	-
Pred										
Age	0	0	-6	0	0	0	0	0	-2	-2
LED	-6	0	0	0	8	0	-10	0	-6	1
ETH	0	0	0	0	0	0	-6	0	0	0
SO	28	32							38	32
SN	0	15							5	15
SP	16	10							19	10
SB	0	14							5	14
SW	32								32	

Males

	S	SW	SO	SD	SN	SP	SF	SB	TES	TESW
N	298	299	0	0	0	316	0	312	-	-
R^2	47	41	0	0	0	2	0	2	-	-
Age	0	0	0	0	0	-14	0	-14	-1	-2
SO	30	30							44	30
SD	0	15							7	15
SN	0	20							9	20
SB	0	14							7	14
SW	47								47	

Females

	S	SW	SO	SD	SN	SP	SF	SB	TES	TESW
N	641	644	0	659	655	0	656	655	-	-
R^2	34	29	0	1	1	0	2	1	-	-
LED	0	0	0	10	12	0	-16	8	-1	1
SO	27	31							34	31
SD	9	0							9	0
SN	0	12							3	12
SP	20	15							24	15
SF	12	9							14	9
SB	0	16							4	16
SW	24								24	

Philippines, De La Salle University

	S	SW	SO	SD	SN	SP	SF	SB	TES	TESW
N	292	292	0	303	306	306	0	0	-	-
R^2	48	39	0	4	1	3	0	0	-	-
Pred										
Sex	0	0	0	-17	-13	0	0	0	-1	-3
Age	0	0	0	0	0	-12	0	0	-2	0
WS	0	-10	0	0	0	0	0	0	-4	-10
LED	0	0	0	-14	0	-12	0	0	-2	0

Philippines, De La Salle University (continued)

	S	SW	SO	SD	SN	SP	SF	SB	TES	TESW
ETH	-9	0	0	0	0	0	0	0	-9	0
SO	22	37							38	37
SN	0	19							8	19
SP	18	0							18	0
SB	0	16							7	16
SW	42								42	

Males

	S	SW	SO	SD	SN	SP	SF	SB	TES	TESW
N	138	138	0	143	0	147	0	0	-	-
R^2	53	41	0	3	0	6	0	0	-	-
Age	0	0	0	0	0	-26	0	0	0	0
LED	0	0	0	-20	0	0	0	0	0	0
ETH	-14	0	0	0	0	0	0	0	-14	0
SO	28	40							48	40
SN	0	33							17	33
SW	51								51	

Females

	S	SW	SO	SD	SN	SP	SF	SB	TES	TESW
N	153	153	0	0	0	0	0	157	-	-
R^2	46	36	0	0	0	0	0	3	-	-
WS	0	0	0	0	0	0	0	19	2	5
SO	21	45							35	45
SP	35	0							35	0
SB	0	27							8	27
SW	31								31	

Philippines, Philippine Normal College

	S	SW	SO	SD	SN	SP	SF	SB	TES	TESW
N	294	297	0	0	0	0	305	305	-	-
R^2	18	23	0	0	0	0	4	1	-	-
Pred										
Sex	0	0	0	0	0	0	-17	0	0	0
Age	0	0	0	0	0	0	13	-13	0	0
WS	0	0	0	0	0	0	-13	0	0	0
SO	23	20							26	20
SD	0	21							3	21
SP	20	20							23	20
SW	14								14	

Females

	S	SW	SO	SD	SN	SP	SF	SB	TES	TESW
N	266	269	0	0	0	0	0	276	-	-
R^2	17	23	0	0	0	0	0	1	-	-
Age	0	0	0	0	0	0	0	-12	0	0
SO	20	20							20	20

Philippines, Philippine Normal College (continued)

	S	SW	SO	SD	SN	SP	SF	SB	TES	TESW
SD	15	21							15	21
SP	18	20							18	20

Philippines, University of the Philippines

	S	SW	SO	SD	SN	SP	SF	SB	TES	TESW
N	356	357	0	0	0	0	0	0	-	-
R^2	50	39	0	0	0	0	0	0	-	-
Pred										
SO	32	33							45	33
SN	0	20							8	20
SB	15	24							24	24
SW	38								38	

Males

	S	SW	SO	SD	SN	SP	SF	SB	TES	TESW
N	134	135	0	0	0	0	0	140	-	-
R^2	43	45	0	0	0	0	0	6	-	-
Age	0	0	0	0	0	0	0	-33	-3	-8
LED	0	0	0	0	0	0	0	27	3	7
SO	26	30							38	30
SD	0	28							11	28
SP	15	0							15	0
SB	0	24							10	24
SW	40								40	

Females

	S	SW	SO	SD	SN	SP	SF	SB	TES	TESW
N	222	222	0	0	0	222	0	0	-	-
R^2	56	36	0	0	0	1	0	0	-	-
LED	0	0	0	0	0	-13	0	0	0	0
SO	31	32							42	32
SD	16	0							16	0
SN	0	22							8	22
SF	10	13							15	13
SB	17	27							27	27
SW	35								35	

Portugal, Technical University of Lisbon

	S	SW	SO	SD	SN	SP	SF	SB	TES	TESW
N	157	163	0	181	0	0	0	0	-	-
R^2	76	75	0	3	0	0	0	0	-	-
Pred										
Age	0	0	0	20	0	0	0	0	-1	3
LED	-9	0	0	0	0	0	0	0	-9	0
SO	29	44							50	44

Portugal, Technical University of Lisbon (continued)

	S	SW	SO	SD	SN	SP	SF	SB	TES	TESW
SD	-13	13							-7	13
SN	19	30							33	30
SB	13	12							19	12
SW	48								48	

Puerto Rico, University of Puerto Rico

	S	SW	SO	SD	SN	SP	SF	SB	TES	TESW
N	276	277	0	0	0	300	0	0	-	-
R^2	45	46	0	0	0	1	0	0	-	-
Pred										
LED	0	0	0	0	0	-12	0	0	-1	-2
SO	32	40							49	40
SN	0	24							10	24
SP	0	18							8	18
SW	43								43	
Males										
N	153	153	166	0	0	166	0	169	-	-
R^2	50	45	2	0	0	4	0	2	-	-
Age	0	0	-17	0	0	0	0	0	-10	-6
LED	0	0	0	0	0	-22	0	-16	-2	-5
SO	41	37							55	37
SN	0	23							9	23
SP	0	22							9	22
SW	39								39	
Females										
N	123	124	0	0	0	0	0	0	-	-
R^2	39	45	0	0	0	0	0	0	-	-
SO	20	46							43	46
SN	0	32							16	32
SW	50								50	

Singapore, National University of Singapore

	S	SW	SO	SD	SN	SP	SF	SB	TES	TESW
N	243	244	255	251	0	253	0	254	-	-
R^2	54	53	4	2	0	4	0	1	-	-
Pred										
WS	0	0	21	0	0	0	0	0	11	7
ETH	0	0	0	16	0	21	0	13	3	5
SO	35	32							50	32
SD	0	17							8	17
SN	0	21							10	21

Singapore, National University of Singapore (continued)

	S	SW	SO	SD	SN	SP	SF	SB	TES	TESW
SB	0	20							9	20
SW	46								46	
Females										
N	203	204	212	210	0	210	0	211	-	-
R^2	52	52	4	4	0	3	0	1	-	-
Age	0	0	0	14	0	0	0	0	1	2
WS	0	0	22	0	0	0	0	0	11	7
ETH	0	0	0	14	0	18	0	14	2	5
SO	35	31							49	31
SD	0	13							6	13
SN	0	22							10	22
SB	0	22							10	22
SW	45								45	

Republic of South Africa, University of Zululand

	S	SW	SO	SD	SN	SP	SF	SB	TES	TESW
N	233	239	0	0	0	0	282	0	-	-
R^2	34	28	0	0	0	0	3	0	-	-
Pred										
LED	0	0	0	0	0	0	20	0	0	0
SO	35	21							40	21
SD	15	0							15	0
SN	0	16							4	16
SP	0	29							7	29
SW	24								24	
Males										
N	104	106	0	0	0	0	123	0	-	-
R^2	40	25	0	0	0	0	3	0	-	-
Age	0	0	0	0	0	0	20	0	-4	0
SO	39	32							49	32
SP	0	31							10	31
SF	-18	0							-18	0
SW	31								31	
Females										
N	129	133	0	0	0	164	159	0	-	-
R^2	34	29	0	0	0	2	5	0	-	-
LED	0	-160	0	0	0	0	23	0	-3	-16
ETH	0	0	0	0	0	16	0	0	1	6
SO	32	0							32	0
SD	25	0							25	0
SN	0	25							5	25

Republic of South Africa, U. of Zululand (continued)

	S	SW	SO	SD	SN	SP	SF	SB	TES	TESW
SP	0	35							7	35
SW	20								20	

Spain, University of Madrid

	S	SW	SO	SD	SN	SP	SF	SB	TES	TESW
N	256	256	0	265	0	0	0	266	-	-
R^2	48	37	0	2	0	0	0	2	-	-
Pred										
Sex	0	11	0	0	0	0	0	0	4	11
WS	0	0	0	-16	0	0	0	-16	-3	0
ETH	0	-13	0	0	0	0	0	0	-5	-13
SO	20	38							35	38
SN	0	17							7	17
SP	13	19							21	19
SB	17	0							17	0
SW	40								40	
Males										
N	128	128	0	134	136	0	0	134	-	-
R^2	54	39	0	5	4	0	0	9	-	-
WS	0	0	0	-25	0	0	0	-31	-7	0
ETH	0	0	0	0	22	0	0	0	0	0
SO	29	50							50	50
SP	0	23							9	23
SB	21	0							21	0
SW	41								41	
Females										
N	128	128	0	0	0	0	0	0	-	-
R^2	39	32	0	0	0	0	0	0	-	-
ETH	0	-18	0	0	0	0	0	0	-8	-18
SO	0	31							13	31
SN	0	19							8	19
SP	33	21							42	21
SW	42								42	

Sweden, University of Uppsala

	S	SW	SO	SD	SN	SP	SF	SB	TES	TESW
N	210	211	0	0	0	260	227	0	-	-
R^2	70	55	0	0	0	1	5	0	-	-
Pred										
Sex	0	0	0	0	0	13	-15	0	3	2
Age	-11	0	0	0	0	0	0	0	-11	0

Sweden, University of Uppsala (continued)

	S	SW	SO	SD	SN	SP	SF	SB	TES	TESW
ETH	0	0	0	0	0	0	-21	0	1	2
SO	12	23							26	23
SN	0	45							27	45
SP	13	0							13	0
SF	0	-10							-6	-10
SB	13	15							22	15
SW	59								59	

Males

	S	SW	SO	SD	SN	SP	SF	SB	TES	TESW
N	109	109	0	0	0	0	119	0	-	-
R^2	70	65	0	0	0	0	11	0	-	-
Age	0	0	0	0	0	0	26	0	0	0
WS	-12	0	0	0	0	0	0	0	-12	0
ETH	0	0	0	0	0	0	-35	0	0	0
SO	33	23							43	23
SN	0	51							23	51
SB	20	21							30	21
SW	45								45	

Females

	S	SW	SO	SD	SN	SP	SF	SB	TES	TESW
N	101	102	0	122	0	0	0	0	-	-
R^2	75	42	0	5	0	0	0	0	-	-
WS	0	0	0	19	0	0	0	0	0	0
ETH	0	0	0	-20	0	0	0	0	0	0
SO	0	24							18	24
SN	0	50							37	50
SB	23	0							23	0
SW	73								73	

Switzerland, University of Freiburg

	S	SW	SO	SD	SN	SP	SF	SB	TES	TESW
N	310	311	0	0	0	345	0	335	-	-
R^2	60	58	0	0	0	1	0	2	-	-
Pred										
Sex	0	0	0	0	0	12	0	15	1	2
ETH	0	8	0	0	0	0	0	0	4	8
SO	13	39							32	39
SD	0	15							7	15
SN	28	17							36	17
SP	0	19							9	19
SF	0	8							4	8
SW	48								48	

Switzerland, University of Freiburg (continued)

	S	SW	SO	SD	SN	SP	SF	SB	TES	TESW
Males										
N	158	158	0	0	0	0	169	0	-	-
R^2	64	56	0	0	0	0	4	0	-	-
LED	0	0	0	0	0	0	22	0	0	0
SO	14	29							28	29
SD	0	16							8	16
SN	30	26							42	26
SP	0	22							10	22
SW	47								47	
Females										
N	153	152	0	0	0	0	0	0	-	-
R^2	54	60	0	0	0	0	0	0	-	-
ETH	0	18	0	0	0	0	0	0	10	18
SO	0	54							31	54
SD	0	16							9	16
SN	26	16							35	16
SW	57								57	

Taiwan

	S	SW	SO	SD	SN	SP	SF	SB	TES	TESW
N	2366	2368	0	2459	2469	2460	2437	0	-	-
R^2	42	38	0	1	1	1	1	0	-	-
Pred										
Sex	0	4	0	4	0	5	-5	0	3	5
Age	0	0	0	0	0	0	-7	0	0	0
WS	0	0	0	5	6	0	0	0	1	2
ETH	0	0	0	0	0	0	-5	0	0	0
SO	22	24							30	24
SD	13	16							18	16
SN	0	15							5	15
SP	14	16							19	16
SB	0	9							3	9
SW	34								34	
Males										
N	1223	1223	0	1272	0	0	1263	0	-	-
R^2	44	37	0	1	0	0	1	0	-	-
Age	0	0	0	0	0	0	-11	0	0	0
WS	0	0	0	6	0	0	0	0	1	1
ETH	0	5	0	0	0	0	0	0	2	5
SO	25	26							34	26
SD	12	19							18	19

Taiwan (continued)

	S	SW	SO	SD	SN	SP	SF	SB	TES	TESW
SN	0	12							4	12
SP	14	15							19	15
SB	0	8							3	8
SW	33								33	

Females

	S	SW	SO	SD	SN	SP	SF	SB	TES	TESW
N	1144	1145	0	0	1191	0	0	0	-	-
R²	40	38	0	0	1	0	0	0	-	-
WS	0	0	0	0	7	0	0	0	0	1
SO	17	22							25	22
SD	14	13							18	13
SN	0	18							6	18
SP	15	17							21	17
SB	0	11							4	11
SW	34								34	

Tanzania, University of Dar Es Salaam

	S	SW	SO	SD	SN	SP	SF	SB	TES	TESW
N	198	200	0	224	225	0	220	223	-	-
R²	22	30	0	6	8	0	3	3	-	-
Pred										
Sex	0	0	0	0	0	0	0	18	3	0
Age	0	0	0	0	-28	0	0	0	0	0
WS	0	16	0	0	0	0	20	0	0	16
LED	0	0	0	-21	0	0	0	0	0	0
ETH	0	0	0	-14	0	0	0	0	0	0
SO	40	37							40	37
SP	0	26							0	26
SB	16	0							16	0

Males

	S	SW	SO	SD	SN	SP	SF	SB	TES	TESW
N	137	139	0	155	154	0	151	154	-	-
R²	27	29	0	5	8	0	3	2	-	-
Age	0	0	0	0	-29	0	0	0	0	0
WS	0	18	0	0	0	0	18	0	0	18
ETH	-20	0	0	-23	0	0	0	-16	-23	0
SO	36	35							36	35
SP	0	26							0	26
SB	17	0							17	0

Thailand

	S	SW	SO	SD	SN	SP	SF	SB	TES	TESW
N	545	549	0	0	0	0	574	577	-	-

Thailand (continued)

	S	SW	SO	SD	SN	SP	SF	SB	TES	TESW
R^2	28	26	0	0	0	0	23	4	-	-
Pred										
Age	0	0	0	0	0	0	-47	18	-2	-4
WS	-9	0	0	0	0	0	0	0	-9	0
LED	0	-10	0	0	0	0	12	-10	-3	-9
SO	16	30							27	30
SD	0	13							5	13
SN	0	12							4	12
SP	13	9							16	9
SF	0	9							3	9
SW	37								37	

Males

	S	SW	SO	SD	SN	SP	SF	SB	TES	TESW
N	245	249	0	0	262	0	260	264	-	-
R^2	26	23	0	0	1	0	18	4	-	-
Age	0	0	0	0	0	0	-37	20	0	0
LED	0	0	0	0	-13	0	17	0	0	0
ETH	-11	0	0	0	0	0	0	0	-11	0
SO	26	35							38	35
SD	0	21							7	21
SW	33								33	

Females

	S	SW	SO	SD	SN	SP	SF	SB	TES	TESW
N	300	300	0	0	0	0	314	313	-	-
R^2	30	26	0	0	0	0	29	2	-	-
Age	-10	0	0	0	0	0	-56	15	-10	0
WS	-15	0	0	0	0	0	0	0	-15	0
LED	0	-12	0	0	0	0	11	0	-5	-12
SO	0	29							13	29
SN	0	20							9	20
SP	16	14							22	14
SW	43								43	

Thailand, Chiang Mai University

	S	SW	SO	SD	SN	SP	SF	SB	TES	TESW
N	279	282	0	0	0	0	0	0	-	-
R^2	24	21	0	0	0	0	0	0	-	-
Pred										
SO	16	28							25	28
SD	0	15							5	15
SP	15	17							20	17
SW	32								32	

Thailand, Chiang Mai University (continued)

	S	SW	SO	SD	SN	SP	SF	SB	TES	TESW
Males										
N	121	124	0	127	0	0	0	127	-	-
R^2	25	21	0	7	0	0	0	7	-	-
WS	0	-20	0	0	0	0	0	31	-4	-20
LED	0	0	0	-37	0	0	0	-21	0	0
ETH	0	0	0	29	0	0	0	0	0	0
SO	25	34							33	34
SP	19	21							24	21
SW	22								22	
Females										
N	158	158	0	0	0	163	163	0	-	-
R^2	24	22	0	0	0	3	3	0	-	-
Age	0	0	0	0	0	0	-20	0	0	0
WS	-15	0	0	0	0	0	0	0	-15	0
ETH	0	0	0	0	0	-19	0	0	-2	-3
SO	0	28							13	28
SD	0	17							8	17
SP	0	18							9	18
SW	48								48	

Thailand, University of Srinakharinwirot

	S	SW	SO	SD	SN	SP	SF	SB	TES	TESW
N	266	267	0	0	0	0	0	0	-	-
R^2	32	30	0	0	0	0	0	0	-	-
Pred										
WS	-10	0	0	0	0	0	0	0	-10	0
LED	0	-13	0	0	0	0	0	0	-5	-13
SO	14	32							27	32
SD	0	15							6	15
SN	14	19							21	19
SW	39								39	
Males										
N	124	125	0	0	0	0	0	0	-	-
R^2	27	29	0	0	0	0	0	0	-	-
SO	0	37							16	37
SD	0	27							12	27
SN	17	0							17	0
SW	43								43	
Females										
N	142	142	0	0	0	0	0	0	-	-
R^2	34	32	0	0	0	0	0	0	-	-

Thailand, University of Srinakharinwirot (continued)

	S	SW	SO	SD	SN	SP	SF	SB	TES	TESW
WS	-15	0	0	0	0	0	0	0	-15	0
LED	0	-21	0	0	0	0	0	0	-9	-21
SO	0	29							13	29
SN	19	24							29	24
SB	0	-16							-7	-16
SW	43								43	

Turkey, University of Uludag

	S	SW	SO	SD	SN	SP	SF	SB	TES	TESW
N	283	283	0	287	289	289	285	288	-	-
R^2	36	39	0	2	1	4	1	2	-	-
Pred										
LED	0	0	0	-14	-13	-20	13	-15	-7	-8
SO	26	28							30	28
SD	15	18							18	17
SP	18	29							22	29
SW	15								15	
Males										
N	196	195	198	198	0	198	196	197	-	-
R^2	38	35	2	2	0	6	2	5	-	-
LED	0	0	-15	-16	0	-26	16	-22	-14	-14
SO	34	29							34	29
SD	14	15							14	15
SP	26	28							26	28

United Kingdom, University of York

	S	SW	SO	SD	SN	SP	SF	SB	TES	TESW
N	216	216	223	0	0	0	221	0	-	-
R^2	48	57	3	0	0	0	2	0	-	-
Pred										
Sex	0	11	16	0	0	0	0	0	10	18
Age	0	-11	0	0	0	0	0	0	-6	-11
WS	0	0	-13	0	0	0	0	0	-3	-6
LED	0	14	0	0	0	0	-14	0	5	14
SO	0	44							23	44
SD	15	0							15	0
SN	0	25							13	25
SP	21	0							21	0
SF	15	0							15	0
SB	0	18							10	18
SW	53								53	

United Kingdom, University of York (continued)

	S	SW	SO	SD	SN	SP	SF	SB	TES	TESW
Males										
N	99	99	0	101	0	104	0	0	-	-
R^2	48	58	0	4	0	6	0	0	-	-
Age	0	0	0	-21	0	0	0	0	0	0
WS	19	0	0	0	0	-22	0	0	13	0
ETH	0	0	0	0	0	-20	0	0	-6	0
SO	0	52							29	52
SN	0	19							11	19
SP	29	0							29	0
SF	17	0							17	0
SB	0	22							12	22
SW	56								56	
Females										
N	117	117	0	0	0	0	118	0	-	-
R^2	47	46	0	0	0	0	3	0	-	-
LED	0	0	0	0	0	0	-20	0	0	0
SO	24	39							39	39
SN	0	28							11	28
SP	21	0							21	0
SB	0	20							8	20
SW	39								39	

United States of America

	S	SW	SO	SD	SN	SP	SF	SB	TES	TESW
N	1266	1273	1327	1314	1325	1327	1320	1318	-	-
R^2	55	47	2	1	1	2	1	2	-	-
Pred										
Sex	0	8	0	0	0	0	0	0	4	8
Age	0	-4	-13	0	0	-16	0	-13	-11	-12
WS	0	0	0	9	8	0	-8	0	1	2
ETH	0	0	0	-9	-10	0	11	0	-1	1
SO	28	43							47	43
SN	0	16							7	16
SP	7	10							11	10
SF	0	-7							-3	-7
SB	9	9							13	9
SW	44								44	
Males										
N	436	441	467	460	465	467	462	460	-	-
R^2	49	44	1	2	2	4	1	4	-	-
Age	0	0	-12	-21	0	-13	13	-20	-8	-9

United States of America (continued)

	S	SW	SO	SD	SN	SP	SF	SB	TES	TESW
LED	0	0	0	15	0	0	0	0	0	0
ETH	0	0	0	0	-14	-11	0	0	-3	-2
SO	28	49							46	49
SN	9	16							15	16
SP	11	0							11	0
SB	0	14							5	14
SW	37								37	

Females

	S	SW	SO	SD	SN	SP	SF	SB	TES	TESW
N	830	832	860	854	860	860	858	858	-	-
R^2	59	48	2	2	1	2	2	1	-	-
Age	0	0	-17	0	0	-15	0	-9	-11	-10
WS	0	0	0	15	11	0	-15	0	1	3
LED	0	0	8	0	0	0	0	0	4	3
ETH	0	0	0	-9	0	0	11	-	0	-1
SO	29	41							49	41
SN	0	16							8	16
SP	0	16							8	16
SF	6	-8							2	-8
SB	13	7							16	7
SW	49								49	

USA, Arizona State University

	S	SW	SO	SD	SN	SP	SF	SB	TES	TESW
N	204	206	216	0	0	217	0	0	-	-
R^2	60	52	2	0	0	2	0	0	-	-
Pred										
Sex	0	12	0	0	0	0	0	0	6	12
Age	-12	0	-16	0	0	0	0	0	-21	-9
ETH	0	0	0	0	0	-14	0	0	-1	-2
SO	30	53							57	53
SD	0	15							8	15
SP	0	17							9	17
SW	51								51	

Females

	S	SW	SO	SD	SN	SP	SF	SB	TES	TESW
N	151	151	157	0	0	0	0	0	-	-
R^2	63	54	2	0	0	0	0	0	-	-
Age	-10	0	-17	0	0	0	0	0	-20	-9
SO	28	51							56	51
SD	0	20							11	20
SP	0	19							11	19
SW	55								55	

USA, Cornell University

	S	SW	SO	SD	SN	SP	SF	SB	TES	TESW
N	104	104	0	108	111	0	109	109	-	-
R^2	54	53	0	3	3	0	3	3	-	-
Pred										
Sex	0	0	0	0	-19	0	0	20	2	4
WS	0	7	0	20	0	0	-21	0	4	7
LED	0	-21	0	0	0	0	0	0	-11	-21
SO	28	39							49	39
SN	0	16							9	16
SB	0	34							18	34
SW	54								54	

USA, Edison Community College

	S	SW	SO	SD	SN	SP	SF	SB	TES	TESW
N	138	138	0	0	144	145	0	0	-	-
R^2	57	47	0	0	4	5	0	0	-	-
Pred										
Age	0	0	0	0	-21	-51	0	0	-7	-14
ETH	0	0	0	0	0	37	0	0	4	7
SO	24	39							44	39
SN	0	18							9	18
SP	0	19							10	19
SF	0	-16							-8	-16
SB	14	0							14	0
SW	51								51	

Females

	S	SW	SO	SD	SN	SP	SF	SB	TES	TESW
N	93	93	0	98	98	99	98	98	-	-
R^2	59	44	0	3	3	11	10	4	-	-
Age	0	0	0	0	-20	-31	0	0	-7	-12
WS	0	0	0	21	0	22	-33	0	5	9
ETH	0	0	0	0	0	0	0	23	0	0
SO	29	36							50	36
SP	0	40							23	40
SW	57								57	

USA, University of Illinois

	S	SW	SO	SD	SN	SP	SF	SB	TES	TESW
N	266	267	0	278	277	277	274	0	-	-
R^2	53	42	0	2	2	2	1	0	-	-
Pred										
Sex	0	10	0	0	0	0	0	0	4	10
Age	0	0	0	0	0	-15	0	0	-1	-2

USA, University of Illinois (continued)

	S	SW	SO	SD	SN	SP	SF	SB	TES	TESW
ETH	0	0	0	-16	-14	0	12	0	-1	-2
SO	24	49							44	49
SD	-13	0							-13	0
SN	15	13							20	13
SP	0	12							5	12
SB	15	0							15	0
SW	40								40	

Males

	S	SW	SO	SD	SN	SP	SF	SB	TES	TESW
N	120	121	0	0	0	0	0	0	-	-
R^2	49	43	0	0	0	0	0	0	-	-
SO	40	64							64	64
SF	0	-14							-5	-14
SW	38								38	

Females

	S	SW	SO	SD	SN	SP	SF	SB	TES	TESW
N	146	146	0	150	0	150	148	0	-	-
R^2	56	40	0	3	0	4	4	0	-	-
Age	0	0	0	0	0	-22	0	0	-3	-5
ETH	0	0	0	-20	0	0	21	0	0	0
SO	0	46							24	46
SN	17	0							17	0
SP	0	24							13	24
SB	23	0							23	0
SW	53								53	

USA, Ohio State University, Newark

	S	SW	SO	SD	SN	SP	SF	SB	TES	TESW
N	253	255	0	0	267	0	268	265	-	-
R^2	47	47	0	0	3	0	1	3	-	-
Pred										
Age	0	0	0	0	0	0	13	-19	-1	-3
WS	0	0	0	0	18	0	0	0	1	3
SO	26	41							42	41
SD	0	15							6	15
SN	0	15							6	15
SP	16	0							16	0
SB	0	14							5	14
SW	38								38	

Males

	S	SW	SO	SD	SN	SP	SF	SB	TES	TESW
N	121	123	130	0	128	130	129	128	-	-
R^2	34	43	6	0	14	9	7	11	-	-
Age	0	0	-26	0	-35	-32	28	-34	-16	-22

USA, Ohio State University, Newark (continued)

	S	SW	SO	SD	SN	SP	SF	SB	TES	TESW
LED	0	0	0	0	28	0	0	0	2	8
SO	37	49							52	49
SN	0	27							8	27
SW	30								30	

Females

	S	SW	SO	SD	SN	SP	SF	SB	TES	TESW
N	132	132	139	136	139	137	0	0	-	-
R^2	60	53	2	4	7	2	0	0	-	-
WS	0	0	17	22	28	17	0	0	10	14
SO	21	48							44	48
SD	0	25							12	25
SF	0	-23							-11	-23
SB	22	0							22	0
SW	47								47	

USA, Sangamon State University

	S	SW	SO	SD	SN	SP	SF	SB	TES	TESW
N	141	143	0	0	149	0	0	0	-	-
R^2	69	48	0	0	2	0	0	0	-	-
Pred										
Sex	0	0	0	0	17	0	0	0	3	6
SO	33	46							52	46
SN	0	35							15	35
SP	23	0							23	0
SW	42								42	

USA, Smith College (Females)

	S	SW	SO	SD	SN	SP	SF	SB	TES	TESW
N	160	160	162	0	0	0	0	162	-	-
R^2	54	50	3	0	0	0	0	5	-	-
Pred										
Age	0	0	-18	0	0	0	0	0	-10	-6
WS	0	15	0	0	0	0	0	0	6	15
LED	0	0	0	0	0	0	0	23	0	0
ETH	0	-12	0	0	0	0	0	0	-5	-12
SO	40	34							54	34
SN	0	25							11	25
SP	0	26							11	26
SW	42								42	

Yugoslavia, University of Zagreb

	S	SW	SO	SD	SN	SP	SF	SB	TES	TESW
N	303	305	0	0	0	327	0	323	-	-
R^2	55	43	0	0	0	3	0	1	-	-
Pred										
Age	-11	0	0	0	0	-17	0	-12	-14	-2
LED	-11	0	0	0	0	0	0	0	-11	0
ETH	11	-10	0	0	0	0	0	0	-7	-10
SO	33	36							47	36
SN	0	29							11	29
SP	11	12							16	12
SW	39								39	
Males										
N	161	161	173	0	0	0	0	0	-	-
R^2	55	44	2	0	0	0	0	0	-	-
WS	0	0	17	0	0	0	0	0	9	7
LED	-21	0	0	0	0	0	0	0	-21	0
ETH	12	-14	0	0	0	0	0	0	6	-14
SO	38	42							55	42
SN	0	20							8	20
SB	0	19							8	19
SW	41								41	
Females										
N	142	144	153	155	0	155	0	152	-	-
R^2	56	45	2	2	0	5	0	3	-	-
Age	0	0	0	0	0	-24	0	0	-9	-6
WS	-12	0	0	0	0	0	0	0	-12	0
ETH	0	0	-16	-16	0	0	0	-19	-6	-4
SO	31	25							38	25
SN	0	29							8	29
SP	32	25							39	25
SF	19	0							19	0
SW	29								29	

Appendix 4 Results of regressions using MDT to explain satisfaction with one's living partner, alphabetically by country and university (decimal points omitted)

Austria, University of Vienna

	S	SW	SO	SD	SN	SP	SF	SB	TES	TESW
N	224	240	284	0	0	0	315	0	-	-
R²	79	79	3	0	0	0	2	0	-	-
Pred										
Sex	0	0	12	0	0	0	-14	0	6	5
LED	0	0	15	0	0	0	0	0	8	7
SO	18	43							50	43
SN	0	21							16	21
SP	0	26							20	26
SB	0	10							6	10
SW	75								75	

Males

	S	SW	SO	SD	SN	SP	SF	SB	TES	TESW
N	96	103	0	0	0	0	0	0	-	-
R²	82	79	0	0	0	0	0	0	-	-
ETH	-11	0	0	0	0	0	0	0	-11	0
SO	0	37							33	37
SN	0	35							31	35
SP	0	35							31	35
SF	0	13							12	13
SW	89								89	

Females

	S	SW	SO	SD	SN	SP	SF	SB	TES	TESW
N	128	137	168	0	169	0	0	0	-	-
R²	79	81	2	0	2	0	0	0	-	-
LED	0	0	16	0	17	0	0	0	7	11
ETH	9	0	0	0	0	0	0	0	9	0
SO	26	48							58	48
SN	0	17							11	17
SP	0	21							14	21
SB	0	14							9	14
SW	67								67	

Bangladesh, Dhaka University

	S	SW	SO	SD	SN	SP	SF	SB	TES	TESW
N	160	161	0	0	0	0	0	0	-	-
R²	69	59	0	0	0	0	0	0	-	-
Pred										
SO	20	36							41	36
SN	15	32							33	32

Bangladesh, Dhaka University (continued)

	S	SW	SO	SD	SN	SP	SF	SB	TES	TESW
SF	0	11							6	11
SB	0	25							14	25
SW	57								57	
Females										
N	105	105	0	0	0	0	0	0	-	-
R^2	74	67	0	0	0	0	0	0	-	-
WS	0	17	0	0	0	0	0	0	10	17
SO	30	59							66	59
SB	0	29							18	29
SW	61								61	

Brazil, Pontifical Catholic University of Minas Gerais

	S	SW	SO	SD	SN	SP	SF	SB	TES	TESW
N	164	178	0	0	0	216	0	219	-	-
R^2	70	69	0	0	0	2	0	2	-	-
Pred										
Sex	0	0	0	0	0	0	0	15	2	0
ETH	0	0	0	0	0	-15	0	0	-1	-3
SO	39	52							60	52
SD	0	26							11	26
SP	0	18							7	18
SB	14	0							14	0
SW	41								41	
Females										
N	104	108	0	0	126	127	132	0	-	-
R^2	75	69	0	0	3	3	3	0	-	-
WS	0	0	0	0	-19	0	0	0	0	0
LED	0	0	0	0	0	0	19	0	0	0
ETH	0	0	0	0	0	-20	0	0	-2	-5
SO	37	48							59	48
SD	0	28							13	28
SP	0	23							10	23
SB	16	0							16	0
SW	45								45	

Cameroon, Yaounde University

	S	SW	SO	SD	SN	SP	SF	SB	TES	TESW
N	115	122	0	0	0	0	159	167	-	-
R^2	55	46	0	0	0	0	3	6	-	-

Cameroon, Yaounde University (continued)

	S	SW	SO	SD	SN	SP	SF	SB	TES	TESW
Pred										
LED	0	0	0	0	0	0	-18	27	0	0
ETH	0	0	0	0	0	0	0	-19	0	0
SO	23	39							33	39
SD	36	36							45	36
SW	26								26	
Males										
N	90	95	126	0	0	0	126	130	-	-
R^2	56	46	2	0	0	0	4	6	-	-
LED	0	0	18	0	0	0	-22	29	6	6
ETH	0	0	0	0	0	0	0	-20	0	0
SO	24	32							32	32
SD	36	44							47	44
SW	26								26	

Canada

	S	SW	SO	SD	SN	SP	SF	SB	TES	TESW
N	790	833	936	950	977	988	1155	0	-	-
R^2	72	66	2	1	1	1	2	0	-	-
Pred										
Sex	0	0	7	0	0	9	0	0	4	3
Age	0	6	12	0	0	0	0	0	9	12
WS	0	0	0	8	8	0	0	0	2	2
LED	0	0	0	0	0	0	6	0	0	0
ETH	0	0	0	0	0	0	11	0	0	0
SO	33	49							54	49
SD	8	10							12	10
SN	8	14							14	14
SB	5	18							13	18
SW	42								42	
Males										
N	292	312	359	367	379	380	453	0	-	-
R^2	73	68	4	2	1	1	1	0	-	-
Age	0	0	21	16	0	12	0	0	15	12
WS	0	0	0	0	13	0	0	0	1	2
ETH	0	0	0	0	0	0	12	0	0	0
SO	33	47							55	47
SD	15	13							21	13
SN	0	15							7	15
SB	0	20							9	20
SW	47								47	

Canada (continued)

	S	SW	SO	SD	SN	SP	SF	SB	TES	TESW
Females										
N	498	521	0	0	0	0	701	0	-	-
R^2	72	64	0	0	0	0	1	0	-	-
ETH	0	0	0	0	0	0	11	0	0	0
SO	34	54							56	54
SN	11	19							19	19
SP	10	0							10	0
SB	0	16							7	16
SW	41								41	

Canada, Dalhousie University

	S	SW	SO	SD	SN	SP	SF	SB	TES	TESW
N	122	132	0	0	153	0	0	0	-	-
R^2	62	62	0	0	3	0	0	0	-	-
Pred										
WS	0	0	0	0	19	0	0	0	0	0
SO	20	62							50	62
SB	19	24							31	24
SW	49								49	

Canada, University of Guelph

	S	SW	SO	SD	SN	SP	SF	SB	TES	TESW
N	176	183	220	224	0	0	267	0	-	-
R^2	75	63	2	2	0	0	4	0	-	-
Pred										
Age	0	0	17	17	0	0	0	0	14	11
WS	10	0	0	0	0	0	0	0	10	0
SO	36	65							63	65
SD	18	0							18	0
SN	0	21							9	21
SW	42								42	

Canada, Mount Saint Vincent University

	S	SW	SO	SD	SN	SP	SF	SB	TES	TESW
N	160	164	174	174	0	0	0	0	-	-
R^2	72	69	2	3	0	0	0	0	-	-
Pred										
Sex	0	0	0	-18	0	0	0	0	-2	-4
WS	-10	17	0	0	0	0	0	0	-2	17
LED	0	0	15	0	0	0	0	0	7	8
ETH	0	-10	0	0	0	0	0	0	-5	-10

Canada, Mount Saint Vincent University (continued)

	S	SW	SO	SD	SN	SP	SF	SB	TES	TESW
SO	21	54							48	54
SD	0	22							11	22
SP	24	0							24	0
SB	0	13							7	13
SW	50								50	
Females										
N	145	149	0	0	0	0	0	0	-	-
R^2	73	70	0	0	0	0	0	0	-	-
WS	-11	16	0	0	0	0	0	0	-3	16
ETH	0	-10	0	0	0	0	0	0	-5	-10
SO	22	65							53	65
SD	0	23							11	23
SP	27	0							27	0
SW	48								48	

Canada, Saint Mary's University

	S	SW	SO	SD	SN	SP	SF	SB	TES	TESW
N	154	163	179	0	0	194	0	0	-	-
R^2	78	71	2	0	0	4	0	0	-	-
Pred										
Sex	0	0	0	0	0	20	0	0	2	6
WS	0	0	15	0	0	0	0	0	9	6
SO	50	41							60	41
SN	13	22							18	22
SP	0	32							8	32
SB	11	0							11	0
SW	24								24	

Canada, Simon Fraser University

	S	SW	SO	SD	SN	SP	SF	SB	TES	TESW
N	135	148	0	0	0	0	214	0	-	-
R^2	83	69	0	0	0	0	3	0	-	-
Pred										
Sex	0	0	0	0	0	0	17	0	0	0
Age	0	12	0	0	0	0	0	0	7	12
LED	11	0	0	0	0	0	0	0	11	0
ETH	-12	0	0	0	0	0	0	0	-12	0
SO	39	41							63	41
SN	0	29							17	29
SP	0	21							12	21
SW	58								58	

Finland, University of Helsinki

	S	SW	SO	SD	SN	SP	SF	SB	TES	TESW
N	146	148	0	0	0	187	211	0	-	-
R^2	64	50	0	0	0	3	2	0	-	-
Pred										
Age	0	0	0	0	0	-19	0	0	-2	-4
LED	0	0	0	0	0	0	-16	0	0	0
SO	17	48							45	48
SN	0	15							9	15
SP	0	21							12	21
SB	17	0							17	0
SW	59								59	

Federal Republic of Germany

	S	SW	SO	SD	SN	SP	SF	SB	TES	TESW
N	528	548	644	0	667	679	678	665	-	-
R^2	79	79	2	0	2	1	3	1	-	-
Pred										
Sex	0	0	12	0	13	10	0	12	10	11
Age	0	7	9	0	0	0	0	0	5	12
WS	0	0	0	0	0	0	-17	0	0	0
SO	27	52							54	52
SD	9	7							13	7
SN	0	18							9	18
SP	0	15							8	15
SB	9	7							13	7
SW	51								51	
Males										
N	285	300	356	335	374	374	373	370	-	-
R^2	80	81	3	2	4	3	3	3	-	-
Age	0	9	17	13	20	16	0	19	21	26
WS	0	0	0	0	0	0	-18	0	0	0
ETH	0	0	0	0	0	-12	0	-12	-2	-2
SO	29	58							62	58
SN	0	22							12	22
SP	0	16							9	16
SB	10	0							10	0
SW	56								56	
Females										
N	243	248	0	279	0	0	305	295	-	-
R^2	76	76	0	2	0	0	4	2	-	-
Age	0	0	0	-14	0	0	0	-14	-3	-2
WS	0	0	0	0	0	0	-12	0	0	0

Federal Republic of Germany (continued)

	S	SW	SO	SD	SN	SP	SF	SB	TES	TESW
ETH	0	0	0	0	0	0	-16	0	0	0
SO	32	48							55	48
SD	15	0							15	0
SN	0	19							9	19
SP	0	17							8	17
SB	0	14							7	14
SW	48								48	

Germany, Federal College of Public Administration

	S	SW	SO	SD	SN	SP	SF	SB	TES	TESW
N	166	171	198	0	206	210	0	200	-	-
R^2	80	83	5	0	3	2	0	4	-	-
Pred										
Sex	0	0	20	0	17	15	0	21	14	14
Age	0	11	0	0	0	0	0	0	8	11
ETH	0	0	22	0	0	0	0	0	11	10
SO	20	44							52	44
SD	0	22							16	22
SN	0	17							12	17
SP	0	16							12	16
SF	-8	9							-2	9
SW	72								72	

Males

	S	SW	SO	SD	SN	SP	SF	SB	TES	TESW
N	100	104	119	116	126	0	0	120	-	-
R^2	85	84	6	5	4	0	0	3	-	-
Age	0	12	0	0	0	0	0	20	13	12
ETH	0	0	27	24	23	0	0	0	20	24
SO	0	51							42	51
SD	0	27							22	27
SN	0	17							14	17
SF	-11	8							-4	8
SB	15	0							15	0
SW	82								82	

Germany, University of Frankfurt

	S	SW	SO	SD	SN	SP	SF	SB	TES	TESW
N	184	192	232	0	240	248	247	247	-	-
R^2	71	77	2	0	3	1	1	3	-	-
Pred										
Sex	0	8	15	0	0	13	-13	13	7	18
Age	0	0	0	0	19	0	0	0	2	5

Germany, University of Frankfurt (continued)

	S	SW	SO	SD	SN	SP	SF	SB	TES	TESW
LED	0	10	0	0	0	0	0	0	4	10
SO	49	67							76	67
SN	0	26							10	26
SW	40								40	
Males										
N	107	113	0	0	146	150	0	151	-	-
R^2	72	77	0	0	8	5	0	2	-	-
Age	0	0	0	0	0	0	0	17	0	0
LED	0	11	0	0	29	23	0	0	5	20
SO	64	60							79	60
SN	0	20							5	20
SP	0	15							4	15
SW	25								25	

Germany, University of Mannheim

	S	SW	SO	SD	SN	SP	SF	SB	TES	TESW
N	177	184	0	0	0	0	0	0	-	-
R^2	85	81	0	0	0	0	0	0	-	-
Pred										
ETH	-7	0	0	0	0	0	0	0	-7	0
SO	27	52							57	52
SN	0	19							11	19
SP	11	25							25	25
SW	57								57	
Females										
N	100	101	116	0	0	0	0	118	-	-
R^2	81	76	3	0	0	0	0	5	-	-
Age	0	0	-20	0	0	0	0	-24	-15	-13
SO	32	37							46	37
SD	13	0							13	0
SN	0	20							8	20
SP	0	17							7	17
SB	15	24							24	24
SW	39								39	

Greece, Aristotelian University of Thessaloniki

	S	SW	SO	SD	SN	SP	SF	SB	TES	TESW
N	202	212	233	0	0	0	0	240	-	-
R^2	69	40	8	0	0	0	0	1	-	-
Pred										
WS	0	0	14	0	0	0	0	13	10	5

Greece, Aristotelian U. of Thessaloniki (continued)

	S	SW	SO	SD	SN	SP	SF	SB	TES	TESW
ETH	9	0	25	0	0	0	0	0	22	9
SO	43	37							52	37
SD	-14	0							-14	0
SP	15	33							23	33
SB	20	0							20	0
SW	24								24	
Males										
N	114	118	133	0	0	138	0	138	-	-
R^2	54	32	16	0	0	3	0	3	-	-
Age	0	0	19	0	0	0	0	0	12	8
WS	0	0	22	0	0	18	0	19	16	14
ETH	0	0	25	0	0	0	0	0	16	11
SO	50	42							64	42
SD	-15	0							-15	0
SF	-18	0							-18	0
SB	0	25							8	25
SW	33								33	

Hungary, University of Economics

	S	SW	SO	SD	SN	SP	SF	SB	TES	TESW
N	138	148	0	181	0	0	0	0	-	-
R^2	81	83	0	2	0	0	0	0	-	-
Pred										
Age	0	0	0	16	0	0	0	0	0	0
SO	20	60							63	60
SN	0	12							9	12
SP	0	25							18	25
SW	72								72	
Females										
N	100	108	0	0	0	0	0	0	-	-
R^2	83	82	0	0	0	0	0	0	-	-
SO	0	65							54	65
SD	13	0							13	0
SP	0	29							24	29
SW	83								83	

Israel, Hebrew University of Jerusalem

	S	SW	SO	SD	SN	SP	SF	SB	TES	TESW
N	299	299	309	309	309	309	0	309	-	-
R^2	73	77	3	2	4	2	0	1	-	-

Israel, Hebrew University of Jerusalem (continued)

	S	SW	SO	SD	SN	SP	SF	SB	TES	TESW
Pred										
Sex	0	0	0	-16	-20	0	0	0	-7	-7
Age	0	0	17	0	0	0	0	0	9	10
ETH	0	0	0	0	0	15	0	12	0	0
SO	23	57							54	57
SD	0	11							6	11
SN	13	28							28	28
SW	55								55	
Males										
N	155	155	0	0	158	158	0	158	-	-
R^2	56	71	0	0	2	4	0	3	-	-
Age	-12	0	0	0	0	0	0	0	-12	0
ETH	0	0	0	0	16	23	0	18	5	5
SO	20	62							47	62
SN	18	29							31	29
SW	44								44	
Females										
N	144	144	151	0	0	0	0	0	-	-
R^2	88	80	4	0	0	0	0	0	-	-
Age	0	0	22	0	0	0	0	0	9	13
SO	27	59							68	59
SN	0	38							27	38
SF	9	0							9	0
SW	70								70	

Japan

	S	SW	SO	SD	SN	SP	SF	SB	TES	TESW
N	686	701	795	795	802	0	825	797	-	-
R^2	66	62	2	1	1	0	2	2	-	-
Pred										
Sex	0	0	15	10	12	0	10	10	11	10
Age	6	0	0	0	0	0	0	0	6	0
WS	0	0	0	0	8	0	-7	0	2	2
LED	0	0	0	0	0	0	0	11	1	0
SO	26	36							40	36
SD	9	11							13	11
SN	9	25							19	25
SP	0	16							6	16
SB	10	0							10	0
SW	38								38	

Japan (continued)

	S	SW	SO	SD	SN	SP	SF	SB	TES	TESW
Males										
N	587	600	0	0	683	673	695	677	-	-
R^2	66	61	0	0	1	1	2	1	-	-
Age	6	0	0	0	0	0	0	0	6	0
WS	0	0	0	0	9	8	-9	0	3	4
LED	0	0	0	0	0	0	0	10	1	0
ETH	0	0	0	0	0	0	11	0	0	0
SO	27	35							41	35
SD	0	12							5	12
SN	14	23							23	23
SP	0	17							7	17
SB	13	0							13	0
SW	39								39	
Females										
N	99	101	118	118	119	0	0	0	-	-
R^2	70	61	11	4	3	0	0	0	-	-
Age	0	0	34	23	0	0	0	0	22	15
WS	-13	0	0	0	0	0	0	0	-13	0
LED	0	0	0	0	20	0	0	0	3	8
SO	31	43							47	43
SD	25	0							25	0
SN	0	41							15	41
SW	36								36	

Japan, Tokai University

	S	SW	SO	SD	SN	SP	SF	SB	TES	TESW
N	153	155	173	173	0	0	185	178	-	-
R^2	61	51	3	2	0	0	2	2	-	-
Pred										
Sex	0	0	0	0	0	0	15	0	0	0
Age	0	0	0	0	0	0	0	17	3	0
ETH	0	0	19	17	0	0	0	0	9	7
SO	27	37							45	37
SN	0	32							15	32
SP	0	16							8	16
SB	20	0							20	0
SW	48								48	
Males										
N	107	108	123	123	0	0	0	125	-	-
R^2	60	53	3	3	0	0	0	5	-	-
ETH	0	0	20	20	0	0	0	0	6	9

Japan, Tokai University (continued)

	S	SW	SO	SD	SN	SP	SF	SB	TES	TESW
SO	0	44							29	44
SN	0	28							19	28
SP	22	16							33	16
SW	66								66	

Japan, Tokai and Denkitsushin Universities

	S	SW	SO	SD	SN	SP	SF	SB	TES	TESW
N	469	480	0	531	0	0	533	0	-	-
R^2	70	61	0	1	0	0	1	0	-	-
Pred										
Sex	0	0	0	0	0	0	-10	0	0	0
WS	0	0	0	11	0	0	0	0	2	1
SO	21	36							36	36
SD	14	11							19	11
SN	11	25							21	25
SP	0	16							7	16
SB	8	0							8	0
SW	41								41	
Males										
N	436	446	0	493	0	0	0	485	-	-
R^2	70	60	0	1	0	0	0	1	-	-
WS	0	0	0	10	0	0	0	0	1	0
LED	0	0	0	0	0	0	0	10	1	0
SO	22	38							37	38
SD	12	0							12	0
SN	13	30							25	30
SP	0	19							7	19
SB	10	0							10	0
SW	39								39	

Jordan, Yarmouk University

	S	SW	SO	SD	SN	SP	SF	SB	TES	TESW
N	103	107	0	143	134	0	0	0	-	-
R^2	51	66	0	2	3	0	0	0	-	-
Pred										
Age	0	0	0	17	20	0	0	0	10	16
SD	0	60							36	60
SN	0	28							17	28
SB	19	0							19	0
SW	60								60	

Kenya, University of Nairobi

	S	SW	SO	SD	SN	SP	SF	SB	TES	TESW
N	164	174	0	0	0	0	0	0	-	-
R^2	57	61	0	0	0	0	0	0	-	-
Pred										
Age	0	12	0	0	0	0	0	0	5	12
ETH	0	-13	0	0	0	0	0	0	-6	-13
SO	17	46							37	46
SD	27	0							27	0
SP	0	38							16	38
SW	43								43	

Korea, Korea University

	S	SW	SO	SD	SN	SP	SF	SB	TES	TESW
N	411	413	0	423	425	0	0	422	-	-
R^2	66	53	0	1	2	0	0	3	-	-
Pred										
WS	0	0	0	0	0	0	0	18	0	0
LED	0	0	0	-10	-21	0	0	-10	-4	-5
ETH	0	0	0	0	-17	0	0	0	-2	-3
SO	14	50							43	50
SD	12	16							21	16
SN	0	15							9	15
SP	9	0							9	0
SW	57								57	
Males										
N	327	327	0	0	0	0	0	334	-	-
R^2	63	52	0	0	0	0	0	1	-	-
WS	0	0	0	0	0	0	0	7	0	0
SO	18	53							46	53
SD	18	26							32	26
SW	53								53	

Mexico, University of Baja California Sur

	S	SW	SO	SD	SN	SP	SF	SB	TES	TESW
N	142	151	177	0	184	0	191	187	-	-
R^2	30	34	6	0	3	0	5	3	-	-
Pred										
Sex	0	0	19	0	18	0	0	0	8	6
WS	16	0	0	0	0	0	-23	19	17	5
ETH	0	0	16	0	0	0	0	0	7	5
SO	34	33							43	33
SP	0	23							6	23

Mexico, University of Baja California Sur (continued)

	S	SW	SO	SD	SN	SP	SF	SB	TES	TESW
SF	0	-20							-5	-20
SW	26								26	
Males										
N	103	110	0	0	0	133	140	138	0	0
R^2	42	33	0	0	0	4	7	5	-	-
Age	17	0	0	0	0	0	0	0	17	0
WS	0	17	0	0	0	21	-28	24	6	21
SO	33	25							40	25
SD	22	20							27	20
SP	0	21							6	21
SW	26								26	

Netherlands, Erasmus University

	S	SW	SO	SD	SN	SP	SF	SB	TES	TESW
N	219	229	279	279	288	294	0	286	-	-
R^2	72	71	3	2	1	5	0	2	-	-
Pred										
Sex	0	0	18	15	14	23	0	17	16	16
SO	26	35							42	35
SD	0	29							13	29
SN	17	17							25	17
SP	0	14							6	14
SB	9	0							9	0
SW	46								46	
Males										
N	116	125	0	0	0	162	0	0	-	-
R^2	78	74	0	0	0	2	0	0	-	-
LED	0	0	0	0	0	16	0	0	1	2
SO	27	38							43	38
SD	0	42							18	42
SN	28	0							28	0
SP	0	15							7	15
SW	43								43	
Females										
N	102	103	122	0	0	0	0	0	-	-
R^2	61	64	4	0	0	0	0	0	-	-
LED	0	0	-22	0	0	0	0	0	-5	-6
SO	26	45							48	45
SN	0	23							11	23
SP	0	17							8	17
SF	0	-17							-8	-17

Netherlands, Erasmus University (continued)

	S	SW	SO	SD	SN	SP	SF	SB	TES	TESW
SB	16	0							16	0
SW	48								48	

Netherlands, University of Leiden

	S	SW	SO	SD	SN	SP	SF	SB	TES	TESW
N	139	153	0	0	217	0	261	0	-	-
R^2	84	76	0	0	5	0	1	0	-	-
Pred										
Age	0	-9	0	0	0	0	0	0	-6	-9
WS	0	0	0	0	16	0	0	0	3	5
ETH	8	0	0	0	-20	0	13	0	4	-5
SO	20	52							54	52
SN	0	32							21	32
SP	16	0							16	0
SF	-8	14							1	14
SB	0	15							10	15
SW	65								65	
Females										
N	90	98	0	0	128	0	0	133	-	-
R^2	84	79	0	0	2	0	0	2	-	-
Age	0	0	0	0	0	0	0	-17	-3	-4
WS	0	11	0	0	18	0	0	0	11	16
SO	16	51							51	51
SN	0	28							19	28
SP	16	0							16	0
SB	0	26							18	26
SW	69								69	

New Zealand, Massey University

	S	SW	SO	SD	SN	SP	SF	SB	TES	TESW
N	150	168	0	0	0	0	0	209	-	-
R^2	79	75	0	0	0	0	0	3	-	-
Pred										
Sex	0	10	0	0	0	0	0	18	6	14
Age	0	14	0	0	0	0	0	0	6	14
SO	37	38							53	38
SN	0	18							7	18
SP	20	18							27	18
SB	0	21							9	21
SW	41								41	

New Zealand, Massey University (continued)

	S	SW	SO	SD	SN	SP	SF	SB	TES	TESW
Females										
N	101	108	0	0	0	0	0	0	-	-
R^2	78	71	0	0	0	0	0	0	-	-
Age	0	15	0	0	0	0	0	0	8	15
SO	32	32							48	32
SN	0	19							10	19
SP	0	26							13	26
SB	14	18							23	18
SW	51								51	

Norway

	S	SW	SO	SD	SN	SP	SF	SB	TES	TESW
N	121	131	167	153	179	0	201	0	-	-
R^2	70	71	6	2	3	0	5	0	-	-
Pred										
Age	0	0	26	16	20	0	-20	0	13	16
ETH	0	0	0	0	0	0	19	0	0	0
SO	27	39							41	39
SN	0	28							10	28
SB	33	32							44	32
SW	35								35	

Philippines

	S	SW	SO	SD	SN	SP	SF	SB	TES	TESW
N	146	162	0	0	0	241	320	0	-	-
R^2	58	64	0	0	0	2	2	0	-	-
Pred										
LED	0	0	0	0	0	15	0	0	3	2
ETH	0	0	0	0	0	0	-16	0	0	0
SO	44	46							56	46
SN	0	15							4	15
SP	17	16							21	16
SB	0	16							4	16
SW	25								25	

Portugal, Technical University of Lisbon

	S	SW	SO	SD	SN	SP	SF	SB	TES	TESW
N	95	99	0	0	0	0	0	0	-	-
R^2	65	57	0	0	0	0	0	0	-	-
Pred										
SO	62	41							76	41

Portugal, Technical University of Lisbon (continued)

	S	SW	SO	SD	SN	SP	SF	SB		TES	TESW
SD	0	22								8	22
SF	21	-17								15	-17
SB	0	25								9	25
SW	35									35	

Puerto Rico, University of Puerto Rico

	S	SW	SO	SD	SN	SP	SF	SB		TES	TESW
N	209	212	0	0	0	245	253	0		-	-
R^2	65	42	0	0	0	1	1	0		-	-
Pred											
Sex	0	0	0	0	0	13	0	0		0	0
LED	0	0	0	0	0	0	13	0		0	0
SO	47	51								69	51
SN	0	21								9	21
SW	43									43	
Males											
N	112	112	0	0	0	0	0	0		-	-
R^2	63	40	0	0	0	0	0	0		-	-
ETH	14	0	0	0	0	0	0	0		14	0
SO	43	50								66	50
SN	0	23								11	23
SW	46									46	
Females											
N	97	100	0	0	0	0	113	0		-	-
R^2	71	44	0	0	0	0	4	0		-	-
LED	0	0	0	0	0	0	21	0		3	0
SO	54	43								72	43
SD	0	30								12	30
SF	16	0								16	0
SW	41									41	

Republic of South Africa, University of Zululand

	S	SW	SO	SD	SN	SP	SF	SB		TES	TESW
N	164	176	0	0	0	0	243	0		-	-
R^2	45	55	0	0	0	0	6	0		-	-
Pred											
Age	0	12	0	0	0	0	16	0		3	12
LED	0	0	0	0	0	0	18	0		0	0
SO	35	47								47	47
SD	16	15								20	15
SP	0	21								6	21

Republic of South Africa, U. of Zululand (continued)

	S	SW	SO	SD	SN	SP	SF	SB	TES	TESW
SW	26								26	

Spain, University of Madrid

	S	SW	SO	SD	SN	SP	SF	SB	TES	TESW
N	146	153	0	0	0	180	0	0	-	-
R^2	64	60	0	0	0	3	0	0	-	-
Pred										
Sex	0	15	0	0	0	18	0	0	12	15
Age	0	31	0	0	0	0	0	0	16	31
ETH	0	-33	0	0	0	0	0	0	-18	-33
SO	0	52							28	64
SD	0	34							18	34
SP	21	0							21	0
SF	-12	0							-12	0
SB	17	0							17	0
SW	53								53	

Sweden, University of Uppsala

	S	SW	SO	SD	SN	SP	SF	SB	TES	TESW
N	133	136	0	192	0	0	0	0	-	-
R^2	87	77	0	3	0	0	0	0	-	-
Pred										
Sex	0	0	0	-19	0	0	0	0	0	0
SO	35	48							59	48
SN	0	23							11	23
SP	16	19							25	19
SF	0	-16							-8	-16
SW	49								49	

Switzerland, University of Freiburg

	S	SW	SO	SD	SN	SP	SF	SB	TES	TESW
N	224	240	0	0	0	0	0	0	-	-
R^2	84	76	0	0	0	0	0	0	-	-
Pred										
SO	31	54							60	54
SD	0	13							7	13
SN	0	25							14	25
SP	13	0							13	0
SF	0	8							4	8
SB	6	0							6	0
SW	54								54	

Switzerland, University of Freiburg (continued)

	S	SW	SO	SD	SN	SP	SF	SB	TES	TESW
Males										
N	109	118	0	0	0	0	0	0	-	-
R^2	84	75	0	0	0	0	0	0	-	-
SO	20	54							49	54
SN	0	39							21	39
SP	12	0							12	0
SF	11	0							11	0
SB	13	0							13	0
SW	53								53	
Females										
N	115	122	138	0	0	0	0	0	-	-
R^2	85	79	4	0	0	0	0	0	-	-
WS	0	0	23	0	0	0	0	0	17	14
ETH	0	9	0	0	0	0	0	0	5	9
SO	38	61							73	61
SD	0	30							17	30
SF	0	11							6	11
SW	58								58	

Taiwan

	S	SW	SO	SD	SN	SP	SF	SB	TES	TESW
N	2245	2266	2388	2406	2419	2414	2390	2415	-	-
R^2	67	69	2	2	3	2	1	2	-	-
Pred										
Sex	-4	0	0	0	0	0	0	0	-4	0
WS	-3	0	-14	-15	-15	-13	11	-14	-16	-9
ETH	0	0	0	0	5	0	0	0	1	1
SO	18	39							36	39
SD	6	25							18	25
SN	8	12							14	12
SP	0	14							7	14
SB	9	0							9	0
SW	47								47	
Males										
N	1164	1177	1241	1251	1258	1257	1242	1259	-	-
R^2	65	67	2	2	2	2	1	2	-	-
WS	-4	0	-14	-15	-15	-13	10	-13	-16	-13
SO	11	33							29	33
SD	9	30							25	30
SN	0	11							6	11
SP	0	13							7	13

Taiwan (continued)

	S	SW	SO	SD	SN	SP	SF	SB	TES	TESW
SB	15	0							15	0
SW	53								53	

Females

	S	SW	SO	SD	SN	SP	SF	SB	TES	TESW
N	1081	1089	1147	1155	1161	1157	1148	1156	-	-
R^2	70	72	2	3	3	2	2	2	-	-
WS	0	0	-15	-15	-15	-14	13	-14	-13	-14
ETH	0	0	0	7	6	0	0	0	2	2
SO	34	46							51	46
SD	0	18							7	18
SN	19	14							24	14
SP	0	13							5	13
SW	37								37	

Tanzania, University of Dar Es Salaam

	S	SW	SO	SD	SN	SP	SF	SB	TES	TESW
N	154	158	0	188	193	0	187	193	-	-
R^2	61	50	0	5	4	0	5	2	-	-
Pred										
Sex	0	0	0	0	0	0	0	16	3	0
LED	0	0	0	-23	-21	0	23	0	0	0
SO	27	56							52	56
SP	0	21							10	21
SB	19	0							19	0
SW	45								45	

Males

	S	SW	SO	SD	SN	SP	SF	SB	TES	TESW
N	104	105	0	127	130	0	124	0	-	-
R^2	67	47	0	8	6	0	5	0	-	-
LED	0	0	0	-30	-26	0	23	0	0	0
SO	26	69							60	69
SB	19	0							19	0
SW	49								49	

Thailand

	S	SW	SO	SD	SN	SP	SF	SB	TES	TESW
N	351	366	0	0	0	0	437	403	-	-
R^2	31	37	0	0	0	0	22	3	-	-
Pred										
Sex	0	9	0	0	0	0	0	13	4	9
Age	0	0	0	0	0	0	-44	14	0	0
ETH	0	0	0	0	0	0	9	0	0	0
SO	12	33							26	33

Thailand (continued)

	S	SW	SO	SD	SN	SP	SF	SB	TES	TESW
SD	11	0							11	0
SN	0	16							7	16
SP	0	26							11	26
SW	43								43	

Males

	S	SW	SO	SD	SN	SP	SF	SB	TES	TESW
N	178	184	0	0	0	0	211	199	-	-
R^2	25	38	0	0	0	0	15	2	-	-
Age	0	0	0	0	0	0	-33	0	0	0
WS	26	0	0	0	0	0	14	0	26	0
LED	-16	0	0	0	0	0	0	-17	-16	0
SO	0	36							14	36
SD	14	0							14	0
SP	0	37							14	37
SW	39								39	

Females

	S	SW	SO	SD	SN	SP	SF	SB	TES	TESW
N	173	182	0	0	0	0	226	0	-	-
R^2	47	35	0	0	0	0	31	0	-	-
Age	0	0	0	0	0	0	-56	0	0	0
SO	34	31							48	31
SN	0	23							10	23
SP	0	19							9	19
SW	45								45	

Thailand, Chiang Mai University

	S	SW	SO	SD	SN	SP	SF	SB	TES	TESW
N	198	208	0	229	0	0	0	0	-	-
R^2	39	36	0	3	0	0	0	0	-	-
Pred										
Age	0	0	0	28	0	0	0	0	0	0
LED	0	0	0	-20	0	0	0	0	0	0
SO	24	31							39	31
SN	0	24							12	24
SP	0	25							12	25
SF	0	16							8	16
SW	48								48	

Males

	S	SW	SO	SD	SN	SP	SF	SB	TES	TESW
N	95	98	0	0	0	0	0	0	-	-
R^2	31	40	0	0	0	0	0	0	-	-
SO	0	29							16	29
SP	0	43							24	43
SW	56								56	

Thailand, Chiang Mai University (continued)

Females

	S	SW	SO	SD	SN	SP	SF	SB	TES	TESW
N	103	110	0	119	0	0	0	0	-	-
R^2	47	29	0	3	0	0	0	0	-	-
Age	0	0	0	20	0	0	0	0	0	0
SO	27	43							46	43
SN	0	27							12	27
SP	17	0							17	0
SF	0	17							7	17
SW	43								43	

Thailand, University of Srinakharinwirot

	S	SW	SO	SD	SN	SP	SF	SB	TES	TESW
N	153	158	0	0	0	0	202	181	-	-
R^2	27	39	0	0	0	0	2	2	-	-
Pred										
Sex	0	0	0	0	0	0	14	16	0	0
SO	0	36							15	36
SD	22	0							22	0
SP	0	37							15	37
SW	41								41	

Turkey, University of Uludag

	S	SW	SO	SD	SN	SP	SF	SB	TES	TESW
N	243	246	266	0	0	0	0	0	-	-
R^2	49	42	2	0	0	0	0	0	-	-
Pred										
Sex	0	0	-15	0	0	0	0	0	-5	-6
SO	20	41							30	41
SD	0	17							4	17
SN	25	0							25	0
SP	16	17							20	17
SW	25								25	

Males

	S	SW	SO	SD	SN	SP	SF	SB	TES	TESW
N	164	167	0	0	0	0	0	181	-	-
R^2	55	36	0	0	0	0	0	2	-	-
Age	14	0	0	0	0	0	0	0	14	0
LED	0	0	0	0	0	0	0	-15	0	0
SO	38	46							49	46
SD	28	23							34	23
SW	24								24	

United States of America

	S	SW	SO	SD	SN	SP	SF	SB	TES	TESW
N	790	845	971	0	0	0	0	959	-	-
R^2	73	69	1	0	0	0	0	1	-	-
Pred										
Age	0	5	0	0	0	0	0	0	2	5
LED	0	0	12	0	0	0	0	8	7	7
SO	29	50							48	50
SD	6	11							10	11
SN	0	12							5	12
SP	10	0							10	0
SF	0	-7							-3	-7
SB	13	17							20	17
SW	38								38	

Males

	S	SW	SO	SD	SN	SP	SF	SB	TES	TESW
N	278	302	356	358	0	0	0	0	-	-
R^2	67	65	2	1	0	0	0	0	-	-
LED	0	0	15	11	0	0	0	0	7	9
SO	30	61							49	61
SN	0	10							3	10
SP	15	0							15	0
SB	17	19							23	19
SW	31								31	

Females

	S	SW	SO	SD	SN	SP	SF	SB	TES	TESW
N	512	543	615	0	0	637	0	0	-	-
R^2	76	71	1	0	0	1	0	0	-	-
Age	-5	0	0	0	0	-10	0	0	-6	0
LED	0	0	11	0	0	0	0	0	6	5
SO	31	45							51	45
SD	0	14							6	14
SN	0	15							7	15
SP	8	0							8	0
SF	0	-7							-3	-7
SB	13	17							21	17
SW	45								45	

USA, Arizona State University

	S	SW	SO	SD	SN	SP	SF	SB	TES	TESW
N	153	159	182	181	0	186	0	178	-	-
R^2	65	66	2	4	0	4	0	4	-	-
Pred										
Sex	12	0	17	0	0	17	0	16	26	15
LED	0	0	0	21	0	16	0	20	5	5

USA, Arizona State University (continued)

	S	SW	SO	SD	SN	SP	SF	SB	TES	TESW
ETH	-10	0	0	0	0	0	0	0	-10	0
SO	29	64							53	64
SP	18	0							18	0
SB	0	23							9	23
SW	38								38	
Females										
N	112	117	0	0	0	0	0	0	-	-
R^2	61	63	0	0	0	0	0	0	-	-
Age	-13	0	0	0	0	0	0	0	-13	0
SO	42	64							63	64
SD	16	0							16	0
SB	0	21							7	21
SW	33								33	

USA, Edison Community College

	S	SW	SO	SD	SN	SP	SF	SB	TES	TESW
N	100	116	0	0	0	0	0	0	-	-
R^2	71	56	0	0	0	0	0	0	-	-
Pred										
SO	22	25							32	25
SD	0	19							7	19
SP	18	0							18	0
SF	0	-24							-9	-24
SB	23	26							33	26
SW	38								38	

USA, University of Illinois

	S	SW	SO	SD	SN	SP	SF	SB	TES	TESW
N	191	194	222	0	0	0	0	0	-	-
R^2	69	62	1	0	0	0	0	0	-	-
Pred										
WS	-12	0	-13	0	0	0	0	0	-18	-8
SO	49	58							49	58
SD	17	0							17	0
SN	0	13							0	13
SB	26	16							26	16
Females										
N	105	105	118	117	117	0	0	116	-	-
R^2	73	64	7	8	3	0	0	8	-	-
Age	0	0	30	30	18	0	0	32	27	18
LED	0	0	-23	-27	0	0	0	-25	-21	-14

USA, University of Illinois (continued)

	S	SW	SO	SD	SN	SP	SF	SB	TES	TESW
ETH	0	-13	0	0	0	0	0	0	0	-13
SO	72	59							72	59
SP	0	27							0	27
SB	17	0							17	0

USA, Ohio State University, Newark

	S	SW	SO	SD	SN	SP	SF	SB	TES	TESW
N	126	141	163	0	166	166	0	0	-	-
R^2	78	79	2	0	2	2	0	0	-	-
Pred										
Sex	12	0	0	0	0	0	0	0	12	0
Age	0	0	17	0	0	0	0	0	5	8
LED	0	0	0	0	17	17	0	0	2	4
SO	19	48							49	48
SN	0	23							14	23
SF	0	-15							-9	-15
SB	14	25							30	25
SW	62								62	

USA, Sangamon State University

	S	SW	SO	SD	SN	SP	SF	SB	TES	TESW
N	107	110	0	0	0	0	0	0	-	-
R^2	83	77	0	0	0	0	0	0	-	-
Pred										
Sex	-9	0	0	0	0	0	0	0	-9	0
SO	34	70							64	70
SN	0	23							10	23
SP	22	0							22	0
SW	43								43	

Yugoslavia, University of Zagreb

	S	SW	SO	SD	SN	SP	SF	SB	TES	TESW
N	202	210	247	0	0	255	265	257	-	-
R^2	70	64	1	0	0	3	2	2	-	-
Pred										
Sex	0	0	0	0	0	0	0	14	1	4
WS	0	0	0	0	0	-16	0	0	-3	0
ETH	0	0	13	0	0	13	15	0	6	6
SO	30	47							41	47
SN	19	18							23	18
SP	20	0							20	0

Yugoslavia, University of Zagreb (continued)

	S	SW	SO	SD	SN	SP	SF	SB	TES	TESW
SF	-11	0							-11	0
SB	0	25							6	25
SW	24								24	
Males										
N	110	114	133	0	0	140	146	144	-	-
R^2	66	57	2	0	0	3	2	2	-	-
LED	0	0	0	0	0	0	18	0	-3	0
ETH	0	0	18	0	0	18	0	17	7	15
SO	41	58							41	58
SD	15	0							15	0
SN	34	0							34	0
SF	-17	0							-17	0
SB	0	24							0	24

Appendix 5 Results of regressions using MDT to explain satisfaction with one's self-esteem, alphabetically by country and university (decimal points omitted)

Austria, University of Vienna

	S	SW	SO	SD	SN	SP	SF	SB	TES	TESW
N	300	301	338	0	335	0	0	0	-	-
R^2	68	62	2	0	1	0	0	0	-	-
Pred										
Sex	0	0	-16	0	-13	0	0	0	-9	-10
ETH	-9	0	0	0	0	0	0	0	-9	0
SO	23	42							46	42
SD	0	14							8	14
SN	0	24							13	24
SP	15	0							15	0
SF	0	-8							-4	-8
SB	0	10							6	10
SW	55								55	

Males

	S	SW	SO	SD	SN	SP	SF	SB	TES	TESW
N	118	129	0	0	0	0	0	0	-	-
R^2	72	66	0	0	0	0	0	0	-	-
ETH	-24	0	0	0	0	0	0	0	-24	0
SO	27	48							51	48
SD	0	24							12	24
SN	0	20							10	20
SP	17	0							17	0
SW	50								50	

Females

	S	SW	SO	SD	SN	SP	SF	SB	TES	TESW
N	182	182	206	0	0	0	0	205	-	-
R^2	68	58	3	0	0	0	0	2	-	-
ETH	0	0	-19	0	0	0	0	-15	-9	-10
SO	21	43							44	43
SN	19	33							37	33
SB	0	14							7	14
SW	53								53	

Bahrain, University College of Arts, Science and Education

	S	SW	SO	SD	SN	SP	SF	SB	TES	TESW
N	219	220	0	0	0	0	248	249	-	-
R^2	34	41	0	0	0	0	2	3	-	-
Pred										
Age	0	0	0	0	0	0	0	18	4	0
LED	0	0	0	0	0	0	0	-13	-3	0

Bahrain, U. C. of Arts, Science and Education (continued)

	S	SW	SO	SD	SN	SP	SF	SB	TES	TESW
SO	18	55							33	55
SD	-16	0							-16	0
SN	23	17							23	17
SB	20	0							20	0
SW	28								28	
Females										
N	178	179	0	205	0	209	202	206	-	-
R^2	32	42	0	6	0	2	3	4	-	-
Age	0	0	0	19	0	14	-19	23	6	0
WS	0	0	0	-18	0	0	0	0	0	0
LED	0	0	0	0	0	0	0	-17	-4	0
SO	18	54							35	54
SN	0	19							6	19
SB	25	0							25	0
SW	32								32	

Bangladesh, Dhaka University

	S	SW	SO	SD	SN	SP	SF	SB	TES	TESW
N	296	296	0	0	311	0	312	0	-	-
R^2	65	58	0	0	2	0	2	0	-	-
Pred										
Sex	8	0	0	0	0	0	0	0	8	0
ETH	0	0	0	0	-15	0	14	0	-3	-5
SO	19	40							41	40
SD	18	0							18	0
SN	0	34							19	34
SB	0	21							12	21
SW	55								55	
Males										
N	126	126	132	130	0	0	0	0	-	-
R^2	63	55	5	3	0	0	0	0	-	-
LED	0	0	25	19	0	0	0	0	14	8
SO	22	33							38	33
SD	25	0							25	0
SN	0	40							19	40
SB	0	23							11	23
SW	48								48	
Females										
N	170	170	181	0	181	0	0	0	-	-
R^2	68	61	4	0	2	0	0	0	-	-
WS	11	0	0	0	0	0	0	0	11	0

Bangladesh, Dhaka University (continued)

	S	SW	SO	SD	SN	SP	SF	SB	TES	TESW
ETH	0	0	-20	0	-16	0	0	0	-4	-14
SO	14	48							44	48
SN	14	25							30	25
SB	0	22							14	22
SW	62								62	

Brazil, Pontifical Catholic University of Minas Gerais

	S	SW	SO	SD	SN	SP	SF	SB	TES	TESW
N	244	245	265	0	0	0	0	274	-	-
R^2	43	31	2	0	0	0	0	2	-	-
Pred										
Sex	-11	0	16	0	0	0	0	13	-2	8
SO	37	39							52	39
SN	0	19							7	19
SB	0	12							5	12
SW	39								39	
Males										
N	95	96	0	0	0	0	0	0	-	-
R^2	43	25	0	0	0	0	0	0	-	-
SO	49	26							57	26
SN	0	36							10	36
SW	29								29	
Females										
N	149	149	0	0	0	0	0	0	-	-
R^2	46	36	0	0	0	0	0	0	-	-
SO	18	52							42	52
SN	18	0							18	0
SB	0	17							8	17
SW	47								47	

Cameroon, Yaounde University

	S	SW	SO	SD	SN	SP	SF	SB	TES	TESW
N	145	147	173	171	170	0	0	179	-	-
R^2	31	45	2	4	2	0	0	3	-	-
Pred										
Sex	0	15	17	22	17	0	0	19	14	25
LED	0	13	0	0	0	0	0	0	4	13
SO	31	34							43	34
SN	0	25							9	25
SP	0	25							9	25
SF	0	20							7	20

Cameroon, Yaounde University (continued)

	S	SW	SO	SD	SN	SP	SF	SB	TES	TESW
SW	34								34	
Males										
N	112	112	0	0	0	0	0	0	-	-
R^2	33	43	0	0	0	0	0	0	-	-
SO	29	36							43	36
SN	0	26							10	26
SP	0	26							10	26
SF	0	20							8	20
SW	38								38	

Canada

	S	SW	SO	SD	SN	SP	SF	SB	TES	TESW
N	1512	1523	1579	1555	1568	1575	1574	1578	-	-
R^2	62	50	4	2	2	1	1	1	-	-
Pred										
Sex	0	7	-10	-12	-11	0	0	0	-5	1
Age	0	0	14	0	0	8	0	0	7	6
WS	0	0	5	6	7	0	0	6	5	5
LED	0	0	0	0	0	-6	0	0	0	0
ETH	0	5	0	0	0	0	11	0	2	5
SO	31	41							49	41
SD	6	7							9	7
SN	5	25							16	25
SB	8	13							14	13
SW	43								43	
Males										
N	584	588	0	0	603	0	605	0	-	-
R^2	64	47	0	0	1	0	1	0	-	-
WS	0	0	0	0	8	0	0	0	1	2
ETH	0	0	0	0	0	0	11	0	0	0
SO	34	45							55	45
SD	6	0							6	0
SN	0	23							11	23
SB	7	13							13	13
SW	46								46	
Females										
N	927	934	968	0	0	968	968	972	-	-
R^2	60	52	4	0	0	1	1	1	-	-
Age	0	0	21	0	0	9	0	11	12	10
ETH	0	6	0	0	0	0	10	0	3	6
SO	29	39							46	39

Canada (continued)

	S	SW	SO	SD	SN	SP	SF	SB	TES	TESW
SD	7	6							10	6
SN	0	29							13	29
SP	7	0							7	0
SB	7	13							13	13
SW	44								44	

Canada, Dalhousie University

	S	SW	SO	SD	SN	SP	SF	SB	TES	TESW
N	253	261	270	265	269	0	0	0	-	-
R^2	59	47	3	3	2	0	0	0	-	-
Pred										
Sex	0	10	0	-19	-14	0	0	0	3	5
Age	0	0	18	0	0	0	0	0	9	8
SO	30	44							52	44
SN	0	33							16	33
SB	11	0							11	0
SW	49								49	
Females										
N	171	171	181	0	0	0	0	0	-	-
R^2	58	47	5	0	0	0	0	0	-	-
Age	0	0	23	0	0	0	0	0	14	10
SO	42	43							61	43
SN	0	34							15	34
SW	43								43	

Canada, University of Guelph

	S	SW	SO	SD	SN	SP	SF	SB	TES	TESW
N	305	310	330	326	0	0	331	0	-	-
R^2	64	53	1	1	0	0	5	0	-	-
Pred										
WS	0	0	0	11	0	0	0	0	1	2
ETH	0	0	12	0	0	0	23	0	6	4
SO	34	35							53	35
SD	0	15							8	15
SN	0	23							12	23
SB	0	17							9	17
SW	53								53	
Males										
N	170	173	0	184	0	0	0	0	-	-
R^2	72	51	0	2	0	0	0	0	-	-
ETH	0	0	0	15	0	0	0	0	1	2

Canada, University of Guelph (continued)

	S	SW	SO	SD	SN	SP	SF	SB	TES	TESW
SO	45	35							62	35
SD	0	16							8	16
SN	0	23							11	23
SB	0	17							8	17
SW	49								49	
Females										
N	133	135	0	0	0	0	141	0	-	-
R^2	53	56	0	0	0	0	16	0	-	-
WS	0	0	0	0	0	0	-16	0	0	0
ETH	0	14	0	0	0	0	38	0	9	14
SO	0	32							20	32
SN	0	34							21	34
SP	16	20							29	20
SW	63								63	

Canada, Mount Saint Vincent University

	S	SW	SO	SD	SN	SP	SF	SB	TES	TESW
N	269	272	276	276	0	0	0	280	-	-
R^2	61	51	6	3	0	0	0	2	-	-
Pred										
Sex	0	0	0	-18	0	0	0	0	0	0
Age	0	0	19	0	0	0	0	15	12	11
LED	0	0	13	0	0	0	0	0	7	6
SO	36	47							57	47
SN	0	24							11	24
SP	10	0							10	0
SB	0	14							6	14
SW	44								44	
Females										
N	249	252	256	0	0	257	0	260	-	-
R^2	62	52	6	0	0	1	0	3	-	-
Age	0	0	19	0	0	13	0	18	14	12
LED	0	0	13	0	0	0	0	0	8	6
SO	37	48							58	48
SN	0	24							10	24
SP	12	0							12	0
SB	0	14							6	14
SW	43								43	

Canada, Saint Mary's University

	S	SW	SO	SD	SN	SP	SF	SB	TES	TESW
N	307	309	316	0	0	315	0	314	-	-
R^2	57	44	3	0	0	3	0	1	-	-
Pred										
Sex	0	10	-11	0	0	0	0	0	-2	6
WS	0	0	14	0	0	18	0	12	9	8
SO	34	41							48	41
SD	15	0							15	0
SN	0	25							9	25
SB	12	17							18	17
SW	34								34	

Males

	S	SW	SO	SD	SN	SP	SF	SB	TES	TESW
N	163	164	169	0	0	0	0	0	-	-
R^2	51	40	3	0	0	0	0	0	-	-
LED	0	0	18	0	0	0	0	0	8	7
SO	28	38							44	38
SD	16	0							16	0
SN	0	18							8	18
SP	0	22							10	22
SW	43								43	

Females

	S	SW	SO	SD	SN	SP	SF	SB	TES	TESW
N	143	144	146	0	0	146	0	0	-	-
R^2	63	51	2	0	0	5	0	0	-	-
WS	0	0	18	0	0	24	0	0	9	3
SO	41	42							52	42
SD	16	0							16	0
SN	0	31							8	31
SP	0	-18							-5	-18
SB	16	29							24	29
SW	27								27	

Canada, Simon Fraser University

	S	SW	SO	SD	SN	SP	SF	SB	TES	TESW
N	278	279	299	289	294	0	297	0	-	-
R^2	68	54	3	2	1	0	1	0	-	-
Pred										
Sex	0	0	0	-14	-12	0	13	0	-3	-3
Age	0	0	19	0	0	0	0	0	9	8
SO	26	43							45	43
SN	14	26							26	26
SP	12	0							12	0
SB	0	17							8	17

Canada, Simon Fraser University (continued)

	S	SW	SO	SD	SN	SP	SF	SB	TES	TESW
SW	45								45	
Males										
N	109	109	0	0	0	0	0	0	-	-
R^2	74	52	0	0	0	0	0	0	-	-
SO	43	73							72	73
SB	17	0							17	0
SW	39								39	
Females										
N	169	170	185	0	0	184	0	0	-	-
R^2	66	60	5	0	0	2	0	0	-	-
Age	0	0	24	0	0	16	0	0	11	7
SO	20	31							35	31
SD	12	14							19	14
SN	0	32							15	32
SP	16	0							16	0
SB	0	19							9	19
SW	47								47	

Chile, Austral University of Chile

	S	SW	SO	SD	SN	SP	SF	SB	TES	TESW
N	226	226	245	0	0	0	250	0	-	-
R^2	49	20	2	0	0	0	2	0	-	-
Pred										
Sex	0	0	0	0	0	0	-16	0	-2	0
ETH	0	0	-15	0	0	0	0	0	-8	-5
SO	45	34							54	34
SD	0	20							5	20
SF	11	0							11	0
SB	17	0							17	0
SW	27								27	
Males										
N	122	122	131	0	0	0	0	0	-	-
R^2	49	18	2	0	0	0	0	0	-	-
ETH	0	0	-18	0	0	0	0	0	-10	-7
SO	45	36							56	36
SN	0	18							5	18
SB	16	0							16	0
SW	30								30	
Females										
N	104	104	0	0	0	0	0	0	-	-
R^2	45	24	0	0	0	0	0	0	-	-

Chile, Austral University of Chile (continued)

	S	SW	SO	SD	SN	SP	SF	SB	TES	TESW
SO	52	36							61	36
SD	0	28							7	28
SW	26								26	

Egypt, Ain Shams University

	S	SW	SO	SD	SN	SP	SF	SB	TES	TESW
N	218	220	0	0	0	0	252	260	-	-
R^2	46	44	0	0	0	0	2	1	-	-
Pred										
Sex	0	0	0	0	0	0	0	-13	-3	0
ETH	0	0	0	0	0	0	14	0	0	0
SO	27	67							51	67
SB	21	0							21	0
SW	35								35	
Males										
N	132	133	0	0	0	0	144	0	-	-
R^2	37	33	0	0	0	0	5	0	-	-
ETH	0	0	0	0	0	0	024	0	0	0
SO	20	58							42	58
SB	20	0							20	0
SW	38								38	

Finland, University of Helsinki

	S	SW	SO	SD	SN	SP	SF	SB	TES	TESW
N	242	245	0	0	0	0	0	269	-	-
R^2	76	66	0	0	0	0	0	2	-	-
Pred										
Sex	0	0	0	0	0	0	0	14	0	0
SO	21	32							40	32
SD	-11	15							-2	15
SN	16	41							41	41
SP	10	0							10	0
SF	0	-9							-5	-9
SW	60								60	
Males										
N	96	97	109	0	0	0	0	0	-	-
R^2	73	65	3	0	0	0	0	0	-	-
LED	0	-17	-19	0	0	0	0	0	-18	-22
ETH	0	16	0	0	0	0	0	0	10	16
SO	20	28							38	28
SD	0	20							13	20

Finland, University of Helsinki (continued)

	S	SW	SO	SD	SN	SP	SF	SB	TES	TESW
SN	0	38							24	38
SP	13	0							13	0
SW	63								63	
Females										
N	146	148	0	0	0	160	0	0	-	-
R^2	80	67	0	0	0	2	0	0	-	-
Age	0	0	0	0	0	17	0	0	0	0
SO	26	37							47	37
SD	-18	0							-18	0
SN	29	55							60	55
SW	57								57	

Federal Republic of Germany

	S	SW	SO	SD	SN	SP	SF	SB	TES	TESW
N	680	680	750	0	757	0	740	757	-	-
R^2	62	56	1	0	1	0	1	1	-	-
Pred										
Sex	0	0	-8	0	-9	0	0	8	-4	-4
Age	6	0	0	0	0	0	0	0	6	0
WS	0	0	0	0	0	0	-12	0	0	0
LED	0	0	0	0	0	0	-9	0	0	0
ETH	5	0	9	0	0	0	0	11	10	5
SO	22	38							40	38
SD	0	8							4	8
SN	15	22							25	22
SP	0	11							5	11
SB	8	14							14	14
SW	46								46	
Males										
N	366	366	409	390	0	0	0	0	-	-
R^2	60	55	1	1	0	0	0	0	-	-
Age	7	0	0	11	0	0	0	0	7	0
LED	0	0	11	0	0	0	0	0	5	4
ETH	0	10	0	0	0	0	0	0	4	10
SO	25	37							41	37
SN	14	28							26	28
SP	0	12							5	12
SB	8	15							15	15
SW	44								44	
Females										
N	314	314	341	0	342	344	0	343	-	-

Federal Republic of Germany (continued)

	S	SW	SO	SD	SN	SP	SF	SB	TES	TESW
R^2	64	58	4	0	1	2	0	3	-	-
LED	0	0	0	0	-12	0	0	0	-4	-3
ETH	11	0	21	0	0	16	0	19	21	13
SO	17	42							39	42
SN	16	26							30	26
SP	0	12							6	12
SB	0	10							5	10
SW	53								53	

Germany, Federal College of Public Administration

	S	SW	SO	SD	SN	SP	SF	SB	TES	TESW
N	234	234	0	0	0	250	0	250	-	-
R^2	68	62	0	0	0	1	0	2	-	-
Pred										
Sex	0	0	0	0	0	13	0	14	3	3
ETH	0	9	0	0	0	0	0	0	4	9
SO	27	44							46	44
SD	15	0							15	0
SN	0	28							12	28
SF	8	8							11	8
SB	12	19							20	19
SW	42								42	
Males										
N	135	135	0	0	0	0	0	0	-	-
R^2	68	65	0	0	0	0	0	0	-	-
ETH	0	11	0	0	0	0	0	0	3	11
SO	29	45							42	45
SD	20	0							20	0
SN	21	33							30	33
SP	0	16							5	16
SF	15	0							15	0
SW	28								28	
Females										
N	99	99	0	0	0	0	0	0	-	-
R^2	76	61	0	0	0	0	0	0	-	-
SO	27	47							54	47
SF	0	20							11	20
SB	13	35							33	35
SW	57								57	

Germany, University of Frankfurt

	S	SW	SO	SD	SN	SP	SF	SB	TES	TESW
N	224	224	261	0	268	0	262	0	-	-
R^2	58	55	5	0	2	0	3	0	-	-
Pred										
Sex	-12	12	0	0	-15	0	0	0	-8	-7
Age	12	0	0	0	0	0	0	0	12	0
LED	0	0	15	0	0	0	-17	0	6	5
ETH	0	0	17	0	0	0	0	0	7	6
SO	24	35							42	35
SN	0	31							16	31
SP	0	25							13	25
SB	11	0							11	0
SW	50								50	

Males

	S	SW	SO	SD	SN	SP	SF	SB	TES	TESW
N	134	134	0	0	0	0	156	0	-	-
R^2	54	54	0	0	0	0	6	0	-	-
LED	0	0	0	0	0	0	-20	0	0	0
ETH	0	0	0	0	0	0	20	0	0	0
SO	31	28							45	28
SN	0	21							11	21
SP	0	19							10	19
SB	0	24							12	24
SW	51								51	

Females

	S	SW	SO	SD	SN	SP	SF	SB	TES	TESW
N	90	90	105	0	0	0	106	0	-	-
R^2	63	64	11	0	0	0	5	0	-	-
Age	19	0	0	0	0	0	0	0	19	0
WS	0	13	0	0	0	0	-23	0	7	13
LED	0	0	25	0	0	0	0	0	7	12
ETH	20	0	24	0	0	0	0	0	27	12
SO	0	49							27	49
SN	21	43							45	43
SW	56								56	

Germany, University of Mannheim

	S	SW	SO	SD	SN	SP	SF	SB	TES	TESW
N	221	221	239	0	0	0	0	0	-	-
R^2	62	53	2	0	0	0	0	0	-	-
Pred										
Sex	0	0	-15	0	0	0	0	0	-6	-6
Age	11	0	0	0	0	0	0	0	11	0

Germany, University of Mannheim (continued)

	S	SW	SO	SD	SN	SP	SF	SB	TES	TESW
SO	18	42							40	42
SN	16	27							30	27
SB	0	17							9	17
SW	53								53	
Males										
N	96	96	0	100	0	0	0	105	-	-
R^2	60	47	0	3	0	0	0	4	-	-
Age	0	0	0	20	0	0	0	21	0	0
SO	28	42							52	42
SN	0	34							20	34
SW	58								58	
Females										
N	124	124	132	0	132	0	0	132	-	-
R^2	61	55	4	0	4	0	0	3	-	-
Age	12	0	0	0	0	0	0	0	12	0
WS	0	0	0	0	-21	0	0	0	-8	-5
ETH	0	0	21	0	0	0	0	20	8	14
SO	0	45							26	45
SN	27	22							40	22
SB	0	21							12	21
SW	58								58	

Greece, Aristotelian University of Thessaloniki

	S	SW	SO	SD	SN	SP	SF	SB	TES	TESW
N	229	232	0	248	249	0	0	251	-	-
R^2	43	22	0	1	4	0	0	3	-	-
Pred										
Age	-14	0	0	0	0	0	0	0	-14	0
ETH	0	0	0	-13	-20	0	0	-19	0	-3
SO	42	39							56	39
SD	-10	0							-10	0
SB	0	18							7	18
SW	36								36	
Males										
N	123	125	0	136	138	0	0	139	-	-
R^2	37	16	0	5	11	0	0	6	-	-
Age	-22	0	0	0	21	0	0	0	-22	0
ETH	0	0	0	-23	-32	0	0	-25	0	0
SO	37	41							51	41
SW	33								33	

Greece, Aristotelian U. of Thessaloniki (continued)

	S	SW	SO	SD	SN	SP	SF	SB	TES	TESW
Females										
N	106	107	0	0	0	0	0	0	-	-
R^2	52	32	0	0	0	0	0	0	-	-
ETH	0	-18	0	0	0	0	0	0	-6	-18
SO	49	43							64	43
SB	0	25							9	25
SW	35								35	

Hungary, University of Economics

	S	SW	SO	SD	SN	SP	SF	SB	TES	TESW
N	204	204	219	0	0	0	0	0	-	-
R^2	45	51	2	0	0	0	0	0	-	-
Pred										
Age	0	0	-15	0	0	0	0	0	-6	-7
SO	29	43							39	43
SN	0	23							6	23
SP	14	18							18	18
SB	16	0							16	0
SW	24								24	
Females										
N	150	150	0	0	0	0	158	0	-	-
R^2	46	46	0	0	0	0	2	0	-	-
Age	0	0	0	0	0	0	16	0	0	0
SO	34	41							51	41
SN	0	21							9	21
SP	0	20							8	20
SW	42								42	

India, University of Delhi

	S	SW	SO	SD	SN	SP	SF	SB	TES	TESW
N	207	211	240	242	0	0	0	238	-	-
R^2	38	27	2	2	0	0	0	1	-	-
Pred										
WS	0	0	15	0	0	0	0	0	8	6
LED	0	-12	0	-14	0	0	0	0	-4	-15
ETH	0	0	0	0	0	0	0	-13	0	0
SO	45	38							55	38
SD	0	20							5	20
SW	26								26	
Males										
N	130	133	0	153	0	0	0	150	-	-

India, University of Delhi (continued)

	S	SW	SO	SD	SN	SP	SF	SB	TES	TESW
R^2	36	27	0	3	0	0	0	3	-	-
Age	0	-15	0	0	0	0	0	0	-5	-15
LED	0	0	0	-19	0	0	0	-19	0	0
SO	39	50							55	50
SW	32								32	

Israel, Hebrew University of Jerusalem

	S	SW	SO	SD	SN	SP	SF	SB	TES	TESW
N	307	307	0	309	0	309	0	0	-	-
R^2	40	23	0	2	0	1	0	0	-	-
Pred										
Sex	0	0	0	0	0	12	0	0	2	0
Age	0	0	0	-14	0	0	0	0	0	0
LED	0	-12	0	0	0	0	0	0	-5	-12
SO	26	38							42	38
SN	0	20							9	20
SP	13	0							13	0
SW	43								43	
Males										
N	157	157	0	158	158	0	0	0	-	-
R^2	35	23	0	4	2	0	0	0	-	-
Age	-14	0	0	0	0	0	0	0	-14	0
WS	0	0	0	-20	0	0	0	0	0	0
LED	0	-14	0	0	0	0	0	0	-6	-14
ETH	0	0	0	0	17	0	0	0	1	3
SO	23	33							38	33
SN	0	18							8	18
SP	0	19							8	19
SW	44								44	
Females										
N	150	150	151	151	0	0	150	0	-	-
R^2	48	24	4	2	0	0	3	0	-	-
Age	0	0	0	-16	0	0	19	0	0	0
WS	0	0	21	0	0	0	0	0	10	9
SO	28	41							46	41
SN	0	16							7	16
SP	22	0							22	0
SW	44								44	

Japan

	S	SW	SO	SD	SN	SP	SF	SB	TES	TESW
N	1122	1129	1192	1179	1187	1183	1191	1189	-	-
R^2	50	49	9	3	5	4	1	6	-	-
Pred										
Sex	0	0	7	0	0	8	0	7	3	3
Age	0	7	14	0	0	0	10	0	7	11
WS	0	0	-8	-9	-12	-10	0	-10	-7	-8
LED	8	0	12	13	17	12	0	17	18	12
SO	15	25							26	25
SD	8	8							12	8
SN	11	31							25	31
SP	0	11							5	11
SB	0	6							3	6
SW	45								45	

Males

	S	SW	SO	SD	SN	SP	SF	SB	TES	TESW
N	920	926	977	968	974	968	976	974	-	-
R^2	47	45	7	2	4	3	2	4	-	-
Age	0	9	14	0	0	0	13	0	7	12
WS	0	0	-8	-8	-11	-10	0	-10	-6	-7
LED	10	0	12	12	15	10	0	15	20	10
SO	13	21							23	21
SD	7	11							12	11
SN	10	32							25	32
SP	0	13							6	13
SW	46								46	

Females

	S	SW	SO	SD	SN	SP	SF	SB	TES	TESW
N	202	203	215	211	213	215	0	215	-	-
R^2	62	61	6	4	7	5	0	7	-	-
Age	0	0	26	21	27	24	0	0	21	22
LED	0	0	0	0	0	0	0	27	0	0
SO	31	50							51	50
SD	18	0							18	0
SN	0	34							13	34
SW	39								39	

Japan, Sophia University

	S	SW	SO	SD	SN	SP	SF	SB	TES	TESW
N	237	240	262	257	256	256	256	257	-	-
R^2	29	43	2	2	3	5	3	3	-	-
Pred										
Sex	0	0	16	14	18	23	-19	18	8	12
LED	-12	0	0	0	0	0	0	0	-12	0

Japan, Sophia University (continued)

	S	SW	SO	SD	SN	SP	SF	SB	TES	TESW
SO	15	29							25	29
SD	13	0							13	0
SN	0	43							14	43
SW	33								33	
Males										
N	158	160	0	173	172	171	0	172	-	-
R^2	21	40	0	3	8	3	0	2	-	-
WS	0	0	0	-19	-20	0	0	0	-7	-10
ETH	0	0	0	0	-20	-19	0	-16	-6	-5
SO	0	21							7	21
SD	0	27							9	27
SN	19	25							27	25
SW	33								33	

Japan, Tokai University

	S	SW	SO	SD	SN	SP	SF	SB	TES	TESW
N	279	280	0	293	0	0	0	0	-	-
R^2	47	49	0	1	0	0	0	0	-	-
Pred										
LED	0	0	0	12	0	0	0	0	0	0
SO	0	22							10	22
SN	29	41							47	41
SP	0	20							9	20
SF	-9	0							-9	0
SW	44								44	
Males										
N	199	200	216	0	215	0	0	211	-	-
R^2	41	49	3	0	2	0	0	2	-	-
Age	0	13	18	0	0	0	0	0	6	13
LED	0	0	0	0	14	0	0	14	8	8
SN	27	45							47	45
SP	0	23							10	23
SF	0	11							5	11
SB	0	15							7	15
SW	44								44	

Japan, Tokai and Denkitsushin Universities

	S	SW	SO	SD	SN	SP	SF	SB	TES	TESW
N	606	609	0	629	0	630	636	638	-	-
R2	49	40	0	1	0	1	1	1	-	-

Japan, Tokai and Denkitsushin Universities (continued)

	S	SW	SO	SD	SN	SP	SF	SB	TES	TESW
Pred										
Age	0	7	0	0	0	0	0	0	4	7
LED	0	0	0	-10	0	0	0	0	-2	-1
ETH	0	0	0	0	0	-10	10	-10	-1	-2
SO	14	24							26	24
SD	18	11							24	11
SN	0	29							15	29
SP	0	11							6	11
SF	0	-7							-4	-7
SW	50								50	
Males										
N	563	566	0	583	587	583	589	591	-	-
R^2	50	41	0	1	1	1	1	1	-	-
Age	0	7	0	0	0	0	0	0	4	7
ETH	0	0	0	-9	-8	-11	10	-10	-4	-5
SO	13	24							26	24
SD	18	11							24	11
SN	0	31							16	31
SP	0	11							6	11
SF	0	-7							-4	-7
SW	52								52	

Jordan, Yarmouk University

	S	SW	SO	SD	SN	SP	SF	SB	TES	TESW
N	270	271	295	0	0	289	0	289	-	-
R^2	35	34	1	0	0	1	0	1	-	-
Pred										
Sex	0	0	0	0	0	13	0	13	2	0
LED	-11	0	-12	0	0	0	0	0	-16	-6
SO	29	49							37	49
SN	14	19							17	19
SF	0	11							2	11
SB	18	0							18	0
SW	17								17	
Males										
N	220	221	0	0	0	0	0	0	-	-
R^2	34	31	0	0	0	0	0	0	-	-
SO	28	44							36	44
SN	0	22							4	22
SB	27	0							27	0
SW	19								19	

Kenya, University of Nairobi

	S	SW	SO	SD	SN	SP	SF	SB	TES	TESW
N	242	249	0	0	270	0	0	0	-	-
R^2	52	46	0	0	3	0	0	0	-	-
Pred										
Sex	-11	0	0	0	0	0	0	0	-11	0
LED	0	0	0	0	18	0	0	0	0	0
SO	40	36							50	36
SD	0	26							7	26
SB	17	20							23	20
SW	28								28	
Males										
N	134	138	0	0	0	0	0	0	-	-
R^2	57	44	0	0	0	0	0	0	-	-
SO	42	29							51	29
SD	0	31							10	31
SP	0	19							6	19
SB	17	0							17	0
SW	32								32	
Females										
N	109	111	0	115	116	0	116	0	-	-
R^2	44	49	0	3	8	0	3	0	-	-
LED	0	0	0	20	29	0	0	0	0	0
ETH	0	0	0	0	0	0	-20	0	0	0
SO	43	52							59	52
SB	0	28							8	28
SW	30								30	

Korea, Korea University

	S	SW	SO	SD	SN	SP	SF	SB	TES	TESW
N	435	435	442	0	441	442	0	0	-	-
R^2	50	48	1	0	1	1	0	0	-	-
Pred										
Sex	0	-11	-10	0	-12	0	0	0	-11	-16
Age	0	0	0	0	0	12	0	0	0	0
SO	30	30							42	30
SD	0	17							7	17
SN	11	20							19	20
SF	0	-10							-4	-10
SB	0	10							4	10
SW	41								41	
Males										
N	346	346	0	0	0	351	0	351	-	-

Korea, Korea University (continued)

	S	SW	SO	SD	SN	SP	SF	SB	TES	TESW
R^2	49	46	0	0	0	2	0	1	-	-
Age	0	0	0	0	0	14	0	0	0	0
ETH	0	0	0	0	0	0	0	12	1	1
SO	34	32							48	32
SD	0	13							6	13
SN	0	20							9	20
SF	0	-11							-5	-11
SB	0	11							5	11
SW	45								45	

Mexico, University of Baja California Sur

	S	SW	SO	SD	SN	SP	SF	SB	TES	TESW
N	189	194	0	0	0	234	235	230	-	-
R^2	42	31	0	0	0	4	2	2	-	-
Pred										
Sex	0	0	0	0	0	13	0	0	0	0
WS	0	0	0	0	0	0	-14	0	-2	0
LED	0	13	0	0	0	0	0	0	2	13
ETH	0	0	0	0	0	16	0	14	5	0
SO	45	42							53	42
SD	0	22							4	22
SF	13	0							13	0
SB	23	0							23	0
SW	18								18	

Males

	S	SW	SO	SD	SN	SP	SF	SB	TES	TESW
N	129	133	0	0	0	165	166	163	-	-
R^2	38	27	0	0	0	3	3	2	-	-
WS	0	0	0	0	0	0	-20	0	0	0
ETH	0	0	0	0	0	18	0	16	3	0
SO	55	36							55	36
SD	0	26							0	26
SB	17	0							17	0

Netherlands, Erasmus University

	S	SW	SO	SD	SN	SP	SF	SB	TES	TESW
N	483	483	508	516	0	511	513	518	-	-
R^2	45	44	1	1	0	1	1	1	-	-
Pred										
Sex	-13	0	0	0	0	0	0	0	-13	0
LED	0	0	11	11	0	12	-11	9	7	6
SO	21	15							28	15

Netherlands, Erasmus University (continued)

	S	SW	SO	SD	SN	SP	SF	SB	TES	TESW
SD	0	43							19	43
SN	0	16							7	16
SP	8	0							8	0
SB	10	0							10	0
SW	44								44	

Males

	S	SW	SO	SD	SN	SP	SF	SB	TES	TESW
N	277	277	0	0	0	0	0	0	-	-
R^2	38	41	0	0	0	0	0	0	-	-
SO	15	21							25	21
SD	0	41							19	41
SN	0	13							6	13
SB	19	0							19	0
SW	45								45	

Females

	S	SW	SO	SD	SN	SP	SF	SB	TES	TESW
N	203	203	0	0	213	0	0	0	-	-
R^2	55	50	0	0	3	0	0	0	-	-
LED	0	0	0	0	17	0	0	0	2	4
SO	27	0							27	0
SD	18	44							36	44
SN	0	26							11	26
SF	0	-12							-5	-12
SW	41								41	

Netherlands, University of Leiden

	S	SW	SO	SD	SN	SP	SF	SB	TES	TESW
N	293	293	345	0	347	0	0	0	-	-
R^2	57	42	3	0	9	0	0	0	-	-
Pred										
Sex	-10	0	-18	0	-31	0	0	0	-23	-13
SO	31	39							49	39
SD	11	12							16	12
SN	0	29							13	29
SW	45								45	

Males

	S	SW	SO	SD	SN	SP	SF	SB	TES	TESW
N	126	126	0	0	0	0	0	0	-	-
R^2	40	25	0	0	0	0	0	0	-	-
SO	40	50							57	50
SW	33								33	

Females

	S	SW	SO	SD	SN	SP	SF	SB	TES	TESW
N	167	167	0	0	0	0	0	0	-	-
R^2	63	54	0	0	0	0	0	0	-	-

Netherlands, University of Leiden (continued)

	S	SW	SO	SD	SN	SP	SF	SB	TES	TESW
SO	25	35							43	35
SD	17	0							17	0
SN	0	49							26	49
SW	52								52	

New Zealand, Massey University

	S	SW	SO	SD	SN	SP	SF	SB	TES	TESW
N	306	307	0	0	318	314	318	318	-	-
R^2	55	47	0	0	1	2	2	2	-	-
Pred										
Sex	0	0	0	0	-12	15	0	0	-2	-4
LED	0	0	0	0	0	0	15	-14	0	0
SO	29	37							42	37
SD	0	11							4	11
SN	17	34							29	34
SP	11	0							11	0
SW	34								34	
Males										
N	110	110	114	0	0	112	0	113	-	-
R^2	54	41	5	0	0	2	0	5	-	-
WS	0	0	0	0	0	-20	0	0	-5	0
LED	0	0	0	0	0	0	0	-24	0	0
ETH	0	0	23	0	0	0	0	0	9	7
SO	26	30							38	30
SN	0	44							18	44
SP	27	0							27	0
SW	40								40	
Females										
N	196	197	0	201	0	0	204	0	-	-
R^2	56	53	0	3	0	0	3	0	-	-
LED	0	0	0	-17	0	0	18	0	-1	-4
SO	30	38							43	38
SD	0	24							8	24
SN	22	26							31	26
SW	35								35	

Norway

	S	SW	SO	SD	SN	SP	SF	SB	TES	TESW
N	196	196	226	205	226	0	227	0	-	-
R^2	73	56	5	3	8	0	2	0	-	-

Norway (continued)

	S	SW	SO	SD	SN	SP	SF	SB	TES	TESW
Pred										
Sex	8	0	-15	-18	-28	0	15	0	-11	-16
Age	-9	-13	0	0	0	0	0	0	-14	-13
WS	0	0	17	0	0	0	0	0	9	7
SO	35	40							50	40
SN	28	35							41	35
SP	0	15							6	15
SW	37								37	
Females										
N	121	121	0	0	0	0	141	0	-	-
R^2	78	63	0	0	0	0	3	0	-	-
Age	0	0	0	0	0	0	-19	0	0	0
SO	31	43							47	43
SN	32	36							45	36
SP	0	15							5	15
SW	36								36	

Norway, University of Oslo

	S	SW	SO	SD	SN	SP	SF	SB	TES	TESW
N	113	113	134	117	133	0	0	0	-	-
R^2	79	62	4	4	11	0	0	0	-	-
Pred										
Sex	0	0	-23	0	-33	0	0	0	-23	-15
WS	0	0	0	22	0	0	0	0	2	4
SO	34	37							50	37
SD	0	19							8	19
SN	25	20							33	20
SP	0	21							9	21
SW	42								42	

Philippines

	S	SW	SO	SD	SN	SP	SF	SB	TES	TESW
N	922	927	966	967	966	967	967	967	-	-
R^2	42	34	1	1	1	2	2	1	-	-
Pred										
Sex	0	7	-11	-9	-7	7	0	0	-3	1
Age	0	0	0	0	0	7	0	0	0	0
LED	0	0	0	0	8	8	-13	7	2	3
SO	26	37							40	37
SN	0	31							12	31
SB	16	0							16	0

Philippines (continued)

	S	SW	SO	SD	SN	SP	SF	SB	TES	TESW
SW	37								37	
Males										
N	297	300	0	0	0	314	0	0	-	-
R^2	51	37	0	0	0	1	0	0	-	-
Age	-9	0	0	0	0	0	0	0	-9	0
WS	0	0	0	0	0	12	0	0	0	0
ETH	0	11	0	0	0	0	0	0	3	11
SO	36	42							49	42
SN	0	26							8	26
SB	19	0							19	0
SW	30								30	
Females										
N	624	627	0	654	654	653	651	655	-	-
R^2	38	33	0	1	2	3	3	1	-	-
Age	0	0	0	0	0	9	0	0	0	0
LED	0	0	0	10	14	13	-16	12	4	5
ETH	0	0	0	0	0	0	9	0	0	0
SO	21	34							35	34
SN	0	33							13	33
SB	14	0							14	0
SW	40								40	

Philippines, De La Salle University

	S	SW	SO	SD	SN	SP	SF	SB	TES	TESW
N	293	296	0	0	306	306	304	304	-	-
R^2	50	44	0	0	2	1	3	3	-	-
Pred										
Sex	0	0	0	0	-14	0	15	0	-3	-3
WS	0	0	0	0	0	13	0	0	0	0
LED	-9	0	0	0	-12	0	12	-17	-13	-6
SO	30	28							38	28
SD	12	0							12	0
SN	13	35							24	35
SF	0	15							5	15
SB	0	23							7	23
SW	30								30	
Males										
N	138	141	146	0	0	147	0	145	-	-
R^2	51	38	2	0	0	4	0	3	-	-
WS	0	0	17	0	0	21	0	0	8	5
LED	0	0	0	0	0	0	0	-18	-1	-40

Philippines, De La Salle University (continued)

	S	SW	SO	SD	SN	SP	SF	SB	TES	TESW
SO	43	30							49	30
SN	25	30							31	30
SF	0	22							4	22
SB	0	22							4	22
SW	20								20	

Females

	S	SW	SO	SD	SN	SP	SF	SB	TES	TESW
N	154	154	0	157	0	0	0	158	-	-
R^2	53	51	0	2	0	0	0	2	-	-
LED	0	0	0	-17	0	0	0	-16	-6	-3
SO	0	23							13	23
SD	28	0							28	0
SN	0	31							17	31
SP	0	16							9	16
SB	0	18							10	18
SW	56								56	

Philippines, Philippine Normal College

	S	SW	SO	SD	SN	SP	SF	SB	TES	TESW
N	277	280	303	0	0	0	303	0	-	-
R^2	20	21	2	0	0	0	2	0	-	-
Pred										
Sex	0	15	0	0	0	0	-16	0	4	15
LED	0	0	14	0	0	0	0	0	3	3
SO	17	19							22	19
SN	0	41							12	41
SB	18	-16							15	-16
SW	28								28	

Females

	S	SW	SO	SD	SN	SP	SF	SB	TES	TESW
N	251	254	273	0	0	0	0	0	-	-
R^2	15	17	1	0	0	0	0	0	-	-
LED	0	0	13	0	0	0	0	0	2	0
SO	15	0							15	0
SN	0	42							11	42
SB	16	0							16	0
SW	25								25	

Philippines, University of the Philippines

	S	SW	SO	SD	SN	SP	SF	SB	TES	TESW
N	354	354	361	362	361	0	363	362	-	-
R^2	54	44	1	2	2	0	1	1	-	-

Philippines, University of the Philippines (continued)

	S	SW	SO	SD	SN	SP	SF	SB	TES	TESW
Pred										
Sex	0	12	-11	-13	-15	0	0	-13	-4	2
LED	0	0	0	0	0	0	-12	0	-1	0
SO	25	48							48	48
SN	0	17							8	17
SF	9	0							9	0
SB	16	13							22	13
SW	47								47	
Males										
N	135	135	0	140	0	0	141	0	-	-
R^2	48	40	0	3	0	0	4	0	-	-
WS	0	0	0	-19	0	0	0	0	0	0
LED	0	0	0	0	0	0	-22	0	0	0
SO	35	52							57	52
SB	0	18							8	18
SW	43								43	
Females										
N	219	219	0	0	0	0	0	0	-	-
R^2	58	45	0	0	0	0	0	0	-	-
SO	20	52							49	52
SN	0	22							12	22
SP	17	0							17	0
SF	15	0							15	0
SW	55								55	

Portugal, Technical University of Lisbon

	S	SW	SO	SD	SN	SP	SF	SB	TES	TESW
N	195	196	217	0	0	0	217	215	-	-
R^2	38	33	2	0	0	0	2	2	-	-
Pred										
Sex	0	0	0	0	0	0	-14	0	0	0
WS	0	0	0	0	0	0	0	14	0	0
LED	0	16	16	0	0	0	0	0	12	16
SO	24	0							24	0
SD	0	20							10	20
SN	0	35							18	35
SP	0	13							7	13
SW	51								51	
Males										
N	113	114	123	0	0	0	0	122	-	-
R^2	43	38	3	0	0	0	0	4	-	-

Portugal, Technical University of Lisbon (continued)

	S	SW	SO	SD	SN	SP	SF	SB	TES	TESW
WS	0	0	0	0	0	0	0	21	0	0
LED	0	26	19	0	0	0	0	0	19	26
SO	18	0							18	0
SD	0	27							16	27
SN	0	27							16	27
SP	0	17							10	17
SW	59								59	

Puerto Rico, University of Puerto Rico

	S	SW	SO	SD	SN	SP	SF	SB	TES	TESW
N	264	266	294	0	0	0	0	0	-	-
R^2	50	41	1	0	0	0	0	0	-	-
Pred										
Sex	0	0	-12	0	0	0	0	0	-5	-5
Age	0	-10	0	0	0	0	0	0	-5	-10
SO	27	38							45	38
SD	0	21							10	21
SP	0	20							9	20
SF	12	0							12	0
SB	11	0							11	0
SW	47								47	
Males										
N	147	147	0	0	0	0	0	0	-	-
R^2	52	39	0	0	0	0	0	0	-	-
ETH	0	-19	0	0	0	0	0	0	-10	-19
SO	34	44							56	44
SD	0	28							14	28
SF	15	0							15	0
SW	50								50	
Females										
N	117	119	0	0	0	0	0	0	-	-
R^2	43	45	0	0	0	0	0	0	-	-
SO	26	35							43	35
SD	0	18							9	18
SP	0	29							14	29
SW	48								48	

Singapore, National University of Singapore

	S	SW	SO	SD	SN	SP	SF	SB	TES	TESW
N	238	239	253	252	0	0	253	0	-	-
R^2	58	53	1	1	0	0	3	0	-	-

Singapore, National University of Singapore (continued)

	S	SW	SO	SD	SN	SP	SF	SB	TES	TESW
Pred										
Sex	0	12	-13	-13	0	0	0	0	-4	5
Age	12	0	0	0	0	0	0	0	12	0
LED	0	0	0	0	0	0	18	0	0	0
ETH	9	0	0	0	0	0	0	0	9	0
SO	31	51							51	51
SD	16	0							16	0
SN	0	32							13	32
SW	39								39	
Females										
N	198	198	0	0	0	0	210	0	-	-
R^2	57	55	0	0	0	0	4	0	-	-
Age	13	0	0	0	0	0	0	0	13	0
LED	0	0	0	0	0	0	21	0	0	0
SO	28	48							49	48
SD	14	0							14	0
SN	0	35							15	35
SW	43								43	

Republic of South Africa, University of Zululand

	S	SW	SO	SD	SN	SP	SF	SB	TES	TESW
N	238	243	0	0	0	0	281	0	-	-
R^2	29	22	0	0	0	0	1	0	-	-
Pred										
LED	0	0	0	0	0	0	12	0	0	0
SO	27	34							36	34
SP	17	22							23	22
SW	27								27	
Males										
N	116	118	0	0	0	0	0	0	-	-
R^2	29	15	0	0	0	0	0	0	-	-
SO	29	40							44	40
SW	37								37	
Females										
N	122	125	0	0	0	0	0	0	-	-
R^2	24	32	0	0	0	0	0	0	-	-
Age	0	15	0	0	0	0	0	0	0	15
SO	36	33							36	33
SP	26	28							26	28
SF	0	-16							0	-16

Spain, University of Madrid

Pred	S	SW	SO	SD	SN	SP	SF	SB	TES	TESW
N	234	236	259	249	253	0	0	0	-	-
R^2	51	43	2	2	2	0	0	0	-	-
Sex	-11	0	0	-15	0	0	0	0	-13	-3
LED	0	15	0	0	0	0	0	0	7	15
ETH	0	-21	15	0	17	0	0	0	-2	-11
SO	23	39							42	39
SD	0	21							10	21
SN	0	26							13	26
SB	14	0							14	0
SW	49								49	

Males

	S	SW	SO	SD	SN	SP	SF	SB	TES	TESW
N	117	119	0	0	129	0	0	0	-	-
R^2	57	44	0	0	4	0	0	0	-	-
Age	0	23	0	0	0	0	0	0	12	23
ETH	0	-43	0	0	23	0	0	0	-18	-35
SO	36	30							51	30
SD	0	20							10	20
SN	0	36							18	36
SW	51								51	

Females

	S	SW	SO	SD	SN	SP	SF	SB	TES	TESW
N	117	117	0	125	0	0	0	0	-	-
R^2	50	42	0	4	0	0	0	0	-	-
LED	0	0	0	21	0	0	0	0	3	7
SO	0	51							22	51
SD	0	34							15	34
SN	28	0							28	0
SB	17	0							17	0
SW	44								44	

Sweden, University of Uppsala

Pred	S	SW	SO	SD	SN	SP	SF	SB	TES	TESW
N	201	201	255	0	255	0	0	0	-	-
R^2	72	56	2	0	4	0	0	0	-	-
Sex	0	0	-15	0	-15	0	0	0	-11	-12
LED	0	0	0	0	-18	0	0	0	-4	-7
SO	34	37							54	37
SN	0	41							22	41
SP	10	0							10	0
SB	0	13							7	13

Sweden, University of Uppsala (continued)

	S	SW	SO	SD	SN	SP	SF	SB	TES	TESW
SW	53								53	
Males										
N	103	103	0	0	133	0	0	0	-	-
R^2	72	53	0	0	6	0	0	0	-	-
LED	0	0	0	0	-26	0	0	0	-8	-14
SO	40	27							55	27
SN	0	55							31	55
SW	56								56	
Females										
N	98	98	0	0	0	0	108	0	-	-
R^2	72	55	0	0	0	0	5	0	-	-
ETH	0	0	0	0	0	0	-24	0	3	0
SO	34	50							61	50
SN	0	38							21	38
SF	-14	0							-14	0
SW	54								54	

Switzerland, University of Freiburg

	S	SW	SO	SD	SN	SP	SF	SB	TES	TESW
N	299	300	334	311	0	0	0	0	-	-
R^2	66	57	2	2	0	0	0	0	-	-
Pred										
Sex	0	0	-15	-12	0	0	0	0	-8	-5
ETH	0	0	0	-11	0	0	0	0	-1	0
SO	27	32							45	32
SD	11	0							11	0
SN	0	33							19	33
SF	0	11							6	11
SB	0	19							11	19
SW	56								56	
Males										
N	152	152	0	158	0	0	0	0	-	-
R^2	74	64	0	2	0	0	0	0	-	-
ETH	0	0	0	-16	0	0	0	0	0	0
SO	31	34							49	34
SN	0	34							18	34
SP	13	0							13	0
SF	0	19							10	19
SB	0	13							7	13
SW	52								52	

Switzerland, University of Freiburg (continued)

	S	SW	SO	SD	SN	SP	SF	SB	TES	TESW
Females										
N	147	148	0	0	0	0	0	0	-	-
R^2	56	49	0	0	0	0	0	0	-	-
SO	22	23							36	23
SN	0	28							17	28
SP	0	18							11	18
SB	0	22							13	22
SW	60								60	

Taiwan

	S	SW	SO	SD	SN	SP	SF	SB	TES	TESW
N	2304	2315	2408	0	2455	2453	2428	0	-	-
R^2	46	34	1	0	1	1	1	0	-	-
Pred										
Sex	-6	0	-10	0	-6	-7	0	0	-11	-4
Age	0	0	0	0	0	0	-8	0	-1	-1
WS	-4	0	0	0	0	0	0	0	-4	0
ETH	0	0	0	0	5	5	-8	0	1	1
SO	29	27							39	27
SD	5	18							12	18
SN	0	12							5	12
SP	7	12							12	12
SF	-4	-8							-7	-8
SB	4	4							6	4
SW	38								38	
Males										
N	1189	1194	0	0	0	0	1253	0	-	-
R^2	44	29	0	0	0	0	2	0	-	-
Age	0	5	0	0	0	0	-10	0	2	4
SO	31	27							41	27
SD	6	16							12	16
SN	0	15							6	15
SP	10	7							13	7
SF	0	-7							-3	-7
SB	0	6							2	6
SW	38								38	
Females										
N	1115	1121	1161	0	0	0	0	1187	-	-
R^2	46	39	1	0	0	0	0	1	-	-
WS	-5	0	0	0	0	0	0	0	-5	0
LED	0	0	6	0	0	0	0	6	2	1

Taiwan (continued)

	S	SW	SO	SD	SN	SP	SF	SB	TES	TESW
SO	28	24							38	24
SD	0	22							9	22
SN	9	10							13	10
SP	8	19							16	19
SF	0	-10							-4	-10
SW	40								40	

Tanzania, University of Dar Es Salaam

	S	SW	SO	SD	SN	SP	SF	SB	TES	TESW
N	185	188	216	216	216	219	211	218	-	-
R^2	61	63	2	5	3	2	6	2	-	-
Pred										
Age	-17	0	0	0	0	0	0	-16	-17	0
WS	0	0	0	0	0	-16	18	0	-3	-3
LED	22	15	-17	-24	-18	0	15	0	16	3
SO	43	68							63	68
SP	14	19							20	19
SW	30								30	
Males										
N	127	130	0	147	0	0	145	0	-	-
R^2	52	66	0	4	0	0	3	0	-	-
WS	0	0	0	0	0	0	19	0	0	0
LED	0	14	0	-22	0	0	0	0	3	11
SO	48	75							69	75
SD	0	16							5	16
SW	28								28	

Thailand

	S	SW	SO	SD	SN	SP	SF	SB	TES	TESW
N	556	558	0	0	578	0	578	578	-	-
R^2	37	33	0	0	1	0	29	18	-	-
Pred										
Age	-10	0	0	0	0	0	-53	39	-10	0
LED	0	0	0	0	-10	0	8	-19	-1	-1
SO	18	45							37	45
SN	0	12							5	12
SP	9	9							13	9
SW	43								43	
Males										
N	253	254	0	266	263	0	262	265	-	-
R^2	38	43	0	2	4	0	24	15	-	-

Thailand (continued)

	S	SW	SO	SD	SN	SP	SF	SB	TES	TESW
Age	0	0	0	0	0	0	-45	33	-2	-4
LED	0	0	0	-14	-20	0	15	-18	-1	-6
SO	16	52							43	52
SN	0	20							10	20
SB	0	-11							-6	-11
SW	51								51	

Females

	S	SW	SO	SD	SN	SP	SF	SB	TES	TESW
N	303	304	311	0	0	0	316	313	-	-
R^2	35	23	1	0	0	0	35	21	-	-
Age	-15	0	-13	0	0	0	-59	46	-20	-5
LED	0	0	0	0	0	0	0	-22	0	0
SO	26	40							42	40
SP	0	15							6	15
SW	39								39	

Thailand, Chiang Mai University

	S	SW	SO	SD	SN	SP	SF	SB	TES	TESW
N	282	283	287	0	289	0	289	289	-	-
R^2	35	33	4	0	1	0	1	2	-	-
Pred										
Sex	0	0	-20	0	-13	0	0	0	-4	-8
Age	0	0	0	0	0	0	-13	0	0	0
LED	0	0	0	0	0	0	0	-25	0	0
ETH	0	0	0	0	0	0	0	17	0	0
SO	0	39							18	39
SD	0	12							6	12
SP	22	17							30	17
SW	47								47	

Males

	S	SW	SO	SD	SN	SP	SF	SB	TES	TESW
N	125	125	0	127	0	127	0	0	-	-
R^2	43	36	0	3	0	6	0	0	-	-
LED	0	0	0	-20	0	-24	0	0	-6	0
ETH	0	0	0	0	0	35	0	0	9	0
SO	0	53							28	53
SP	25	0							25	0
SF	0	-17							-9	-17
SW	52								52	

Females

	S	SW	SO	SD	SN	SP	SF	SB	TES	TESW
N	157	158	0	0	0	0	163	0	-	-
R^2	27	30	0	0	0	0	4	0	-	-
Age	0	0	0	0	0	0	-22	0	0	0

Thailand, Chiang Mai University (continued)

	S	SW	SO	SD	SN	SP	SF	SB	TES	TESW
SO	0	28							12	28
SD	0	18							7	18
SP	20	23							29	23
SW	41								41	

Thailand, University of Srinakharinwirot

	S	SW	SO	SD	SN	SP	SF	SB	TES	TESW
N	274	275	0	0	289	0	0	0	-	-
R^2	39	33	0	0	1	0	0	0	-	-
Pred										
LED	0	0	0	0	-12	0	0	0	-1	-2
SO	31	50							52	50
SN	0	14							6	14
SW	41								41	
Males										
N	128	129	0	0	137	0	0	0	-	-
R^2	36	50	0	0	5	0	0	0	-	-
LED	0	0	0	0	-24	0	0	0	-3	-4
SO	0	53							32	53
SN	0	18							11	18
SF	0	15							9	15
SW	60								60	
Females										
N	146	146	0	0	0	0	0	151	-	-
R^2	44	20	0	0	0	0	0	2	-	-
LED	0	0	0	0	0	0	0	-17	0	0
SO	42	45							58	45
SW	36								36	

Turkey, University of Uludag

	S	SW	SO	SD	SN	SP	SF	SB	TES	TESW
N	283	284	0	285	0	0	287	0	-	-
R^2	39	34	0	1	0	0	2	0	-	-
Pred										
Age	13	0	0	0	0	0	0	0	13	0
LED	0	0	0	-13	0	0	15	0	0	0
SO	32	36							46	36
SN	0	16							6	16
SP	0	20							8	20
SW	38								38	

Turkey, University of Uludag (continued)

	S	SW	SO	SD	SN	SP	SF	SB	TES	TESW
Males										
N	194	194	0	0	0	0	0	0	-	-
R^2	39	39	0	0	0	0	0	0	-	-
SO	26	32							39	32
SN	0	29							12	29
SP	0	18							7	18
SF	-13	0							-13	0
SW	41								41	

United Kingdom, University of York

	S	SW	SO	SD	SN	SP	SF	SB	TES	TESW
N	200	200	218	0	0	0	0	0	-	-
R^2	53	52	2	0	0	0	0	0	-	-
Pred										
Age	0	-14	0	0	0	0	0	0	-7	-14
LED	0	0	-16	0	0	0	0	0	-8	-7
SO	27	42							47	42
SN	0	33							16	33
SP	0	16							8	16
SB	14	0							14	0
SW	48								48	
Males										
N	96	96	103	100	101	0	0	0	-	-
R^2	57	55	6	9	6	0	0	0	-	-
WS	0	0	0	-31	-25	0	0	0	-3	-8
LED	0	-18	-26	0	0	0	0	0	-22	-31
SO	33	48							55	48
SN	0	30							14	30
SP	-18	0							-18	0
SB	24	0							24	0
SW	45								45	
Females										
N	104	104	0	110	0	0	0	0	-	-
R^2	51	49	0	3	0	0	0	0	-	-
Age	0	-17	0	0	0	0	0	0	-9	-17
ETH	0	0	0	-19	0	0	0	0	0	0
SO	23	33							40	33
SN	0	39							20	39
SP	15	22							26	22
SW	50								50	

United States of America

	S	SW	SO	SD	SN	SP	SF	SB	TES	TESW
N	1243	1249	1325	1304	1323	0	1314	1315	-	-
R^2	63	56	2	2	2	0	1	1	-	-
Pred										
Sex	0	0	-8	-13	-15	0	9	0	-7	-8
Age	0	0	0	7	0	0	0	7	1	1
WS	0	0	0	0	0	0	0	6	1	1
LED	0	4	10	0	0	0	0	0	7	9
ETH	0	0	0	-10	0	0	7	0	0	0
SO	34	50							54	50
SN	9	20							17	20
SP	0	9							4	9
SF	0	-6							-2	-6
SB	9	8							12	8
SW	39								39	

Males

	S	SW	SO	SD	SN	SP	SF	SB	TES	TESW
N	428	429	0	457	0	0	461	0	-	-
R^2	56	50	0	1	0	0	1	0	-	-
ETH	0	0	0	-10	0	0	12	0	0	0
SO	43	49							58	49
SN	0	16							5	16
SP	0	19							6	19
SB	15	0							15	0
SW	30								30	

Females

	S	SW	SO	SD	SN	SP	SF	SB	TES	TESW
N	814	820	860	847	861	0	0	857	-	-
R^2	66	58	1	1	1	0	0	2	-	-
Age	-6	0	0	0	0	0	0	10	-5	1
WS	0	0	0	8	9	0	0	9	3	3
LED	0	0	12	0	0	0	0	0	7	6
SO	31	53							55	53
SN	12	21							22	21
SF	0	-7							-3	-7
SB	8	13							14	13
SW	45								45	

USA, Arizona State University

	S	SW	SO	SD	SN	SP	SF	SB	TES	TESW
N	197	199	0	209	0	0	0	0	-	-
R^2	69	60	0	6	0	0	0	0	-	-
Pred										
Sex	0	0	0	-19	0	0	0	0	0	0

USA, Arizona State University (continued)

	S	SW	SO	SD	SN	SP	SF	SB	TES	TESW
LED	0	0	0	14	0	0	0	0	0	0
ETH	-11	0	0	0	0	0	0	0	-11	0
SO	33	64							68	64
SN	0	12							7	12
SB	0	12							7	12
SW	55								55	

Females

	S	SW	SO	SD	SN	SP	SF	SB	TES	TESW
N	144	146	0	153	0	0	154	158	-	-
R^2	69	59	0	2	0	0	3	3	-	-
Age	0	0	0	0	0	0	-19	0	0	0
WS	0	0	0	0	0	0	0	20	4	3
LED	0	0	0	16	0	0	0	0	0	0
ETH	-15	0	0	0	0	0	0	0	-15	0
SO	30	68							65	68
SB	11	16							19	16
SW	52								52	

USA, Cornell University

	S	SW	SO	SD	SN	SP	SF	SB	TES	TESW
N	97	97	0	0	0	0	108	0	-	-
R^2	66	64	0	0	0	0	11	0	-	-
Pred										
Age	0	0	0	0	0	0	-34	0	3	5
SO	0	39							28	39
SD	0	26							19	26
SP	0	21							15	21
SF	0	-14							-10	-14
SB	17	0							17	0
SW	71								71	

USA, Edison Community College

	S	SW	SO	SD	SN	SP	SF	SB	TES	TESW
N	136	136	0	0	142	0	0	0	-	-
R^2	59	46	0	0	2	0	0	0	-	-
Pred										
Sex	-13	0	0	0	-17	0	0	0	-15	-4
SO	17	52							39	52
SD	17	0							17	0
SN	0	25							11	25
SB	19	0							19	0
SW	43								43	

USA, Edison Community College (continued)

	S	SW	SO	SD	SN	SP	SF	SB	TES	TESW
Females										
N	93	93	0	0	0	0	0	0	-	-
R^2	59	47	0	0	0	0	0	0	-	-
WS	16	0	0	0	0	0	0	0	16	0
SO	24	53							46	53
SN	20	24							30	24
SW	42								42	

USA, University of Illinois

	S	SW	SO	SD	SN	SP	SF	SB	TES	TESW
N	264	263	0	276	274	274	273	0	-	-
R^2	68	58	0	3	2	1	3	0	-	-
Pred										
Age	0	0	0	0	0	-12	0	0	0	0
ETH	0	0	0	-17	-15	0	18	0	-1	-4
SO	50	54							66	54
SN	0	29							8	29
SB	13	0							13	0
SW	29								29	
Males										
N	118	119	0	128	0	126	0	0	-	-
R^2	63	49	0	3	0	4	0	0	-	-
Age	0	0	0	0	0	-21	0	0	0	0
ETH	0	0	0	-18	0	0	0	0	0	0
SO	70	51							70	51
SN	0	28							0	28
SB	17	0							17	0
Females										
N	144	144	0	0	148	0	147	0	-	-
R^2	70	63	0	0	2	0	5	0	-	-
ETH	0	0	0	0	-17	0	23	0	-2	-5
SO	45	56							70	56
SN	0	30							13	30
SW	44								44	

USA, Ohio State University, Newark

	S	SW	SO	SD	SN	SP	SF	SB	TES	TESW
N	255	256	268	264	268	0	0	0	-	-
R^2	58	53	7	3	3	0	0	0	-	-
Pred										
Sex	0	0	-20	-17	-18	0	0	0	-15	-14

USA, Ohio State University, Newark (continued)

	S	SW	SO	SD	SN	SP	SF	SB	TES	TESW
Age	0	0	22	0	0	0	0	0	12	11
LED	-10	0	0	0	0	0	0	0	-10	0
SO	41	49							55	49
SN	17	22							23	22
SF	0	-11							-3	-11
SB	0	13							4	13
SW	29								29	

Males

	S	SW	SO	SD	SN	SP	SF	SB	TES	TESW
N	122	122	0	0	129	0	0	0	-	-
R^2	52	52	0	0	6	0	0	0	-	-
Age	0	0	0	0	-23	0	0	0	0	-4
LED	0	0	0	0	19	0	0	0	0	4
SO	66	45							66	45
SN	0	19							0	19
SP	0	23							0	23
SF	-20	0							-20	0

Females

	S	SW	SO	SD	SN	SP	SF	SB	TES	TESW
N	133	134	139	0	0	138	0	137	-	-
R^2	63	54	6	0	0	2	0	2	-	-
Age	0	0	26	0	0	17	0	18	14	16
LED	-12	0	0	0	0	0	0	0	-12	0
SO	30	50							50	50
SN	18	22							27	22
SB	0	18							7	18
SW	40								40	

USA, Sangamon State University

	S	SW	SO	SD	SN	SP	SF	SB	TES	TESW
N	138	140	0	0	0	0	0	0	-	-
R^2	50	50	0	0	0	0	0	0	-	-
Pred										
SO	41	49							59	49
SP	0	29							11	29
SW	37								37	

USA, Smith College (Females)

	S	SW	SO	SD	SN	SP	SF	SB	TES	TESW
N	158	158	0	0	0	0	0	162	-	-
R^2	70	64	0	0	0	0	0	3	-	-
Pred										
Age	0	0	0	0	0	0	0	18	2	3

262

USA, Smith College (Females) (continued)

	S	SW	SO	SD	SN	SP	SF	SB	TES	TESW
SO	28	52							55	52
SN	15	26							28	26
SF	0	-11							-6	-11
SB	0	16							8	16
SW	51								51	

Yugoslavia, University of Zagreb

	S	SW	SO	SD	SN	SP	SF	SB	TES	TESW
N	275	277	319	0	0	310	0	312	-	-
R^2	51	35	2	0	0	3	0	3	-	-
Pred										
Age	0	0	0	0	0	0	0	-17	-2	0
LED	-15	0	-13	0	0	-19	0	0	-21	-7
ETH	0	0	0	0	0	15	0	0	0	0
SO	31	53							47	53
SD	16	15							21	15
SB	10	0							10	0
SW	31								31	
Males										
N	146	147	170	0	0	167	0	170	-	-
R^2	49	35	2	0	0	6	0	2	-	-
LED	-19	0	-15	0	0	-21	0	-17	27	-9
ETH	0	0	0	0	0	25	0	0	0	0
SO	36	60							53	60
SD	18	0							18	0
SW	29								29	
Females										
N	129	130	0	146	141	0	0	142	-	-
R^2	51	33	0	3	11	0	0	3	-	-
Age	0	0	0	0	0	0	0	-19	0	0
WS	-14	0	0	0	0	0	0	0	-14	0
SO	33	48							49	48
SD	17	19							24	19
SW	34								34	

Appendix 6 Results of regressions using MDT to explain happiness and satisfaction in all domains for married students, males and females (decimal points omitted)

Satisfaction and Happiness with Life as a Whole

	S	H	SW	SO	SD	SN	SP	SF	SB	TES	TEH	TESW
N	652	646	659	749	0	745	0	732	739	-	-	-
R^2	57	55	46	1	0	2	0	1	1	-	-	-
Pred												
Sex	0	0	9	12	0	14	0	7	0	10	6	15
WS	0	0	0	0	0	0	0	0	-11	-2	-5	-2
LED	0	-9	0	0	0	0	0	9	0	0	-9	-1
ETH	-8	-6	0	0	0	0	0	0	0	-8	-6	0
SO	20	20	34							35	30	34
SN	8	0	14							14	4	14
SP	9	0	16							16	5	16
SF	0	0	-9							-4	-3	-9
SB	11	40	17							19	45	17
SW	44	28								44	28	

Males

	S	H	SW	SO	SD	SN	SP	SF	SB	TES	TEH	TESW
N	342	341	345	0	0	391	0	380	0	-	-	-
R^2	62	59	50	0	0	1	0	3	0	-	-	-
WS	0	0	0	0	0	10	0	0	0	1	0	2
LED	0	-8	0	0	0	0	0	17	0	-1	-8	-2
ETH	-13	0	0	0	0	0	0	0	0	-13	0	0
SO	21	17	36							38	26	36
SD	0	8	0							0	8	0
SN	0	0	15							7	4	15
SP	10	0	22							20	6	22
SF	0	0	-9							-4	-2	-9
SB	16	44	13							22	47	13
SW	46	25								46	25	

Females

	S	H	SW	SO	SD	SN	SP	SF	SB	TES	TEH	TESW
N	310	305	314	0	0	0	0	0	351	-	-	-
R^2	52	50	40	0	0	0	0	0	2	-	-	-
WS	0	0	0	0	0	0	0	0	-15	-1	-6	-3
LED	0	-9	0	0	0	0	0	0	0	0	-9	0
SO	27	21	30							41	30	30
SD	0	0	14							6	4	14
SN	14	0	0							14	0	0
SP	0	0	12							6	4	12
SF	0	0	-10							-5	-3	-10
SB	0	35	21							10	41	21

Satisfaction and Happiness with Life as a Whole (continued)

	S	H	SW	SO	SD	SN	SP	SF	SB	TES	TEH	TESW
SW	46	29								46		29

Satisfaction with One's Health

	S	SW	SO	SD	SN	SP	SF	SB	TES	TESW
N	681	686	0	0	0	768	0	0	-	-
R^2	52	39	0	0	0	1	0	0	-	-
Pred										
Sex	0	6	0	0	0	0	0	0	3	6
ETH	-8	0	0	0	0	8	0	0	-7	1
SO	24	36							41	36
SD	7	11							12	11
SN	10	16							18	16
SP	0	15							7	15
SW	47								47	

Males

	S	SW	SO	SD	SN	SP	SF	SB	TES	TESW
N	354	356	0	0	0	401	0	0	-	-
R^2	50	34	0	0	0	2	0	0	-	-
LED	0	0	0	0	0	-13	0	0	-1	-2
ETH	0	0	0	0	0	10	0	0	1	2
SO	23	35							40	35
SD	0	12							6	12
SN	13	14							20	14
SP	0	15							7	15
SW	49								49	

Females

	S	SW	SO	SD	SN	SP	SF	SB	TES	TESW
N	327	330	0	0	0	0	0	0	-	-
R^2	55	42	0	0	0	0	0	0	-	-
Age	9	0	0	0	0	0	0	0	9	0
ETH	-12	0	0	0	0	0	0	0	-12	0
SO	23	38							40	38
SD	10	11							15	11
SN	10	18							18	18
SP	0	14							6	14
SW	45								45	

Satisfaction with One's Finances

	S	SW	SO	SD	SN	SP	SF	SB	TES	TESW
N	693	697	763	753	768	763	753	764	-	-
R^2	63	55	4	3	3	2	1	3	-	-
Pred										
Sex	0	0	16	16	16	12	0	10	14	13

Satisfaction with One's Finances (continued)

	S	SW	SO	SD	SN	SP	SF	SB	TES	TESW
Age	0	6	0	0	0	0	0	0	3	6
WS	0	0	13	0	0	9	0	10	7	7
LED	0	0	9	9	0	0	8	11	6	4
SO	23	43							41	43
SD	10	0							10	0
SN	11	30							23	30
SP	0	14							6	14
SB	11	0							11	0
SW	41								41	
Males										
N	365	366	399	399	404	400	394	402	-	-
R^2	61	51	6	1	2	2	2	5	-	-
Age	0	8	0	0	0	0	0	0	3	8
WS	0	0	23	12	16	14	0	19	18	17
LED	0	0	12	0	0	0	15	14	8	7
ETH	0	0	11	0	0	0	0	0	5	5
SO	26	43							44	43
SD	15	0							15	0
SN	0	29							12	29
SB	15	13							21	13
SW	42								42	
Females										
N	328	331	0	0	0	363	0	0	-	-
R^2	64	57	0	0	0	1	0	0	-	-
Age	9	0	0	0	0	0	0	0	9	0
LED	0	0	0	0	0	12	0	0	2	2
SO	20	44							38	44
SN	20	29							32	29
SP	12	16							19	16
SW	41								41	

Satisfaction with One's Family Relations

	S	SW	SO	SD	SN	SP	SF	SB	TES	TESW
N	672	680	758	0	0	0	747	0	-	-
R^2	53	48	1	0	0	0	1	0	-	-
Pred										
Sex	0	0	0	0	0	0	9	0	0	0
WS	0	0	0	0	0	0	8	0	0	0
ETH	-7	0	-9	0	0	0	0	0	-11	-4
SO	24	49							44	49
SD	7	11							11	11

Satisfaction with One's Family Relations (continued)

	S	SW	SO	SD	SN	SP	SF	SB	TES	TESW
SN	8	0							8	0
SP	0	22							9	22
SB	8	0							8	0
SW	40								40	
Males										
N	349	353	0	0	0	0	391	0	-	-
R^2	48	41	0	0	0	0	1	0	-	-
LED	0	0	0	0	0	0	10	0	0	0
SO	30	53							51	53
SN	13	0							13	0
SP	0	19							7	19
SW	39								39	
Females										
N	323	327	363	0	0	0	0	362	-	-
R^2	58	54	1	0	0	0	0	1	-	-
LED	9	0	0	0	0	0	0	12	9	0
ETH	-8	0	-13	0	0	0	0	0	-13	-6
SO	21	48							42	48
SD	11	13							17	13
SP	14	26							25	26
SW	43								43	

Satisfaction with One's Paid Employment

	S	SW	SO	SD	SN	SP	SF	SB	TES	TESW
N	435	458	553	544	554	577	619	571	-	-
R^2	63	53	9	3	5	5	1	7	-	-
Pred										
Sex	0	0	0	12	0	0	0	0	0	0
Age	0	0	12	0	0	0	0	0	5	5
WS	0	0	26	16	24	22	0	27	23	23
LED	0	0	0	0	0	0	11	0	1	0
ETH	-8	0	0	0	0	0	0	0	-8	0
SO	25	40							42	40
SN	17	22							27	22
SP	0	10							4	10
SF	7	0							7	0
SB	8	19							16	19
SW	43								43	
Males										
N	261	271	322	320	327	339	348	331	-	-
R^2	60	49	14	7	13	6	2	14	-	-

Satisfaction with One's Paid Employment (continued)

	S	SW	SO	SD	SN	SP	SF	SB	TES	TESW
Age	0	0	20	0	0	0	0	0	10	10
WS	0	0	30	26	36	25	0	37	27	28
LED	0	0	0	0	0	0	17	0	0	0
ETH	-9	0	0	0	0	0	-11	0	-9	0
SO	26	49							50	49
SN	14	19							23	19
SB	0	18							9	18
SW	49								49	

Females

	S	SW	SO	SD	SN	SP	SF	SB	TES	TESW
N	174	187	231	0	0	238	0	240	-	-
R^2	67	60	5	0	0	3	0	2	-	-
WS	14	0	23	0	0	18	0	14	25	12
SO	21	28							30	28
SN	27	28							36	28
SP	0	18							6	18
SF	0	-11							-4	-11
SB	14	16							19	16
SW	32								32	

Satisfaction with One's Friendships

	S	SW	SO	SD	SN	SP	SF	SB	TES	TESW
N	694	698	0	0	762	0	751	0	-	-
R^2	53	43	0	0	1	0	1	0	-	-
Pred										
Sex	0	0	0	0	8	0	0	0	1	1
WS	0	0	0	0	0	0	10	0	0	0
LED	0	0	0	0	-10	0	0	0	-2	-1
ETH	-9	0	0	0	0	0	0	0	-9	0
SO	30	45							47	45
SN	11	10							15	10
SP	0	12							5	12
SB	9	11							13	11
SW	38								38	

Males

	S	SW	SO	SD	SN	SP	SF	SB	TES	TESW
N	364	366	0	0	402	0	389	403	-	-
R^2	57	47	0	0	1	0	1	1	-	-
WS	0	9	0	0	0	0	0	12	4	11
LED	0	0	0	0	-10	0	0	0	-2	-1
ETH	-9	0	0	0	0	0	-10	0	-9	0
SO	40	49							56	49
SN	14	14							19	14

Satisfaction with One's Friendships (continued)

	S	SW	SO	SD	SN	SP	SF	SB	TES	TESW
SB	0	17							6	17
SW	33								33	
Females										
N	330	332	0	0	0	0	362	0	-	-
R^2	49	39	0	0	0	0	1	0	-	-
WS	0	0	0	0	0	0	11	0	0	0
ETH	-10	-11	0	0	0	0	0	0	-15	-11
SO	19	47							39	47
SP	11	23							21	23
SB	12	0							12	0
SW	43								43	

Satisfaction with One's Housing

	S	SW	SO	SD	SN	SP	SF	SB	TES	TESW
N	694	700	764	759	764	770	0	764	-	-
R^2	65	53	4	3	4	4	0	2	-	-
Pred										
Sex	0	0	13	15	16	15	0	9	12	12
Age	0	6	0	0	0	0	0	0	2	6
WS	0	0	0	0	7	0	0	0	1	1
LED	0	0	14	11	11	13	0	7	11	11
ETH	-6	0	0	0	0	0	0	-8	-6	0
SO	29	47							46	47
SD	0	9							3	9
SN	13	15							18	15
SP	15	11							19	11
SW	36								36	
Males										
N	365	368	402	398	404	403	394	402	-	-
R^2	68	52	4	3	3	2	1	1	-	-
WS	0	0	14	16	16	11	0	13	12	11
LED	0	0	17	12	11	10	11	0	11	12
ETH	-7	0	0	0	0	0	0	0	-7	0
SO	31	46							49	46
SN	0	22							9	22
SP	16	14							22	14
SB	11	0							11	0
SW	40								40	
Females										
N	329	332	362	361	360	367	0	0	-	-
R^2	62	52	1	1	1	2	0	0	-	-

Satisfaction with One's Housing (continued)

	S	SW	SO	SD	SN	SP	SF	SB	TES	TESW
Age	0	8	0	0	0	0	0	0	3	8
LED	9	0	12	12	12	16	0	0	20	9
SO	26	59							44	59
SD	11	19							17	19
SN	13	0							13	0
SP	11	0							11	0
SF	7	0							7	0
SW	31								31	

Satisfaction with One's Recreation Activity

	S	SW	SO	SD	SN	SP	SF	SB	TES	TESW
N	672	682	0	0	0	0	739	0	-	-
R^2	56	53	0	0	0	0	1	0	-	-
Pred										
LED	0	0	0	0	0	0	10	0	1	0
ETH	-6	0	0	0	0	0	0	0	-6	0
SO	28	41							47	41
SD	0	9							4	9
SN	13	20							22	20
SP	0	7							3	7
SF	6	0							6	0
SB	0	11							5	11
SW	45								45	
Males										
N	348	357	397	0	0	401	385	0	-	-
R^2	59	52	2	0	0	1	1	0	-	-
LED	0	0	15	0	0	0	12	0	8	7
ETH	-8	0	0	0	0	10	0	0	-8	0
SO	31	45							52	45
SD	11	12							17	12
SN	0	18							9	18
SB	7	11							12	11
SW	47								47	
Females										
N	324	325	0	356	0	0	0	0	-	-
R^2	53	55	0	1	0	0	0	0	-	-
LED	0	0	0	-11	0	0	0	0	0	0
ETH	0	11	0	0	0	0	0	0	4	11
SO	25	40							41	40
SN	20	26							30	26
SP	0	10							4	10

Satisfaction with One's Recreation Activity (continued)

	S	SW	SO	SD	SN	SP	SF	SB	TES	TESW
SB	0	13							5	13
SW	39								39	

Satisfaction with One's Religion

	S	SW	SO	SD	SN	SP	SF	SB	TES	TESW
N	529	533	0	609	622	631	619	637	-	-
R^2	63	50	0	1	1	2	2	1	-	-
Pred										
WS	0	0	0	0	0	0	11	0	0	0
LED	0	0	0	0	0	0	11	0	0	0
ETH	0	0	0	9	11	15	0	10	4	5
SO	33	44							53	44
SN	0	25							12	25
SP	12	12							18	12
SW	46								46	
Males										
N	273	274	0	0	324	326	317	0	-	-
R^2	68	51	0	0	1	3	5	0	-	-
LED	0	0	0	0	0	0	16	0	0	0
ETH	0	0	0	0	11	18	-16	0	5	6
SO	35	42							51	42
SN	0	25							10	25
SP	15	16							21	16
SB	10	0							10	0
SW	38								38	
Females										
N	256	259	0	290	0	0	302	307	-	-
R^2	60	49	0	2	0	0	1	1	-	-
WS	0	-10	0	0	0	0	13	0	-5	-10
ETH	0	0	0	15	0	0	0	13	0	0
SO	33	48							58	48
SN	0	29							15	29
SW	52								52	

Satisfaction with One's Self-Esteem

	S	SW	SO	SD	SN	SP	SF	SB	TES	TESW
N	665	670	0	0	0	0	733	0	-	-
R^2	56	42	0	0	0	0	2	0	-	-
Pred										
WS	0	0	0	0	0	0	12	0	0	0
LED	0	-7	0	0	0	0	11	0	-3	-7

Satisfaction with One's Self-Esteem (continued)

	S	SW	SO	SD	SN	SP	SF	SB	TES	TESW
ETH	-8	0	0	0	0	0	0	0	-8	0
SO	31	46							51	46
SD	7	0							7	0
SN	0	27							12	27
SB	9	0							9	0
SW	43								43	

Males

	S	SW	SO	SD	SN	SP	SF	SB	TES	TESW
N	350	353	0	0	0	0	381	0	-	-
R^2	56	42	0	0	0	0	2	0	-	-
WS	0	0	0	0	0	0	12	0	0	0
LED	0	0	0	0	0	0	11	0	0	0
ETH	-7	0	0	0	0	0	0	0	-7	0
SO	35	46							54	46
SN	0	28							12	28
SP	11	0							11	0
SW	41								41	

Females

	S	SW	SO	SD	SN	SP	SF	SB	TES	TESW
N	315	317	0	0	0	0	352	0	-	-
R^2	55	40	0	0	0	0	2	0	-	-
WS	0	0	0	0	0	0	14	0	-	-
ETH	-10	0	0	0	0	0	0	0	-10	0
SO	27	46							49	46
SN	0	26							12	26
SB	13	0							13	0
SW	47								47	

Satisfaction with One's Transportation

	S	SW	SO	SD	SN	SP	SF	SB	TES	TESW
N	684	687	758	747	758	756	740	755	-	-
R^2	68	54	2	2	5	2	1	2	-	-
Pred										
Sex	0	0	11	12	17	9	0	11	11	10
Age	7	7	0	0	0	0	0	0	10	7
WS	0	-5	14	10	18	13	0	12	11	7
LED	0	0	0	0	0	0	8	0	0	0
ETH	-6	0	0	0	0	0	0	0	-6	0
SO	30	46							48	46
SN	18	17							25	17
SP	9	13							14	13
SF	5	-5							3	-5
SB	0	9							4	9

Satisfaction with One's Transportation (continued)

	S	SW	SO	SD	SN	SP	SF	SB	TES	TESW
SW	39								39	
Males										
N	355	357	398	395	401	396	0	397	-	-
R^2	67	49	6	4	7	3	0	6	-	-
WS	0	0	21	21	26	18	0	23	19	17
LED	0	0	15	0	0	0	0	12	6	6
SO	26	39							41	39
SN	22	19							29	19
SP	9	21							17	21
SF	0	-8							-3	-8
SW	39								39	
Females										
N	329	330	0	0	0	0	0	0	-	-
R^2	70	59	0	0	0	0	0	0	-	-
Age	10	11	0	0	0	0	0	0	14	11
ETH	-7	0	0	0	0	0	0	0	-7	0
SO	39	57							60	57
SN	17	17							23	17
SB	0	13							5	13
SW	37								37	

Satisfaction with One's University Education

	S	SW	SO	SD	SN	SP	SF	SB	TES	TESW
N	670	673	761	753	758	770	732	766	-	-
R^2	51	39	1	1	2	4	3	6	-	-
Pred										
Sex	0	0	0	8	10	0	0	0	1	2
Age	0	0	0	0	0	7	0	11	3	3
WS	6	0	0	0	0	0	9	-10	4	-2
LED	0	0	0	0	0	-9	14	-13	-4	-3
ETH	0	0	10	10	10	15	0	14	10	10
SO	23	32							37	32
SN	0	22							10	22
SP	14	11							19	11
SB	8	18							16	18
SW	45								45	
Males										
N	354	355	401	0	400	406	385	404	-	-
R^2	58	42	3	0	2	6	4	6	-	-
Age	0	0	0	0	14	0	0	12	2	2
WS	0	0	0	0	0	0	0	-10	-2	-2

Satisfaction with One's University Education (continued)

	S	SW	SO	SD	SN	SP	SF	SB	TES	TESW
LED	0	0	12	0	0	0	20	-11	5	5
ETH	0	0	13	0	0	24	0	15	11	10
SO	30	34							47	34
SD	0	17							8	17
SP	0	13							6	13
SF	0	-12							-6	-12
SB	12	17							20	17
SW	49								49	
Females										
N	316	318	0	359	358	364	347	362	-	-
R^2	42	36	0	2	2	1	1	5	-	-
Age	0	0	0	-10	-15	0	0	0	-2	-4
WS	10	0	0	0	0	0	12	0	12	0
LED	0	0	0	0	0	-11	0	-14	-3	-3
ETH	0	0	0	15	0	0	0	16	1	3
SO	19	31							32	31
SN	0	19							13	29
SP	20	0							20	0
SB	0	19							8	19
SW	43								43	

Appendix 7 Results of regressions using MDT to explain happiness and satisfaction in all domains for unmarried students, males and females (decimal points omitted)

Satisfaction and Happiness with Life as a Whole

	S	H	SW	SO	SD	SN	SP	SF	SB	TES	TEH	TESW
N	6995	6800	7076	0	7693	7789	7758	7696	7700	-	-	-
R^2	44	41	39	0	1	1	1	1	1	-	-	-
Pred												
Sex	-2	0	8	0	4	4	7	0	6	3	4	8
Age	-3	0	0	0	-9	-10	-6	5	-4	-7	-3	-4
WS	4	0	-2	0	0	0	4	0	-3	4	-1	0
LED	-4	-6	-2	0	0	0	0	4	0	-5	-7	-2
ETH	-3	0	4	0	0	4	6	-4	0	0	5	6
SO	19	20	29							30	27	29
SD	6	4	15							12	8	15
SN	5	5	16							11	9	16
SP	9	9	14							14	12	14
SF	0	0	-4							-2	-1	-4
SB	10	26	10							14	28	10
SW	37	23								37	23	
Males												
N	3543	3402	3586	0	3928	3974	3961	3923	3940	-	-	-
R^2	45	39	39	0	1	2	1	1	1	-	-	-
Age	-4	0	0	0	-9	-11	-8	6	-5	-8	-4	-5
WS	0	0	0	0	0	0	3	0	-5	0	-2	0
LED	0	-5	0	0	0	0	0	5	-3	0	-6	0
ETH	-3	0	6	0	6	6	7	-6	0	2	3	9
SO	21	20	29							32	27	29
SD	8	5	16							14	9	16
SN	0	0	16							6	4	16
SP	9	10	15							15	14	15
SF	0	0	-4							-2	-1	-4
SB	10	26	8							13	28	8
SW	38	23								38	23	
Females												
N	3452	3398	3490	0	3765	3815	3797	0	0	-	-	-
R^2	43	43	38	0	1	1	1	0	0	-	-	-
Age	-3	0	0	0	-9	-9	-5	0	0	-6	-2	-4
WS	7	0	-3	0	0	0	5	0	0	6	0	-2
LED	-6	-7	-3	0	0	0	0	0	0	-7	-8	-3
ETH	0	0	3	0	0	0	6	0	0	2	2	4
SO	17	20	29							28	26	29
SD	4	4	15							10	7	15
SN	9	9	15							15	12	15

Satisfaction and Happiness with Life as a Whole (continued)

	S	H	SW	SO	SD	SN	SP	SF	SB	TES	TEH	TESW
SP	9	10	13							14	13	13
SF	0	0	-4							-2	-1	-4
SB	10	25	12							14	28	12
SW	37	22								37	22	

Satisfaction with One's Health

	S	SW	SO	SD	SN	SP	SF	SB	TES	TESW
N	7339	7364	0	7752	7928	7867	7819	7914	-	-
R^2	51	43	0	1	1	1	1	1	-	-
Pred										
Sex	-3	4	0	3	0	4	-3	3	0	5
Age	-3	0	0	-6	-7	-6	5	-6	-6	-3
WS	5	0	0	4	4	4	-4	-4	6	1
LED	0	0	0	3	0	0	0	0	0	0
ETH	-2	3	0	5	3	6	-6	0	1	5
SO	21	34							36	34
SD	6	12							11	12
SN	3	19							12	19
SP	6	11							11	11
SF	0	-2							-1	-2
SB	7	9							11	9
SW	45								45	
Males										
N	3732	3745	0	3957	4059	4021	3997	4046	-	-
R^2	52	43	0	1	1	1	1	1	-	-
Age	-3	0	0	-5	-7	-6	4	-8	-6	-3
WS	5	0	0	4	5	0	-5	-5	6	1
LED	0	0	0	0	0	0	4	0	0	0
ETH	0	5	0	8	8	8	-9	5	6	9
SO	23	35							39	35
SD	7	14							13	14
SN	0	17							8	17
SP	4	13							10	13
SB	9	7							12	7
SW	46								46	
Females										
N	3607	3619	0	0	3869	0	0	0	-	-
R^2	50	42	0	0	1	0	0	0	-	-
Age	-4	0	0	0	-8	0	0	0	-5	-2
WS	6	0	0	0	4	0	0	0	7	1
LED	0	0	0	0	5	0	0	0	1	1

Satisfaction with One's Health (continued)

	S	SW	SO	SD	SN	SP	SF	SB	TES	TESW
ETH	-3	0	0	0	0	0	0	0	-3	0
SO	20	33							35	33
SD	6	10							11	10
SN	5	21							15	21
SP	8	10							13	10
SB	4	11							9	11
SW	45								45	

Satisfaction with One's Finances

	S	SW	SO	SD	SN	SP	SF	SB	TES	TESW
N	7163	7234	7842	7733	7874	7821	7784	7810	-	-
R^2	53	44	1	1	1	2	1	1	-	-
Pred										
Sex	0	2	0	5	3	7	0	2	3	4
Age	0	3	-10	-8	-9	-10	6	-9	-7	-5
WS	0	-6	0	0	0	5	0	6	-1	-5
LED	0	0	5	0	0	2	4	3	3	2
ETH	-3	2	0	4	0	0	-4	0	-2	3
SO	25	29							35	29
SD	6	13							10	13
SN	12	25							20	25
SP	11	10							14	10
SF	5	-7							-3	-7
SB	8	6							10	6
SW	33								33	
Males										
N	3680	3705	4008	3955	4029	4006	3893	4002	-	-
R^2	51	41	1	2	1	1	1	1	-	-
Age	0	3	-11	-10	-9	-8	5	-10	-8	-5
WS	0	-4	0	0	0	6	0	4	0	-3
LED	0	0	7	0	0	0	5	0	3	2
ETH	-3	4	4	7	4	5	-6	0	2	7
SO	25	29							34	29
SD	8	13							12	13
SN	12	22							19	22
SP	11	10							14	10
SF	4	-7							2	-7
SB	9	6							11	6
SW	31								31	
Females										
N	3483	3529	3834	0	3845	3815	3791	3808	-	-

Satisfaction with One's Finances (continued)

	S	SW	SO	SD	SN	SP	SF	SB	TES	TESW
R^2	55	48	1	0	1	1	1	1	-	-
Age	0	4	-7	0	-8	-10	8	-7	-5	-2
WS	0	-8	-4	0	0	5	0	9	-3	-7
LED	0	0	4	0	0	4	0	4	2	2
ETH	-3	0	-6	0	0	0	0	-5	-6	-2
SO	26	28							36	28
SD	4	12							8	12
SN	12	28							22	28
SP	12	10							16	10
SF	5	-7							3	-7
SB	7	6							9	6
SW	35								35	

Satisfaction with One's Family Relations

	S	SW	SO	SD	SN	SP	SF	SB	TES	TESW
N	7204	7251	7848	7778	7871	7842	7814	7851	-	-
R^2	55	47	1	1	1	1	1	1	-	-
Pred										
Sex	0	0	0	0	0	5	0	7	1	1
Age	0	0	-10	-8	-7	-4	0	0	-6	-6
WS	0	0	-3	-3	-4	-4	6	-7	-3	-3
LED	0	-2	6	0	0	0	5	0	2	1
ETH	-4	4	-4	0	0	0	-3	0	-4	-2
SO	27	43							44	43
SD	5	8							8	8
SN	7	15							13	15
SP	6	7							9	7
SB	5	12							10	12
SW	40								40	
Males										
N	3615	3641	3999	3958	4004	3988	3979	4008	-	-
R^2	54	46	1	1	1	1	1	1	-	-
Age	0	3	-12	-9	-8	-5	0	-5	-7	-5
WS	0	0	-5	0	-5	-5	5	-9	-4	-5
LED	0	-4	7	0	0	0	7	0	2	-1
ETH	-4	5	0	0	0	4	-4	0	-2	5
SO	26	45							45	45
SD	5	8							8	8
SN	6	13							11	13
SP	6	4							8	4
SB	5	14							11	14

Satisfaction with One's Family Relations (continued)

	S	SW	SO	SD	SN	SP	SF	SB		TES	TESW
SW	41									41	
Females											
N	3589	3610	3859	3820	0	0	3835	0		-	-
R^2	55	47	1	1	0	0	1	0		-	-
Age	0	0	-8	-9	0	0	0	0		-4	-4
WS	0	0	0	0	0	0	7	0		0	0
LED	0	0	5	4	0	0	0	0		3	2
ETH	-4	4	-6	0	0	0	0	0		-5	2
SO	27	40								43	40
SD	4	8								7	8
SN	7	13								13	16
SP	6	10								10	10
SF	3	0								3	0
SB	6	10								10	10
SW	40									40	

Satisfaction with One's Paid Employment

	S	SW	SO	SD	SN	SP	SF	SB		TES	TESW
N	3240	3526	4475	4433	4553	4583	5375	4562		-	-
R^2	65	57	7	5	5	5	2	6		-	-
Pred											
Sex	0	0	0	3	0	3	0	3		1	1
Age	3	5	20	21	21	19	-11	18		22	23
WS	6	4	14	0	5	8	5	11		16	10
LED	0	0	-6	-8	-8	-8	10	-3		-8	-6
ETH	-3	3	-6	-8	-8	-8	0	-11		-11	-3
SO	30	28								39	28
SD	8	16								13	16
SN	9	23								16	23
SP	10	9								13	9
SF	5	-6								3	-6
SB	6	8								9	8
SW	31									31	
Males											
N	1640	1849	2348	2339	2408	2411	2754	2404		-	-
R^2	64	57	6	4	5	4	2	5		-	-
Age	5	6	16	19	19	17	-10	14		21	21
WS	6	4	15	0	0	9	5	11		15	10
LED	0	0	0	-5	-6	-6	10	0		3	3
ETH	-4	4	-5	-8	-10	-8	0	-11		-9	-2
SO	34	30								42	30

Satisfaction with One's Paid Employment (continued)

	S	SW	SO	SD	SN	SP	SF	SB	TES	TESW
SD	7	17							12	17
SN	10	21							16	21
SP	12	8							14	8
SF	4	-6							2	-6
SB	0	7							2	7
SW	28								28	

Females

	S	SW	SO	SD	SN	SP	SF	SB	TES	TESW
N	1550	1677	2127	2094	2146	2172	2621	2158	-	-
R^2	66	56	8	6	6	6	2	7	-	-
Age	0	5	24	24	24	22	-11	22	22	25
WS	7	4	14	0	5	7	5	10	16	10
LED	0	0	-10	-11	-11	-10	10	-7	-9	-9
ETH	0	0	-7	-8	-7	-7	0	-11	-7	-6
SO	26	25							35	25
SD	9	14							14	14
SN	8	25							17	25
SP	10	10							13	10
SF	4	-5							2	-5
SB	8	8							11	8
SW	34								34	

Satisfaction with One's Friendships

	S	SW	SO	SD	SN	SP	SF	SB	TES	TESW
N	7338	7371	7870	7805	7899	7887	7813	7854	-	-
R^2	50	44	1	1	1	1	1	1	-	-
Pred										
Sex	0	0	0	0	0	3	0	4	1	1
Age	-3	4	-6	-6	-8	-7	4	-5	-6	-1
WS	0	0	-3	0	-4	-2	4	-5	-2	-3
LED	0	-3	4	0	0	0	3	0	-1	-2
ETH	0	7	0	4	0	3	-6	0	3	8
SO	27	36							41	36
SD	0	8							3	8
SN	6	15							12	15
SP	7	14							13	14
SF	2	0							2	0
SB	5	9							9	9
SW	40								40	

Males

	S	SW	SO	SD	SN	SP	SF	SB	TES	TESW
N	3710	3728	4019	3976	4029	4025	3982	4018	-	-
R^2	48	43	1	1	1	1	1	1	-	-

Satisfaction with One's Friendships (continued)

	S	SW	SO	SD	SN	SP	SF	SB	TES	TESW
Age	0	0	-7	-5	-8	-8	0	-7	-6	-6
WS	0	0	-4	0	-4	-5	4	-6	-3	-3
LED	0	0	6	0	0	0	6	0	3	2
ETH	0	8	0	5	0	3	-7	0	3	9
SO	29	37							43	37
SD	0	10							4	10
SN	6	12							11	12
SP	8	13							13	13
SF	3	0							3	0
SB	6	9							9	9
SW	38								38	

Females

	S	SW	SO	SD	SN	SP	SF	SB	TES	TESW
N	3628	3643	0	0	3870	0	3831	0	-	-
R^2	51	45	0	0	1	0	1	0	-	-
Age	-4	0	0	0	-8	0	4	0	-5	-2
WS	0	0	0	0	-4	0	4	0	-1	-1
LED	0	-3	0	0	0	0	0	0	-1	-3
ETH	-3	5	0	0	0	0	-4	0	-1	5
SO	25	34							40	34
SD	0	6							3	6
SN	5	19							13	19
SP	7	16							14	16
SB	5	8							8	8
SW	43								43	

Satisfaction with One's Housing

	S	SW	SO	SD	SN	SP	SF	SB	TES	TESW
N	7203	7251	7850	7782	7891	7835	7816	7811	-	-
R^2	54	47	2	1	1	2	1	1	-	-
Pred										
Sex	3	3	6	6	5	8	0	5	9	8
Age	-2	0	-10	-10	-11	-10	5	-3	-10	-8
WS	0	-4	0	0	0	4	0	0	-1	-4
LED	0	0	6	4	3	5	4	6	4	4
ETH	0	2	-3	0	3	2	-3	-2	2	2
SO	27	32							38	32
SD	5	11							10	11
SN	9	22							17	22
SP	8	9							11	9
SF	3	-4							2	-4
SB	6	9							9	9

Satisfaction with One's Housing (continued)

	S	SW	SO	SD	SN	SP	SF	SB	TES	TESW
SW	35								35	

Males

	S	SW	SO	SD	SN	SP	SF	SB	TES	TESW
N	3674	3699	4012	3975	4035	4007	3991	0	-	-
R^2	54	47	1	1	1	1	1	0	-	-
Age	0	0	-10	-8	-10	-9	6	0	-8	-7
WS	0	-3	0	0	0	4	0	0	-1	-3
LED	0	0	5	0	0	0	5	0	2	2
ETH	0	5	0	5	3	4	-4	0	3	7
SO	29	34							41	34
SD	6	13							11	13
SN	10	22							18	22
SP	5	7							8	7
SF	2	-4							1	-4
SB	5	7							8	7
SW	36								36	

Females

	S	SW	SO	SD	SN	SP	SF	SB	TES	TESW
N	3529	3552	3838	3807	3856	3828	0	3800	-	-
R^2	52	46	1	1	1	1	0	1	-	-
Age	-3	0	-11	-10	-11	-10	0	0	-11	-8
WS	0	-6	0	-3	0	3	0	-4	-2	-6
LED	0	0	7	6	5	7	0	7	6	5
ETH	0	0	-6	0	0	0	0	-4	-3	-2
SO	26	29							36	29
SD	4	9							7	9
SN	8	22							16	22
SP	11	11							15	11
SF	4	-4							3	-4
SB	7	11							11	11
SW	34								34	

Satisfaction with One's Living Partner

	S	SW	SO	SD	SN	SP	SF	SB	TES	TESW
N	4039	4267	5060	5067	5222	5261	5631	5195	-	-
R^2	67	63	1	1	1	1	1	1	-	-
Pred										
Sex	0	3	4	0	0	5	0	8	5	6
Age	0	4	7	10	9	7	-7	6	8	11
WS	0	0	0	0	-5	0	0	0	-1	-1
LED	0	0	5	0	0	3	6	4	3	3
ETH	0	4	0	3	0	3	-5	0	2	5
SO	31	42							48	42

Satisfaction with One's Living Partner (continued)

	S	SW	SO	SD	SN	SP	SF	SB	TES	TESW
SD	0	11							5	11
SN	5	14							11	14
SP	8	14							14	14
SB	7	9							11	9
SW	41								41	
Males										
N	2133	2268	2701	2696	2787	2795	2994	2783	-	-
R^2	64	60	1	1	1	1	1	1	-	-
Age	0	5	5	10	8	6	-8	6	8	11
WS	0	0	0	0	-7	-5	7	-5	-2	-2
LED	0	0	6	0	0	0	0	0	3	3
ETH	0	4	0	0	0	0	-6	0	2	4
SO	27	45							46	45
SD	6	12							11	12
SN	0	15							6	15
SP	10	11							15	11
SB	7	7							10	7
SW	42								42	
Females										
N	1906	1999	2359	2371	2435	2466	0	2412	-	-
R^2	70	66	1	1	1	1	0	1	-	-
Age	0	0	10	10	10	9	0	8	9	9
WS	3	0	0	0	0	0	0	0	3	0
LED	0	0	5	0	0	0	0	0	3	2
ETH	0	4	0	0	0	0	0	0	2	4
SO	35	40							51	40
SD	0	9							4	9
SN	4	14							10	14
SP	6	18							13	18
SB	7	12							12	12
SW	41								41	

Satisfaction with One's Recreation Activity

	S	SW	SO	SD	SN	SP	SF	SB	TES	TESW
N	7210	7274	0	7774	7873	7846	7805	0	-	-
R^2	51	47	0	1	1	1	1	0	-	-
Pred										
Sex	0	3	0	0	0	0	0	0	1	3
Age	-3	0	0	-4	-7	-6	6	0	-5	-2
WS	2	0	0	0	0	0	-3	0	2	0
LED	0	0	0	-3	0	0	4	0	0	-1

Satisfaction with One's Recreation Activity (continued)

	S	SW	SO	SD	SN	SP	SF	SB	TES	TESW
ETH	0	5	0	7	4	7	-8	0	4	8
SO	25	34							39	34
SD	4	14							10	14
SN	3	17							10	17
SP	11	11							16	11
SF	3	-3							2	-3
SB	3	7							6	7
SW	41								41	
Males										
N	3679	3704	4011	3969	4027	4016	3990	4015	-	-
R^2	52	49	1	1	1	1	2	1	-	-
Age	0	0	-5	-5	-8	-6	7	-4	-4	-5
LED	0	0	0	0	0	0	6	-4	0	0
ETH	0	8	7	7	6	9	-8	7	9	14
SO	25	37							41	37
SD	4	14							10	14
SN	0	17							7	17
SP	13	10							17	10
SB	0	7							3	7
SW	42								42	
Females										
N	3531	3570	0	3805	0	3830	3815	0	-	-
R^2	51	45	0	1	0	1	1	0	-	-
Age	-4	0	0	-4	0	-5	4	0	-5	-1
WS	4	0	0	0	0	0	-4	0	4	0
ETH	0	0	0	7	0	6	-7	0	2	2
SO	26	31							38	31
SD	5	13							10	13
SN	5	17							12	17
SP	11	13							16	13
SF	3	-3							2	-3
SB	0	8							3	8
SW	39								39	

Satisfaction with One's Religion

	S	SW	SO	SD	SN	SP	SF	SB	TES	TESW
N	5038	5132	6129	5751	5930	5955	5950	5985	-	-
R^2	63	53	1	1	2	2	2	2	-	-
Pred										
Sex	0	3	3	5	3	5	-3	6	4	6
Age	-3	0	9	10	11	12	-12	11	5	9

Satisfaction with One's Religion (continued)

	S	SW	SO	SD	SN	SP	SF	SB	TES	TESW
WS	0	0	-5	-4	-7	-5	6	-6	-4	-5
LED	0	-3	0	0	-3	-4	6	0	-2	-4
ETH	-2	2	-7	0	-6	0	0	-5	-5	-2
SO	32	37							46	37
SD	4	10							8	10
SN	0	19							7	19
SP	8	10							12	10
SB	5	9							9	9
SW	39								39	

Males

	S	SW	SO	SD	SN	SP	SF	SB	TES	TESW
N	2508	2561	3095	2918	3000	2990	2998	3030	-	-
R^2	61	52	1	1	2	2	2	1	-	-
Age	-3	-4	10	11	12	-15	-13	11	3	3
WS	0	0	-5	0	-7	-5	5	-6	-4	-4
LED	0	0	0	0	0	-6	7	-5	-1	-1
ETH	0	4	0	0	-4	0	0	0	1	3
SO	35	38							48	38
SD	5	11							9	11
SN	6	18							12	18
SP	6	9							9	9
SB	5	10							9	10
SW	35								35	

Females

	S	SW	SO	SD	SN	SP	SF	SB	TES	TESW
N	2530	2571	3034	2833	2930	2965	2952	2955	-	-
R^2	66	53	2	1	2	1	1	2	-	-
Age	-3	0	7	8	9	8	-12	12	4	7
WS	0	0	-4	-4	-7	-5	7	-6	-4	-5
LED	0	0	0	0	0	0	4	0	0	0
ETH	0	0	-11	0	-8	0	0	-8	-7	-6
SO	28	35							43	35
SD	0	10							4	10
SN	6	21							15	21
SP	12	13							18	13
SB	5	8							9	8
SW	44								44	

Satisfaction with One's Self-Esteem

	S	SW	SO	SD	SN	SP	SF	SB	TES	TESW
N	7096	7144	7791	7650	7770	0	7744	0	-	-
R^2	52	45	1	1	2	0	1	0	-	-

Satisfaction with One's Self-Esteem (continued)

	S	SW	SO	SD	SN	SP	SF	SB	TES	TESW
Pred										
Sex	-3	2	-6	-5	-7	0	0	0	-6	-3
Age	-3	-4	-4	-8	-10	0	4	0	-9	-8
WS	0	0	-4	-5	-5	0	3	0	-3	-3
LED	0	0	6	3	5	0	3	0	3	3
ETH	-2	3	-5	-3	0	0	-5	0	-3	1
SO	27	39							43	39
SD	0	8							3	8
SN	7	18							14	18
SP	4	12							9	12
SB	8	6							10	6
SW	40									40
Males										
N	3600	3629	3968	3900	3951	0	3941	3972	-	-
R^2	48	42	1	1	2	0	1	1	-	-
Age	0	-5	-5	-9	-12	0	4	0	-6	-10
WS	0	0	-4	-5	-6	0	0	-8	-3	-4
LED	0	0	7	0	5	0	5	0	4	4
ETH	0	5	0	0	0	0	-7	0	2	5
SO	26	37							41	37
SD	0	10							4	10
SN	6	17							11	17
SP	4	12							9	12
SB	8	6							11	6
SW	41									41
Females										
N	3496	3515	3823	3750	3819	0	0	0	-	-
R^2	56	47	1	1	1	0	0	0	-	-
Age	-4	-3	0	-6	-9	0	0	0	-7	-5
WS	3	0	-5	-5	-5	0	0	0	0	-3
LED	0	0	0	0	4	0	0	0	1	1
ETH	-2	0	-9	-6	-6	0	0	0	-7	-5
SO	27	41							43	41
SD	4	7							7	7
SN	8	18							15	18
SP	4	12							9	12
SB	8	7							11	7
SW	40									40

Satisfaction with One's Transportation

	S	SW	SO	SD	SN	SP	SF	SB	TES	TESW
N	7105	7155	0	7629	7764	7707	7718	0	-	-
R^2	60	50	0	1	1	1	1	0	-	-
Pred										
Sex	0	2	0	0	0	4	0	0	1	2
Age	0	3	0	-6	-5	-6	5	0	1	0
WS	2	0	0	5	5	7	0	0	5	2
LED	0	-2	0	0	0	0	3	0	-1	-2
ETH	0	0	0	4	5	6	-6	0	2	3
SO	25	32							37	32
SD	5	14							10	14
SN	11	23							20	23
SP	10	7							13	7
SF	4	-5							2	-5
SB	5	7							8	7
SW	38								38	
Males										
N	3641	3663	3957	3907	3974	3957	3952	0	-	-
R^2	59	50	1	1	1	2	1	0	-	-
Age	0	0	-5	-8	-7	-8	7	0	-5	-5
WS	0	0	6	5	6	10	0	0	5	5
LED	0	0	0	0	0	0	4	0	0	0
ETH	-3	0	4	0	4	5	-7	0	0	3
SO	25	36							39	36
SD	5	15							11	15
SN	13	19							20	19
SP	7	7							10	7
SF	3	-6							1	-6
SB	5	6							7	6
SW	38								38	
Females										
N	3464	3492	0	0	0	3750	0	0	-	-
R^2	61	51	0	0	0	1	0	0	-	-
Age	0	3	0	0	0	-4	0	0	2	3
WS	0	0	0	0	0	4	0	0	1	0
ETH	0	0	0	0	0	7	0	0	1	1
SO	24	28							35	28
SD	5	13							10	13
SN	9	29							20	29
SP	13	8							16	8
SF	4	-4							2	-4
SB	5	7							8	7

Satisfaction with One's Transportation (continued)

	S	SW	SO	SD	SN	SP	SF	SB	TES	TESW
SW	39								39	

Satisfaction with One's University Education

	S	SW	SO	SD	SN	SP	SF	SB	TES	TESW
N	7231	7262	0	7826	7899	7906	7696	7813	-	-
R²	49	42	0	1	1	2	2	1	-	-
Pred										
Sex	0	0	0	4	3	6	0	0	2	2
Age	-3	-4	0	-9	-10	-7	4	0	-8	-8
WS	0	-4	0	0	0	0	0	-3	-2	-4
LED	0	0	0	0	0	-3	5	-7	-1	0
ETH	0	2	0	5	5	7	-10	8	5	6
SO	17	27							29	27
SD	5	13							11	13
SN	4	19							12	19
SP	10	13							16	13
SF	0	-4							-2	-4
SB	11	11							16	11
SW	43								43	
Males										
N	3687	3701	4040	3992	4040	4043	3933	3999	-	-
R²	51	43	1	1	1	1	2	1	-	-
Age	-3	-4	-7	-10	-9	-7	4	0	-10	-10
WS	0	0	0	0	0	0	4	0	0	0
LED	0	0	4	0	0	-3	7	-8	-1	-3
ETH	-3	5	3	4	5	7	-10	8	4	10
SO	17	29							30	29
SD	6	13							12	13
SN	4	18							12	18
SP	12	10							16	10
SF	0	-5							-2	-5
SB	10	13							16	13
SW	43								43	
Females										
N	3544	3561	0	3834	3859	3863	3763	3815	-	-
R²	47	40	0	1	1	1	1	1	-	-
Age	-4	-3	0	-9	-10	-8	0	0	-9	-8
WS	0	-6	0	0	0	0	0	-4	-3	-6
LED	0	0	0	0	0	0	5	-6	-1	-1
ETH	0	0	0	7	6	8	-9	8	4	4
SO	16	26							27	26

288

Satisfaction with One's University Education (continued)

	S	SW	SO	SD	SN	SP	SF	SB	TES	TESW
SD	3	12							8	12
SN	5	21							14	21
SP	8	16							15	16
SF	0	-4							-2	-4
SB	11	8							14	8
SW	43								43